NIGHT
IN TH

DANNY COLLINS

NIGHTMARE IN THE SUN

THEIR DREAM OF BUYING A HOME IN SPAIN ENDED IN THEIR BRUTAL MURDER

JOHN BLAKE

Published by John Blake Publishing Ltd,
3 Bramber Court, 2 Bramber Road,
London W14 9PB, England

www.blake.co.uk

First published in hardback in 2007

ISBN 978 1 84454 489 9

British Library Cataloguing-in-Publication Data:

A catalogue record for this book is available from the British Library.

Design by www.envydesign.co.uk

Printed and bound in Great Britain by William Clowes Ltd, Beccles, Suffolk

1 3 5 7 9 10 8 6 4 2

Papers used by John Blake Publishing are natural, recyclable products
made from wood grown in sustainable forests. The manufacturing processes
conform to the environmental regulations of the country of origin.

Every attempt has been made to contact the relevant copyright-holders,
but some were unobtainable. We would be grateful if the appropriate
people could contact us.

*This book is dedicated to the memory of Linda
and Anthony O'Malley, for whom a dream in the sun
became a nightmare.*

'GIVE ME THE LIBERTY TO KNOW, TO UTTER, AND
TO ARGUE FREELY ACCORDING TO MY CONSCIENCE,
ABOVE ALL OTHER LIBERTIES.'
John Milton, Aeropagitica

'WILL YOU WALK INTO MY PARLOUR?' SAID THE
SPIDER TO THE FLY, ''TIS THE PRETTIEST LITTLE PARLOUR
THAT EVER YOU DID SPY.'
Mary Howitt 1799 – 1888, Welcome to My Parlour

'MANY PEOPLE THINK THAT WHEN A
SPANIARD SAYS 'MAÑANA' IT MEANS TOMORROW.
IT DOESN'T. IT MEANS 'NOT TODAY'.'
The author in a *GMTV* interview, Alicante, March 2006

FOREWORD

When I first considered writing this story of the investigation into the infamous Costa Blanca house-hunter murders of Anthony and Linda O'Malley I wondered how many friends I'd have left when it was all over.

The O'Malley investigation lasted from October 2002 to the discovery of the bodies on March 25 2003. Many mistakes were made and the wrong conclusions drawn. Witnesses misplaced timelines and some vital evidence was ignored.

More especially, all investigation for the police of two national forces ended with the disinterment of two decomposed corpses on that miserable March night. The Spanish police were satisfied and the Welsh police could wrap up a six month missing persons inquiry with honour but there were still, for me, faces out there in the shadow.

I believe at least two more persons were involved in the

plot that led to the kidnap and deaths of the victims. The fact is that nothing is ever neatly tied up and every investigation finishes up with annoying loose ends. The solution for investigators is to find the tidiest ending and close the file.

The kidnap and murders of Linda and Anthony O'Malley were crimes that shocked Spain. The realisation that such a fate could befall a pleasant middle-aged couple engaged in nothing more ominous than the search for a holiday home in the foothills of the Spanish sierras invaded the comfort zone of thousands of British expatriates who had emigrated to the Spanish Costas for a life of retirement in the sun. Mortal danger, it appeared, lurked in even these idyllic surroundings.

Spain is regarded as a comparatively safe country in which to live – look no further than the 'white flight' syndrome recorded in Britain as many emigrate to the shores of the Mediterranean from a crowded country awash with crime and unfettered immigration.

In Spain on the sun-kissed Costas crime certainly exists but it is the crime inherent in all western societies. Street muggings, burglary, credit card fraud, and that crime peculiar to Mediterranean resorts from Málaga to Naples, the infamous motorised bag-snatch known as el tirón.

All of these crimes find their roots in acquisitive, materialistic societies. What the affluent majority possesses, the poorer minority wants. The under-achievers rob the achievers. It is a history as old as Man.

But, given the odd crooked developer, blatant property fraud in Spain is rare given the good advice offered by lawyers and real estate agents, and murder for gain is rarer still. Yet while murder most foul undoubtedly took place in the O'Malley case, this is more a tale of unrelenting tragedy and a progression of events that were directed by fate into a pattern they were never meant to take.

In this way, the story of Linda and Anthony O'Malley is unique. It evolved through startling coincidences in time and place and needed the intervention of others who never dreamed what the outcome would be. The truth is it startled all of us, and even the professionals involved in the investigation and those they sought and finally arrested couldn't have imagined the tragic outcome in a decade of what-ifs and maybes.

My involvement in the case came with my introduction to the relatives who came to Spain to animate the search for their loved ones and to the police officers who accompanied them, the dedicated Welshmen who would see a missing persons' inquiry on foreign soil through to a murder inquiry and its tragic end.

The case intrigued me. As an investigative journalist I found myself filling in the gaps and following up clues as the hunt grew more intense, my interest was encouraged by my sympathy for the imagined plight of the Linda and Anthony O'Malley and the very tangible distress of their families.

The story as it developed took on all the mystery of a first class thriller that captured the attention of two nations and focussed the spotlight of Europe on the Costa Blanca. At my news desk I received calls from media as far away as South Africa begging for the latest news on the search. Suddenly Linda and Anthony O'Malley were everybody's sister and brother, parents, and grandparents. Their imagined fate was the topic of conversation in bars and cafeterias across Spain. Where had they gone? Who had taken them?

Looking back on my files over those six months of the hunt, I see my preoccupation with small details, notes reminding me to ask questions that would turn out to be irrelevant to the mystery and here and there a name or telephone number that would later prove of the highest importance.

There are photographs too, scores of them, of deserted farmhouses and barren landscapes, of faces and locations accompanied by hastily scribbled notes that at the time were intelligent comments and now need thought in their translation.

They were never originally intended to form the basis of a book. At first I toyed with the idea of writing something for a Sunday supplement, a cautionary tale for naïve travellers, but there was too much to tell, too many words born over 43 months and my story was unique. I had interviewed witnesses who were never questioned by the Spanish police, one of whom was probably the last person to see the O'Malleys alive other than their killers.

And who were the killers? I had also witnessed a hijacked investigation whose thoroughness would be ignored, even unmentioned in court. I heard no mention by a vengeful prosecution of a mysterious third man whose name was raised by the defence but rejected as inadmissible. I listened to fanciful submissions cobbled together by a desperate defence. Yet I would trace the third man to the UK and contact both him and his family.

This was a story that had never been imagined and much of it never became part of the police investigation. Many of my findings and interviews are reproduced here for the first time.

Relating the history of a crime such as murder is a grisly

business and gruesome details often cannot be avoided, nor should they be if the tale is to be told with any regard for the truth. It is easy enough to obliterate a surname or change the identity of a witness who wishes for anonymity but details shouldn't be overlooked when they are crucial to the plot.

Certainly this story has its dark side; how else could such a heinous tale of kidnap, torture, and murder be told? But it is also a recounting of love and devotion, of how two people who loved together died together within moments of each other; and of the devotion of a brother, sister, and daughters, and of the Welsh detectives who were determined to see justice done right through to the end.

It is also a cautionary tale for those who see only good in their fellow men, for the victims of these multiple crimes were trusting people who confided their dreams too many times to the wrong people and paid for their naivety with their lives.

I first considered writing this book soon after the arrests in 2003 but shelved it when I realised the whole story had not reached the end without the trial and imprisonment of a swaggering self-seeking conman and his unsavoury acolyte. Following the trial there were appeals but these too have now been heard.

As always the time-honoured delaying tactics of the professional writer came to the fore. Other business, telephone calls, a television series that couldn't be missed, long walks to clear the mind and books and magazines to fill it up again. But behind it all was the nagging feeling that I was putting aside something that had to be done. The O'Malley story had to be told and I was the only one who could tell it. I owed a debt to two people I had never met.

I didn't doubt that in the telling I would ruffle authority and upset some acquaintances because I would find myself writing harsh truths. I was also aware that a family that has seen such tragedy might wish to guard its privacy and not want its story told to the world. Sadly, that privacy disappears with the first photograph and the first interview. A relationship to tragedy gives us all our unwanted 15 minutes of fame.

I knew it would be difficult to record the police investigation – in Spain the police never talk to journalists and in the UK there isn't the freedom of information as doled out to some of my true crime writer contemporaries by small town sheriffs' offices in the USA.

However, in this I reckoned without the unstinting help given by each of the detectives who played a major role in the investigation. Each and every one took time to explain the various stages of Operation Nevada and was suitably modest about the parts they played. They have already been named but I mention them here again. Alan Jones, Steve Lloyd, and Dave James are men who should make their fellow Welshmen proud to breathe the same air. Relatives of Anthony and Linda O'Malley owe them a great debt of which I'm sure they are aware.

But another false start had been made and abandoned before I finally blew dust off the files and read them again. That reading confirmed in me the belief that this was a story with heroes yet to be recognised in a world where heroes are few.

Sometimes in its writing over the months I would pause and recollect that I must have walked many of the paths of Linda and Anthony O'Malley when they first arrived in Benidorm and I wonder how near those paths were to crossing? Would their fate have been different if, as people often did, they had come to the newspaper office to inquire about the wording of the advertisement and the almost incredible cheapness of the villa in Alcoy? If when they ate in a pizzeria or Chinese restaurant did our eyes meet through a window as I passed? These are questions that will never leave me as the anniversary of their murders comes around each fall. They were people I came to know so well but never met.

In their violent exit from this world, they have left their mark on Spain and on those who live here, expatriate and national alike, for the moral of their story is never to trust the man who offers assistance or the one who speaks kindly. There are no free lunches in this sad world we have created and must now inhabit. None discovered the truth of this more than Anthony and Linda O'Malley.

This is their story.

PROLOGUE

Murder Most Foul
Baradello Gelat, Alcoy, September 13, 2002

She had heard no sound from the villa above since they had left that morning. The cellar where she and Anthony were incarcerated was directly under the stone veranda and stretched the width of the building. A redbrick wall separated the space from the villa's foundations and the outer wall had a barred window at ceiling height that looked out onto an adjoining property and land. Light filtered through the wire mesh that had been attached to the bars and through the slatted grill at the top of the metal door that opened onto steps that led up to ground level. Now she was alone and she knew she must take the chance for their lives' sake.

The exhausted woman sobbed in frustration as she struggled to push the bed across the uneven concrete floor, straining emaciated muscles wasted by almost a week of deprivation to place the metal frame nearer to the barred and netted window.

PROLOGUE

Linda O'Malley's throat seared with thirst but she had wasted the meagre supply of water the man Matthew had brought to the cellar this morning when she had fallen in a dizzy faint and overturned the bucket. She had come to stretched on the concrete floor with her torn and sweat soaked rag of a dress sopping wet. 'So what?' she had thought wearily. It would cool her in the cloying late summer heat of the cellar.

The small window was on a level with the ground outside and the bone dry earth of the garden was constantly blown in with the wind. Her husband Anthony suffered from the grit that hung in the air, his eyes red-rimmed from particles that had become trapped behind his now abandoned contact lenses. He was almost blind without the lenses and she had bathed his eyes with water soaked into a piece of material she had ripped from the skirt of her dress but they still caused him pain. To hide the damage, Matthew and David had brought him sunglasses when they came to take him that morning.

The villa was quiet and she had guessed she was alone. She had tried calling out but she knew her voice was weak. The cellar was 20 metres from the road and the urbanisation of Baradello Gelat was located in thick woodland four kilometres from Alcoy town centre and seldom saw visitors on foot. The window faced inward onto the plot and the house beyond seemed to be unoccupied. But perhaps today would be different. Perhaps today someone would hear her and bring help and a blessed relief from her husband's and her own suffering.

David had promised them both they would be free today. He had said all he and Matthew wanted was the money from England. They were welcome to it if it meant freedom. But David had lied to them when they came to view the villa, claiming it was his to sell. Anthony had told her it was only rented or why else would she and he have been thrown down into this reeking cavern, locked away from the world outside while David and Matthew plundered their bank account? Why oh why had Anthony been so boastful about the money, chatting as if they were all lifelong, best friends? He was usually so withdrawn with strangers but the euphoria of finding the villa had made him garrulous, too talkative and trusting by half whereas she hadn't liked these people from the start.

Acquaintances of Linda O'Malley would swear she was a woman who had never demonstrated ill will towards a living soul but God, how she hated both these men. But tonight she and Anthony had been promised their freedom if David kept his word.

She would call her daughters, Nicola and Jenny, and they would cry together on the phone. Then they would take a flight back home and never venture abroad from Llangollen again.

The men had taken Anthony upstairs to the villa to wash, shave and dress that morning. They had given him a blue T-shirt and a clean pair of trousers to replace his sweat stained and grubby shorts.

He had insisted on coming back down to kiss her goodbye and she had noticed the T-shirt was large and how it draped on his wasted frame. He had lost weight as had she during the five days of their incarceration.

Linda thought the T-shirt may have belonged to the fat man who called himself David. The gross, demanding torturer who had used the cattle prod on her until Anthony had screamed out the bank card PINs and begged them to take the money. All of it, for God's sake, but to leave her in peace. The other, the tall, slim man called Matthew whom David had introduced as his brother-in-law, who had been gardening when they had come to view the villa, he of the woman's eyes and the quiet voice that spoke in whispers, had smiled at that.

She hadn't liked either of them when she and Anthony had arrived late on Saturday afternoon in answer to the advertisement and she had been especially unhappy at her husband's ready acceptance of David's offer that they should move into the villa with their suitcases the following morning, to get to know their new home before they put down the cash. 'To get the feel of the place,' as Matthew had added, smiling. They had been in captivity since the following Sunday – just five days that seemed like an eternity.

The villa had seemed cheap enough, no doubt about that. At thirty thousand euros, just £20,000 for so much ground for the dogs to run, so much space for visiting family and the grandchildren to play in the sun. There was even a swimming pool. But she hadn't liked the men. There was something wrong about them. Too many smiles, too welcoming. Won't you walk into my parlour, said the spider to the fly...

She had seen Anthony's eyes widen at the sight of the gun but she had felt woozy and disorientated after just that one small glass of wine as they sat on the veranda that Sunday lunchtime. She was sure she had been drugged. She had hardly known what was happening as they were both bundled down the narrow cellar steps at the side of the house.

David had handcuffed them to the single bed frames set

head to foot in the narrow confines of the rock and brick-walled cellar and she had cried herself to sleep as Anthony broke off his angry drugged railing against their captors and tried to comfort her as she wept.

She thought again of the tearful welcome they would get from their family. But what if it was all another lie? Why should they trust these men who had already tricked and tortured them and stolen their bank cards and passports, who had even twisted her wedding ring from her finger? Better to take this opportunity to call for help than to sit and await her fate. Anthony would do the same in her circumstances, she knew.

She wasn't sure how much time she had before they returned when the cellar door would be flung open to admit her husband and his captors. Once again they would chain him to the other single bed frame placed in line ahead of hers, both of which served as their only refuge from the damp and gritty floor.

She pulled at the handcuffs that held her left arm to her own bed frame. These had been placed in such a manner as to allow her to manoeuvre herself onto the waste bucket that seemed hardly ever emptied and which reeked from under the metal bed frame. Not that anything passed through her very often with the scant food passed down to them by their captors.

Her wrist was raw and bleeding again. She had stuffed cloth between her flesh and the metal cuff from the thin blanket that Anthony had torn with his teeth for her. She had wept again at the sight of his eyes, red and weeping from the infection caused by his unwashed contact lenses and the eternal wind-borne grit.

She heaved at the bed again and it grated against the

rough stone wall beneath the window. The effort of leaning across the bed checked by the handcuffs made her feel dizzy and she rested a moment before struggling up to kneel half-crouched on the sagging springs, dropping her left shoulder to compensate for the check of the handcuffs. The concrete ceiling was tight against the crown of her head as she struggled to focus her eyes through the close mesh of the wire.

In front of her across the open space of the front yard she saw a chain-linked wire fence that bordered the back of the lot. Behind that was another villa. She thumped on the wire mesh of the cellar window and called as loudly as she could. Even if the people in the villa opposite didn't speak English they'd understand a cry for help. She called again, making herself dizzy as she expelled the air from her lungs.

As she wavered, looking sideways out of the half-obstructed window with the dirt and fallen pine needles at eye level, she thought she heard a car turning into the drive from her left. She rolled her eyes that way and saw a flash of blue coachwork from their hired Seat Stilo that the fat David now drove. They were back. She threw back her head and screamed in desperation. 'Help! Help! Please God help us!' But no one heard.

No one that is, except the three men exiting the car. Anthony, newly cuffed to Matthew for the exit and David, who was pocketing the 9mm converted semi-automatic pistol that had lain between his thighs on the drive back from Benidorm. He left the car at a waddling run followed by Anthony's shout of warning to his wife. Stumbling in his haste between the rear of the villa and the pierced stone wall that bordered the road and then left and down the side steps to the cellar, cursing the woman as he fumbled for the cellar key.

A moment of hesitation at the lock and then he burst in and caught the woman's right arm, somersaulting her back off the bedsprings. The back of her head hit the opposite wall of the narrow cellar, barely two metres across, with a dull thwack and she lay limp, trapped between the frame and the wall and held from falling completely by her handcuffed wrist, now stretched across the grimed mattress.

David picked her up and even he was amazed at her lightness. After a week of captivity her already spare frame had dropped to less than 45 kilos. He threw her onto the bed, his hand smeared with blood from the wound to the rear of her skull. He pulled a handkerchief from his jacket pocket and fastidiously wiped his hand, telling the woman she was a stupid cow in his thick South American accent. Then, overcome with anger at one who would flout his plan and put him and his accomplice in danger of discovery, he punched her angrily several times in the face and neck before he turned to the door.

Outside in the well of the steps, the handcuffed Anthony struggled with Matthew and called his wife's name. On the bed in the cellar, Linda began to convulse from the head wound.

Alone, with the shouts of love and encouragement from her husband coming to her through the closed cellar door, she felt the iron glove grip her chest and squeeze and the pain was momentarily unbearable. It relaxed and then came again in a stronger wave, pulverising her thin chest as she gasped for air and called on God to help her. Please God. No. Surely she wasn't going to die and leave

Anthony like this. He needed her. She gasped for breath as another tremor shook her and she lifted her bleeding head from the foul-smelling mattress before collapsing back into the darkness.

The final, crushing pain hit her like a thunderbolt and her last thoughts were of her family so far away and unaware of her and Anthony's captivity and torture. There was one last convulsion as she died with Anthony's cries ringing in her ears.

In the late afternoon of Friday, September 13, 2002, after five days of hunger and deprivation, the tortured soul of Linda O'Malley, fled free.

★ ★ ★

Handcuffed to Matthew, Anthony O'Malley, who that afternoon had been made to enter the CAM Bank on the corner of Avenida L'Ametlla de Mar in Benidorm to withdraw the last £18,000 from his and Linda's joint UK bank account, needed no urging to enter the cellar, dragging Matthew with him. His cry of anguish on seeing his wife's limp form was pitiable but there was no pity in his captor's hearts.

Despite his weakened state, he threw Matthew aside as he spun on David.

'You fat fucking evil bastard, you've killed her!'

David raised podgy hands and tried to placate him. 'She fell, Anthony. I didn't touch her, I swear.'

Anthony O'Malley rushed at him, dragging Matthew behind him like a rag, 'Then get an ambulance, you bastard. Call an ambulance now!'

David shook his head. 'There's no point, Anthony. She's gone. Can't you see?'

Anthony collapsed in grief over the still body of his wife, ignoring the weight of Matthew, who was now pulled with him into an unwilling obeisance to the soul of the woman in whose torture and robbery he had collaborated over the past five days.

David stooped and unlocked the handcuff attaching his brother-in-law to Anthony and beckoned him outside, leaving their anguished captive inside to mourn his dead wife. He locked the door behind them.

David took the lead. 'He's got to go now. This is a fucking murder rap we're facing here. It's all gone to shit.'

Matthew, ever led by his older brother-in-law, nodded nervously.

'Will you shoot him?'

David gave him a contemptuous smile. 'Is there no limit to your stupidity, little Pepe? A shot would bring the neighbours out of their boxes. Go upstairs and get a plastic bag. We'll need some parcel tape as well. Go now while he's still occupied with howling over his wife.'

As Matthew left on his errand, David fingered the pistol in his pocket and unlocked the door with his right hand. Anthony was lodged between the interior cellar wall and the narrow bed frame, embracing his wife's body and uttering a low crooning of grief.

David paused near the door and spoke softly.

'I'm so sorry, Anthony. I meant what I said this morning about leaving you here in the cellar and calling the police to find you. Once we had the money it would have been over. This is a tragedy for all of us.'

He turned to the door as Matthew arrived and moved his podgy bulk to block O'Malley's view of the colourful green and black plastic carrier bag the man held. Taking the bag from his brother-in-law, he suddenly lunged at Anthony's kneeling form and brought the bag down over his victim's head, clasping a fat arm around the man's neck to restrain his sudden struggles. The kneeling man exploded upwards, ripping at the arm around his throat as the reflexes of asphyxiation kicked in.

Fearing O'Malley's surge of desperate strength might allow him to break free, the hyperventilating David screamed to Matthew to assist him and the trembling younger man scrambled onto the bed, narrowly missing trampling Linda's corpse as he fought his way past the struggling bodies to reach the other side. There his weight added to that of the fat man as the scant oxygen trapped in the bag was exchanged for carbon dioxide and re-breathed into Anthony O'Malley's oxygen-starved lungs. It was then that fate played its last eccentric card of the day.

As the victim's struggles became more frantic and as his head whipped from side to side, there was an audible crack as two vertebrae in his upper spine parted. At the trial 43 months later, forensic officers would give evidence that Anthony O'Malley died either from asphyxiation or the severing of his spinal column at the third and fourth vertebrae coupled with a fracture of the hyoid bone of the throat.

A neck is broken when the skull is sheared off the atlas, the first cervical vertebrae of the spinal column that supports the head, in a twisting motion. Lower broken vertebrae coupled with signs of asphyxiation point to the desperate, tremendous forces generated by Anthony O'Malley against the combined weight of his attackers as they fought to suffocate him. A fracture of the hyoid bone, a small protuberance attached to the base of the tongue at the entrance to the windpipe, is an indication of death by or during strangulation.

Anthony O'Malley sagged and a rank odour invaded the cellar as his body voided.

The two double murderers removed the bag and left the bodies of their victims where they lay. They would later bury them below the cellar floor but first they taped the bag they had used to smother Anthony over Linda's head and sealed it at the neck. There was no other bag available for Anthony so Matthew supported the head while David bound the tape over the mouth, ears, eyes, and nose. They would return to bury the bodies that night, before insects invaded other unmasked body cavities and set off a precipitous cycle of corruption in the heat of the late summer. They were also fulfilling a subconscious wish founded on a superstition of their homeland; never to look into the face of a dead victim for fear the vengeful soul will recognise its murderer.

'I need a drink,' said Matthew.

David smiled. 'Todo menos la sangría, Pepito,' he said. 'Anything but the sangría, little Pepe.'

ACKNOWLEDGEMENTS

So many people helped me in the preparation for this book that it would be impossible to name them all. Some in any event prefer to remain anonymous and for my part so they shall. Deserving of a special mention for his part in the investigation that led to the writing of this book is CBN reporter Tom Cain who accompanied me during many of my earlier out of office inquiries. My thanks also go to those members of the Costa Blanca News staff who recalled events or helped me trace relevant copy in their spare time. They know who they are.

In the UK I am especially indebted to Det Supt Alan Jones of the North Wales Police and I wish him well in his retirement. That debt also extends to DS Steve Lloyd for his tremendous help with chronology and his total recall of facts that had sometimes escaped me, and to that other hero of the investigation, DC Dave James, and to the CID

North Wales East Division at Wrexham in general. Thanks guys and girls.

My old mate Arthur Mills, late retired of the Shropshire Star, and his partner Sylvia answered many of my pleas for help on local information unavailable to me from my lofty perch on a Spanish mountain and my thanks goes across the seas to George and Jackie Tipping and Sue Beske of Henderson, Nevada, who helped me in chasing up a particularly vital clue. I also mustn't forget my good friend Alberto García Román of Freecom SA in Benidorm for his invaluable expertise in the photo lab. A special debt of thanks also goes to my fellow scribe, best-selling author Wensley Clarkson, whose advice has been invaluable, and to my gracious editors Lucian Randall and Clive Hebard at John Blake Publishing for their help and guidance. In closing, a posthumous 'gracias amigo' to Nigel Bowden, old Slippery of the Costas himself, for a generous tip off that put me on a scene at the right time and place and finally my everlasting thanks to my wife Nikki for her indefatigable and diligent reading of a long manuscript, her constant words of encouragement, and her very practical advice when I suffered the writers' perennial fear of missed deadlines.

While this book is a true and accurate account of events that took place between September 2002 and April 2006, some conjecture has been based on evidence later recovered. I believe these assumptions are logical and are supported by both spoken and written statements entered into evidence and by the findings and conclusions of forensic pathologists.

Every effort has been made to faithfully reproduce the timetable of events, but time often plays tricks on the memory and impressions gained in haste are not always accurate on recall.

I have been greatly assisted by Welsh investigators in reporting the order of events but inevitably any mistakes are mine.

All of the protagonists are real people and are so identified with the exception of those whose names have been changed or omitted to protect the innocent as well as the guilty.

CONTENTS

1

FIRST ALARM

At 11.00pm in the late evening of 13 September, Jenny Stewart, Linda's youngest daughter from her first marriage, stood with her son John before the board in the Arrivals Hall of Manchester Airport. They had come to meet the Thomson JMC charter flight carrying her mother and her stepfather back to the UK from their fortnight's house search on Spain's Costa Blanca. The aircraft was due to land at 11.20pm and they had travelled the 60 miles to the airport from Llangollen with time to spare.

The night was cold and Jenny imagined how the couple would ape mock shivers to make her and their grandson smile as they exited from the carousel. She hadn't heard from them since the previous week, on the evening of 4 September, when Linda had called her at the terrace house in Market Street where she looked after her mother and stepfather's Labrador and Alsatian. Linda had reminded her to get birthday cards for two relatives and told her they

1

had had no luck with their search for a holiday home, but they hadn't given up hope and were still looking.

Now Jenny waited to hear the news of their holiday in Benidorm. She knew the car would be filled with conversation on the way home to Llangollen with details about the house search and plans for their next trip abroad to continue the hunt if there had been no luck with this one.

Anthony – Jenny and her sister Nicola actually preferred to call him Tony, although Bernard and Christine, his brother and sister, and his mother Jo always used his full name – and Linda were dedicated sun-worshippers and had long dreamed of retiring to Spain. Jenny hoped they were now a little nearer their dream, having worked so hard for it.

Other flights were landing and passengers streaming out from the baggage-claim area were being greeted by friends and relatives waiting within Arrivals.

11.20pm came and the Arrivals board indicated that the Málaga flight had landed, so Jenny moved to a spot nearer the exit doors from the Customs area to make it easier to spot her mother and stepfather when they emerged with those customary big smiles on their faces. Finally, the stream of passengers pushing their luggage trolleys through the doors and greeting smiling relatives thinned, and still there was no sign of Linda and Tony.

Sure that they would have telephoned her before she left Llangollen if they knew they were going to miss their flight, Jenny was determined to stay until she saw them emerge from the baggage hall. That was probably the answer – they were stuck at the carousel waiting for their luggage to arrive from the aircraft. The hands of her watch ticked inexorably on. Midnight came and went.

As the hour approached 1.00am, the doors of the baggage hall swung open again and more passengers began to pour through. This had to be them. But there was no sign of Linda and Anthony O'Malley that night. The newly arrived flight was from Alicante and Jenny felt a sick feeling of anti-climax. Linda and Tony had been scheduled to fly from Málaga but yet another arrival from Spain seemed a bad omen.

A word with the information desk confirmed that the aircraft had left Málaga Airport without the O'Malleys. The two empty seats had remained vacant.

Jenny made a call from her mobile to alert the family that Mum and Tony hadn't made the flight and would no doubt ring home any time soon to explain the delay. Then she made her way back to the car park for the long, silent journey home with John sitting quietly beside her.

Whatever had happened, she hoped it wasn't serious. It was so unlike them not to call.

★ ★ ★

Saturday came and went with no news of Linda or Anthony. Calls to either of their mobile phones resulted in a message that the phone was out of service. Anxiety and paranoia began to settle in. No one had any idea where the couple had stayed in Benidorm or when they had planned to leave for the journey home, other than that they had planned to rent a hire car for use during their stay on the Costa.

Thoughts of an unforeseen delay or an alteration to travel plans turned to more sinister events, perhaps an accident. A call was planned to the British Consulate in Alicante for the following Monday. Again, the worry was magnified by the knowledge that both Anthony and Linda were responsible people who would never willingly put their family through any sort of anxiety.

As the weekend closed with no news, Linda's married sister, Barbara Murphy, took it upon herself to report the couple's disappearance to North Wales Police at Wrexham, the police station that served Llangollen.

At first, the police weren't sure how to deal with the situation of a holiday couple vanishing 1,000 miles away in a foreign city. The Costa Blanca was an area unfamiliar to the officers at Wrexham and, after all, was 48 hours such an unreasonably long time for a middle-aged couple to decide to prolong their holiday in the sun, however responsible they might normally be?

The North Wales Police also knew any request for the Spanish police in Benidorm to make enquiries about the missing couple would have to be made through Interpol in London, the ponderous international police body whose new eight-storey HQ is located in the fashionable Paris suburb of Saint-Cloud. From there, the request would be passed to Spanish Interpol in Madrid and, from there, eventually to Benidorm. The wheels would grind exceedingly slowly and any answers to their questions would have to come back the same way.

The request was finally made through the official channels and everyone knew that there was nothing more to do but wait for a response from the Spanish.

The Spanish treated the enquiry with typical shakes of the head and a hunching of the shoulders. Wasn't it obvious that here were another two visitors who found the Mediterranean sunshine a better alternative to the cloudy skies of Britain? Reports of missing friends and relatives on holiday arrived on their desks every day. Very few involved anything particularly alarming.

In the case of accidents involving foreign nationals, hospitals in Spain are obliged to inform the police who, in turn, inform the relevant consuls. But the names of Linda and Anthony O'Malley appeared on no emergency registers. 'Give it a fortnight,' the Spanish police told Wrexham through Interpol. 'They'll turn up by then. People usually do.'

But a week later, the circumstances of the O'Malley's disappearance took on a more sinister tone when Jenny Stewart opened a letter from the couple's Chester-based bank listing card purchases and withdrawals from the day of the couple's arrival in Benidorm up to 11 September, two days before they failed to make their flight home.

From a simple hotel booking on 31 August to a petrol purchase in Benidorm on 7 September, the card usage was normal, but from 8 September withdrawals had gone wild with hourly cash extractions and purchases totalling nearly €2,228 on 10 September alone. Goods had been purchased in Benidorm, Finestrat, Alicante and Valencia that included computer equipment, a Dictaphone, a burglar alarm, oversize clothing, shoes, video games, and there had even been an attempt to buy an expensive laptop computer on 11 September, the purchase of which was blocked by the worried bank manager in Chester. The credit card receipts ran into three pages.

As Jenny was to remark in an interview before the *Tonight* cameras nearly a year later, 'Tony and Linda's credit card purchases never ran to more than one page with one or two items. They were so careful and sensible. This was just so out of character.'

The family agreed that the bank should continue to block the account, but worse was yet to come. Unbeknown to the family in England and Wales, Anthony and Linda had opened a foreign resident's account with the CAM Bank in Benidorm soon after their arrival.

On the day of the removal of card status by the UK bank, four attempts were made to withdraw cash from cash points in Alicante using the Yorkshire Bank card. Later on that same day, a man identifying himself as Anthony O'Malley contacted the Yorkshire Bank branch in Chester by fax and arranged for the total remaining balance to be transferred to Spain.

By close of business on 12 September, €28,186.20, the equivalent of a little over £20,000, was deposited in the Spanish CAM account from Chester. By 19 September, the balance remaining would be just €13.

At the police station in Wrexham, officers previously merely perplexed at the O'Malley's disappearance sat up and took notice. It was plain from the cash card purchases and withdrawals, labelled as 'out of character' by the couple's family, that the O'Malleys had either had their credit cards stolen or had fallen victim to an even more desperate fate. Detective Inspector Nick Crabtree was assigned to the case and immediately began to make renewed contact with the Spanish law enforcement agencies through Interpol.

The mystery of the missing couple was presented to the British public by BBC TV's *Crimewatch*, which resulted in some reports of sightings by the viewers. As concern grew and the mystery deepened, the Welsh police force prepared to open its own missing persons' inquiry in Spain.

The man chosen to head this part of the investigation

was a dedicated, long-serving officer whose steady rise through the ranks had been assured by a dogged dedication to detail. Det Supt Alan Jones had an unassuming and courteous manner that marked him as a gentleman among his colleagues, yet he was renowned among his criminal adversaries for having the tenacity of a bulldog.

Married with a grown-up daughter, Jones was in his late forties and just three years off retirement after 30 years in the force. Alan Jones was the man chosen by fate and circumstances to lead the inquiry that would break the case and bring two evil murderers to justice.

For the O'Malley family, he was to be a white knight. For the Spanish police, he would become a tedious thorn in their side providing a much-needed energy boost to the slow-starting Spanish inquiry. The half-hearted investigation had already stalled in Benidorm due to the national force's reluctance to expend hard-stretched manpower on finding two middle-aged holidaymakers who had probably chosen to prolong their vacation in the sun and had omitted to phone home.

The Welsh inquiry, codenamed Nevada, which would be fully launched in February 2003 when events would cause even the reluctant Spanish authorities to sit up and pay attention, began in Llangollen with a painstaking investigation into the O'Malley's lifestyle. Did they owe money? Were they in any kind of trouble?

Friends and family were questioned at length; their work backgrounds and their finances were the subject of intensive study but each investigating detective returned to Wrexham Police Station with the same impression: Linda and Anthony O'Malley were a couple beyond reproach, loved by their immediate family and respected in the community. Linda was known as an intelligent and competent mother and housewife who held down a responsible administrative position in large retail store.

As for Anthony, he had lovingly restored cars that he had sourced himself, and demonstrated a professional pride that spoke of the old values of craftsmanship and skill now so sadly absent in many of today's industries. The purchasers of these hand-restored classics told of a man dedicated to his work who drove a hard bargain, but who was renowned for his business sense of fairness and honesty. Suppliers also spoke of Anthony's straight dealing, and of bills being paid promptly.

The total picture was of a responsible and intelligent middle-aged couple with the support of a loving circle of relatives. That they would take off into the sunset without a word to a soul was unthinkable to everyone who knew them.

As the reports on the missing couple's lifestyle became monotonously repetitive, Alan Jones realised that the focus of the inquiry should move away from Llangollen and across to Spain.

2

THE WELSH
DRAGON STIRS

Barbara Murphy hadn't been very happy about
reporting the failure of her sister and brother-in-law
to catch their flight back to Manchester after a fortnight's
house-hunting in Spain. True enough, they were a
responsible couple and it was unlikely that the
conscientious Linda would take extra time off work
without a very good reason, but still Barbara had wondered
whether she was over-reacting. But was she?

Linda and Anthony had been due back three days earlier
and there had been no word from them. All of the family
were worried and there had been frantic exchanges of
telephone calls between Barbara's home in Liverpool and
her nieces Jenny and Nicola in Chester and Aldershot. She
had spoken with Anthony's brother Bernard in Widnes and
he had made it plain that he felt something was amiss.

'Anthony wouldn't go off somewhere like that without
phoning home,' he had told her, 'and Lin certainly

9

wouldn't let her bosses down. I think we should make the call, even if it's just to be on the safe side.'

She picked up the telephone and dialled the telephone number of North Wales Police Eastern Divisional Headquarters in Bodhyfryd, Wrexham. Her call was answered almost immediately.

'North Wales Police... how can I help you?'

'Hello? I'd like to report two missing persons,' Barbara said.

★ ★ ★

DS Steve Lloyd was no stranger to September tragedies. In 2001, he had been sent from Wrexham to New York as a family liaison officer to assist grieving British and Commonwealth relatives of the victims of 9/11. He would spend 18 days working in the city between the NYPD information centre at Pier 94 and John F Kennedy Airport, where he and Detective Richard Adamson, a colleague from the Surrey force, would assist 210 grief-stricken relatives of the 58 victims from countries as diverse as Australia, Bermuda, Ireland, India, Pakistan, Sudan and Nigeria.

In 2002, on the anniversary of the tragedy, he had returned to New York again to assist at a memorial service organised by the Red Cross, and had only recently arrived back in Wrexham.

The sadness of that horrific September day in 2001 must have been in his mind on 27 September when he heard that he was assigned as family liaison to the relatives of Anthony and Linda O'Malley. He recalls that his first contact with the family was 'stressful'. With their intimate knowledge of the ultra responsible Linda and

Anthony, the family were already convinced that a great tragedy had befallen them. Steve Lloyd gave thanks for the presence of Bernard O'Malley, whose calm ·and commonsense approach to the mystery helped the detective to prepare the younger family members for what lay ahead.

On the following Monday, Steve Lloyd heard that the investigation was now being viewed as serious by the North Wales Constabulary. In the light of large cash withdrawals and purchases being made on the missing couple's credit cards, the case had been transferred to Det Supt Alan Jones, a senior officer whom Lloyd had long admired. Alan Jones was, Lloyd believed, the man to drive the investigation forward.

Jones was a firm believer in the exploitation of public and media interest in such a case and his first step was to call a press conference at North Wales Police Headquarters in Colwyn Bay. The conference was a huge media draw, with full attendance by both provincial and national press, with eager hacks attracted by the thought of the public interest engendered by a respectable middle-aged couple disappearing on the often luridly portrayed Spanish Costas. This coverage was followed by a *GMTV* live broadcast set up by Wrexham CID from Bernard O'Malley's house in Widnes and a link to the Meliá Hotel in Benidorm where Spanish Property Auctions representative Joanne Miles gave an interview.

On the next day, Tuesday, 30 September, one month exactly after Anthony and Linda O'Malley landed at Málaga airport, DS Steve Lloyd with WPS Sharon McCairn acting as interpreter flew to Alicante to accompany Bernard O'Malley and Linda's eldest daughter Nicola

Welch. The purpose of their visit was to attend a press conference arranged by my newsdesk at *Costa Blanca News* with the co-operation of Benidorm Town Hall press office. The conference, again held at the Meliá Hotel, was attended by both UK and Spanish media and TV cameras from Spain's national Canal One, Valencia's Canal Nueve and the UK's BBC, ITV and *GMTV*.

Meanwhile, DS Lloyd had been accompanied by WPS McCairn for another very good reason. As a fluent speaker of Spanish, the young female officer's job would be to interpret for Lloyd in his mission to open up a line of communication with Spanish national police in Benidorm in tandem with his role as family liaison officer to the two members of the O'Malley family during their stay.

Lloyd's first meeting took place with DCI José (Pepe) Bernal of the Benidorm police force, who was not initially a supporter of the theory that Anthony and Linda O'Malley had been the victims of criminal activity. DCI Bernal's response to the concerns of the Welsh police was that there was no firm evidence that a crime had taken place; the significance of the withdrawals on the bank accounts could be minimised until proved otherwise. People could do what they liked with their own money, couldn't they? This attitude prevailed until a startling breakthrough by the Welsh police over the ensuing six months would cause a dramatic change of heart. But until then, the Spanish police remained adamant that there was little for them to investigate, while they paid partial lip service to DS Lloyd's requests for co-operation.

Although I noticed the absence of the Spanish police at the day of the press conference, I was told by my reporter who was acting as interpreter for Bernard and Nicola that the Spanish police had rather churlishly declared that they were not invited. Perhaps they hadn't received the call but the idea that the Spanish police wouldn't go anywhere they weren't invited was a concept totally alien to me. I would later learn that they had formally refused DS Lloyd's invitation to attend the press conference and meet with Bernard and Nicola.

From their arrival until their return to the UK on 8 October – when they were relieved by DI Nick Crabtree and DC Dave James – DS Lloyd and WPS McCairn spent their days in numerous meetings with Spanish police officers in their efforts to gain local collaboration as the missing persons' inquiry unfolded.

Visits were also made to talk with Hella Henneberke, director of the CAM Bank's international office in Benidorm where Linda and Anthony had opened their non-residential account. They had been assisted on that occasion by Joanne Miles, who had been helping the couple prepare for a bid on an embargoed property advertised in the Spanish Property Auctions' circular, the main incentive for their visit to Spain.

Steve Lloyd would report that he found Ms Henneberke 'initially helpful', an opinion I would be able to verify from my own later experience, but it should be remembered that no one in Spain was obliged to speak to either the Welsh police or me during our often parallel investigations.

Steve Lloyd's warrant card with its *Uned Gwasanaethau Trosedd* announcement that he was a Welsh Criminal Services Division detective was probably of less use in Benidorm than my press card when it came to collaborating with the indigenous population – and nobody was very inclined to speak to me either.

3

ESCAPE TO THE SUN

E very year, approximately 2.1 million people fly into Alicante's El Altet Airport, the gateway to the Costa Blanca. Others arrive further south, at the newly refurbished Pablo Ruiz Picasso Airport of Málaga, which serves the Costa del Sol. Choice of arrival between the two can depend on the cheapest flight or the holidaymaker's charter company, but business is brisk and the highly profitable turnover adds to Spain's impressive tourism revenue of around US$28 billion a year, equivalent to 5.32 per cent of the country's GDP.

Spain has the highest tourism revenues pro rata among the larger EU economies but also possesses the lowest per capita GDP of that sector, although substantially higher than those of Greece or Portugal. Unemployment stands at around 20 per cent.

Charter tourism originated in the 1970s when an average-sized family of two adults and two kids could enjoy a ten-day full board holiday in the then knotted-hanky resorts of Benidorm or Torremolinos for less than £7 a day, including flights from Luton. Now those holidays cost a minimum of £700 as holidaymakers have become more sophisticated in their tastes and expectations have risen.

Along with those changes, the nature of the tourism has become a little more international, with visitors willing to learn a smattering of the language, to shop at the local supermarket and cater for themselves. Out of that scenario has sprung an even more adventurous style of tourist – the expatriate resident.

Since the late 1990s, when Spain's membership of the European Union made it easier for the newly arrived foreigner from within an EU member state to find employment, take out a mortgage, import household goods and buy a car, expatriate residency on the Costa Blanca has risen to an official 200,000. The actual figure is more than double that as some of the more paranoid arrivals avoid becoming part of the system. But the system is welcoming, especially for retirees.

Reciprocal agreements with other EU member states provide free health care for expatriate pensioners and many of the country's 17 autonomous regional governments provide subsidised travel and holidays for the older resident. The climate is warm, food, fuel and alcohol cheap, and the people are generally welcoming. Family and friends in the UK, who might once have been a cause of extreme homesickness, are just a two-hour flight away.

According to the promotional holiday shows and constant TV documentaries, if there's a better place to spend those autumn years together, it appears to around

450,000 expatriates that no one has yet discovered it. Added to this is the bonus that the sale of a property in England, Scotland or Wales will nearly always cover the purchase price of a retirement apartment on the sunny Spanish Costas, which could cost the discerning buyer no more than €150,000 (around £100,000) and leave a comfortable nest egg in the bank.

But life on the Spanish Costas can be frenetic, with the summer population in towns often doubling in the high season, causing house-hunters to try their luck further inland where, despite spiralling land costs due to Spain's ongoing construction boom, small farms and holdings in the Costa's arid rural foothills can be bought for as little as the equivalent of £60,000–£80,000. For the O'Malleys, it would serve as the ideal location for family holidays, and perfect for exercising their dogs.

Many of these rural farming or homestead properties are no longer in commercial use, due to an exodus of rural workers to the factories and offices of the cities. The owners are therefore more than willing to rid themselves of a dusty millstone around their ageing necks for a considerable amount of foreign currency which will allow them to join their offspring in the cities and live comfortably off their windfall.

For the new owner, the bug-filled orange trees become a delight, the stone well a curiosity, the eternal rasp of the cicadas a drowsy symphony. It's called heaven, Costa style, where petrol costs 95c a litre and the sandy beach lapped by warm blue waters is just 5km away. Even better for ageing bones, the sun is always warm and, apart from the months of October and March, there's hardly ever a rain cloud in sight.

Areas of particular interest to would-be buyers are the coastal tracts around Torrevieja, south of Alicante, where the constructors' love of identical house façades must sorely test a drinker trying to find his own front door in the dark. But Torrevieja is already paying a price for its undoubted attractions – the rising crime rate – for the arrival of resident expatriates has drawn hundreds of immigrant malefactors who enjoy rich pickings from the comparatively prosperous newcomers.

Even more attractive for some buyers than the crowded terraces of large modern apartment blocks is the isolated home in the country, bought for a comparative song and offering the tranquillity that everyone seeks in the later years – the bottle of local wine, the balmy night air, the scent of jasmine and the shelter of bougainvillaea-clad walls.

It's hardly a wonder that Anthony and Linda O'Malley, sun lovers and regular visitors to Benidorm and its environs, set their hearts on this area as the ideal site for their eventual retirement. In their case, searching more thoroughly than most, they had discovered the advantages of the stringent Spanish system of property embargo and auction.

Banks that embargo properties for unpaid debts in Spain act within a wide spectrum of a very permissive law. Once embargoed by a court, a property can be seized pending auction and the locks changed, effectively depriving the debtor of access to any personal effects within, including even clothing or a car in the driveway. The only items exempt from embargo are tools necessary for the displaced owner to continue to earn his or her living.

Once bought, many properties continue to be the focus

of court actions against the new owner for the return of personal effects that should not have been included in the sale.

Continuing the roughshod approach, the bank has the legal right to reclaim only its debt of money owed, which may be far less than the property's worth. Bargains abound, but the banks have that sewn up, too. A word to a professional bidder might see other bids warned off and the property sold for a song to be later resold for a massive profit with pockets filled all round, barring those of the original and now dispossessed owner.

Despite the bureaucracy and legal loopholes, thousands of British expatriates have trod this well-worn path without mishap. Anthony and Linda's mistake – if they can be accused of having made one at all – was founded in their good natures and an unfailing trust in their fellow man.

Let's not be cynical in the knowledge of hindsight. 'There but for the grace of God go I... ' might well be one of those phrases that links directly to the lessons surrounding Anthony and Linda's trip, and readers would do well to heed those lessons about trust and apparent bargains that seem just too good to be true. The result of ignoring the warning signs, and choosing to trust rather than to proceed with caution, allowed this ill-fated middle-aged couple to embark on a journey that led them unwittingly to a horrific nightmare in the sun.

4

A DEVOTED COUPLE

A visitor to Llangollen in the picturesque county of Denbighshire, North Wales, might wonder why anyone should choose to leave this small, peaceful Welsh township to settle amid the hustle and bustle of the Mediterranean resorts of southern Spain, or indeed anywhere that didn't enjoy the same rolling green landscape and gentle hills of the Dee Valley.

Llangollen is a small town, almost a village, of barely 3,000 inhabitants. The area is steeped in myth and Arthurian legend, with the hilltop remains of Crow Castle – Castell Dinas Bran to the locals – holding the mystery of being yet another supposed burial site of the Holy Grail, as well as the stronghold of princes and bishops.

In the town's centre stands the scheduled ancient monument of the 14th-century Dee Bridge, and close by is Market Street and the end-of-terrace house at number 38 which the O'Malleys left on their fateful journey to Spain.

Their journey would end on an urbanisation close to the bustling Valencian industrial township of Alcoy which, with its population of almost 70,000, ranks as the sixth most populous town in Alicante Province.

Alcoy also has its legends. In the local countryside one finds the ruins of Iberian settlements and the traveller may well stumble upon prehistoric rock paintings that have survived almost since the birth of mankind.

It's doubtful that Anthony and Linda O'Malley had ever heard of this busy municipality that forms the financial, commercial and cultural centre of the surrounding area. Like most visitors, they would have been more familiar with the popular resorts of Benidorm, Villajoyosa, Altea and Albir. Yet a few kilometres east of the town, they would find a location that, at first, seemed to offer the perfect setting for their dream retirement in the sun.

Baradello (or Varadello) Gelat – the 'B' and 'V' have the same hard phonetic B sound in Spanish and are interchangeable – means 'frozen ledge' in the regional Valencian dialect and forms part of the Sierra Mariola within the Font Roja Nature Park. Alcoy lies at an altitude of nearly 600m above sea level and the Sierra Mariola ascends to nearly 800m. The winter temperature can sink as low as 0°C although it is more likely to be between 5°C and 15°C. In the summer, the extremes of 40°C are usually tempered by the mountain breezes to a much more manageable 30°C; still perhaps too high for Northern European tastes, but enjoyable enough to the sun-loving O'Malleys. Some years, it snows in the city and quite often in the surrounding mountains.

The housing development of Baradello Gelat was developed towards the end of the 20th century, and the emerging environmental lobby made itself felt in the preservation orders served to the developers with regard to the lush pines and evergreen oaks that cover the area. Most villas, therefore, enjoy a literal forest almost up to their verandas and the trees cannot be removed by design-conscious landscapers without special permission from the council and regional Department of the Environment.

But Anthony and Linda O'Malley were drawn to the area not by its beauty but by a weird coincidence – a newspaper advertisement that brought them back into contact with a confidence trickster they had been introduced to by telephone within minutes of their plane landing at Málaga Airport.

The journey that would lead Anthony and Linda O'Malley to their violent deaths in Spain began many years before in the Liverpool area, 1,000 miles to the north. Anthony was born on 19 June 1960 in the suburb of Widnes, which lies south of the famous city near the banks of the Mersey River. His brother Bernard and his sister Christine still live in the area.

Linda O'Malley – née Bishop – was Anthony's elder by 14 years but his equal in her zest for life and in their joint desire to retire eventually to the Spanish Costa Blanca. She was born in the city of Liverpool on 26 February 1946. Perhaps it was the austere regime of food and clothes rationing in the post-war years of her adolescence that awakened in her the desire to live life to the full and enjoy every moment of her existence. Certainly, those who knew her would recall a lively and aware woman, always ready with a smile and a word of comfort or encouragement for her family and for those around her.

By the time they met in 1977 through their work as cashiers at Burtonwood Services in Cheshire, Linda was 31 and Anthony an unworldly yet emotionally mature teenager of 17. Linda was at that time married to Kenneth Stewart, and the couple had two daughters – nine-year-old Nicola, and five-year-old Jenny.

Despite the age gap, Linda and the younger Anthony found peace and solace in each other's company. In Anthony, Linda found a quiet and intelligent young man always ready with a sympathetic ear to listen to her problems and her dreams. In Linda, Anthony, in turn, found a vivacious woman who encouraged his ambition to become a vintage car restorer and shared his hopes and beliefs for the future. To quote those who knew them well at that time, Anthony and Linda 'fitted together like a hand in a glove'.

Linda and her then husband Kenneth Stewart divorced and soon after Linda married Anthony. In 1988, the newly married couple moved in to live with Josephine O'Malley, Anthony's widowed mother in Widnes. By this time, the couple's shared love of the nearby North Wales countryside had led them to plan to set up home in the beautiful Eisteddfod country around the riverside town of Llangollen.

The Eisteddfod of Wales is an annual national festival of folk singing, visual arts, poetry, music, dance, drama, Welsh language, science and technology, elocution and literature, with a changing location each year. The Llangollen International Musical Eisteddfod takes place every year in the town during the second week of July.

In that one week, thousands of singers, dancers and instrumentalists dressed in their national costumes and representing around 50 countries descend on Llangollen to perform on a large stage decorated with 50,000 flowers.

It was in such a setting that those who knew Linda and Anthony O'Malley recall a devoted couple, with Anthony assuming his role as stepfather to Linda's two daughters, both often seen hanging on their new 'dad's' arms as he proudly paraded them, accompanied by a smiling Linda, among the summer crowds visiting the Llangollen Eisteddfod. The girls would remember their stepfather as the 'quiet man', solid and dependable but with a dry sense of humour who, when the fancy took him, could reduce his company to laughter with a wink and a subtle word.

Never forgetting their early wish to retire to the sun, Anthony and Linda became regular travellers to the Mediterranean and their favourite resort of Benidorm. Through sheer hard work and ability, by 1995, the ever-conscientious Linda had found herself promoted to store manager at the Ellesmere Port establishment of TJ Hughes at Mercer Walk. Self-employed car restorer and salesman Anthony had extended his hobby of restoring classic and vintage cars into a full-blown business and was doing well. The time was nearing for that longed-for move south to the sun.

By this time, the industrious couple owned a cottage on the picturesque Horseshoe Pass that curls around the Dee Valley above the market town of Llangollen. As the 20th century gave way to the 21st, they decided on a change of direction. Nicola was now married with her own children and living in Hampshire. The younger Jenny was with her partner John and their children in Chester, and capably in charge of her own life, so perhaps the time had come to look to their own future?

A joint decision was taken to sell the cottage in Horseshoe Pass and move to a more modest home in Llangollen itself, with the profit from the sale going into their jokingly named 'Retirement in the Sun' fund, blissfully unaware that their dream of a blissful retirement would end so suddenly in a horrific nightmare.

The sale of the cottage and the purchase of the end-terrace property at 38 Market Street, Llangollen, left a profit of nearly £50,000 in their joint account with the Yorkshire Bank in Chester. It would be enough, in their opinion, for the down-payment on the purchase of a rural property on the Costa Blanca where inland prices for a modest small farm, or *finca*, were rarely more than £85,000.

Their main concern was to find sufficient land to exercise their two beloved dogs – a Labrador named Blackie and a long-haired Alsatian named Prince – who would share their retirement home. But the down-to-earth O'Malleys had no illusions of early retirement at this stage. The Spanish property would be for family use as a holiday home and they estimated it would be five years before they would contemplate a permanent move from the UK.

During their time at Market Street, Anthony and Linda became well known in the small town, always ready with a smile and a word of greeting for any neighbours they encountered when out walking their dogs.

Anthony was, by nature, a quiet, retiring man, who kept his own counsel. His blue-grey eyes had a piercing quality that some found challenging as they seemed to demand openness and honesty. It was not a bad characteristic for a used-car salesman, but even those qualities would not serve him well in Spain.

He was a popular regular at the bar of the Abbey Grange Hotel just outside Llangollen, where, after a few beers alongside Linda, he would proudly describe his latest vintage acquisition and pass on advice to any in the company who needed to tap into his encyclopaedic knowledge of all things mechanical.

By late summer of 2002, the O'Malleys would spend their weekends poring over estate agents' brochures advertising property on the Costa Blanca, and Linda had taken out a subscription to a newssheet distributed by a Leeds-based company called Spanish Property Auctions. The company based its information on upcoming auctions of property embargoed by Spanish courts for mortgage defaults or other similar debts. Under Spanish law, the properties would be auctioned off at a price to cover only the outstanding debt, which often could be fairly minimal. This meant that there were often bargains to be had. Unfortunately, the process also had pitfalls – the O'Malleys would not be aware of these until later.

One property in particular caught their eye. It was a *finca*, or smallholding, with 3,000 square metres of rural farmland at Cami de Hospital in the area of Partida Chica Moratella, in the arable but arid flatlands between the sierras and the coastal town of Villajoyosa. The reserve price was set at 200,000 pesetas, equivalent to £80,000, and they would need to lodge 30 per cent of the reserve price, around £26,000, with the court-appointed bankers before the auction, scheduled for 23 September, took place.

They were both aware that prices were beginning to rise in southern Spain as the constructors moved in, borne on the tidal wave of the residential tourism boom. The opportunity was too good to miss. The excess on the property would be paid for by the sale of the Market Street home.

The dogs were inoculated in preparation for their eventual trip to Spain, a veterinary process that had to be carried out six months prior to the move. Daughter Jenny and her partner John moved into the end-terrace dwelling at 38 Market Street with their two young sons to look after the animals. A telephone call was made to Spanish Property Auctions, who arranged a meeting for the O'Malleys with the Benidorm representative, Joanne Miles, for 2 September. The flights were booked on a Thomas Cook JMC overnight charter to Málaga for 30 August, where the couple planned to hire a car and drive to Benidorm, taking advantage of the 500km journey to look at other possible properties on the route.

At a *bon voyage* drink in the bar of the Abbey Grange Hotel the night before their departure, an exuberant Anthony O'Malley lifted his glass and told the company he would see them in a fortnight 'with the keys'. Cheers of encouragement greeted his toast.

It was the last time their family and neighbours would see the couple alive. Within a week of their arrival at Málaga's Pablo Ruiz Picasso Airport, Linda and Anthony O'Malley would literally disappear off the face of the Earth.

5

THE SEARCH BEGINS

B efore September 2002, I'd never heard of Anthony and Linda O'Malley; over the next seven months, I would eat, drink and breathe their disappearance. It would take me into the underworld of the Costa Blanca's best-known and best-loved resort of Benidorm and up into the lonely *sierras* beyond. I would pace out lonely farm trails and examine rusting water tanks; I would work with mediums. My life and that of my wife would be repeatedly threatened. All of these are undeniably stressful events, but occurrences common enough in my daily working life. I am a freelance investigative journalist working crime-ridden southern and eastern Spain from Gibraltar to Valencia.

When the O'Malley story broke, I was holding down the twin jobs of deputy to the CB News Group Executive Editor and that of News Editor at *Costa Blanca News*, the leading weekly of the news group in southern Spain.

Located on a commercial estate in Finestrat on the southern border of Benidorm, the two-storey offices and print room received a regular daily supply of the joy and misery of expatriate life on the Costa. Birthdays, weddings, anniversaries, robberies, murder, burglaries and property scams – I had seen them all, including hungover Brits who simply missed the flight home. Some of these eventually turned up alive and well after waking up on a beach in Marbella or in a Barcelona fleshpot, while their family worried at home. Some were never seen alive again, appearing only as decomposed corpses discovered by walkers in the rugged coastal countryside. How did they die? Who knew? And, increasingly, the hard-pressed national constabulary seemed to care less and less about another missing foreigner. It was the Costa Blanca's regular headache.

Every year, police statistics show that, even in the UK, a quarter of a million people go missing and 16,000 of them are never heard of again. Many of those who don't return are suicides. In Spain, the number is only slightly lower in a nation that has only two thirds of the total of the combined population of England, Scotland and Wales; this anomaly is due to the transient expatriate population. Sun, sea, sand and sex are a heady combination in which to lose one's self and forget the problems of Blighty.

I still have cases on file that relate to young men who never returned to the UK after a week or two on the Costas and of expatriates who disappeared after driving a friend to the airport. Most have never been solved.

Leicester single parent Derek Cross never returned from a night on the town in Benidorm on 18 November 1996. His travelling companions spoke of a wild, drunken night of carousing in which Cross was last seen asleep in a rubbish skip. Their stories were discounted by the police and all were questioned under caution. Someone, somewhere, knows what happened to Derek Cross, yet he has never been traced, despite his parents distributing more than 100,000 leaflets along the Costa del Sol and Costa Blanca. His son Spencer, now fourteen-years-old, sits at home pining for his dad and waiting for the telephone to ring and announce his homecoming.

Mentally handicapped Jeffrey Hodgson from Stockport was 38 when he went missing on a dark, windy night in rock-rimmed Calla Llonga, Ibiza, after an argument with his parents. Jeffrey had supposed his long-suffering parents would take him to his much loved resort of Benidorm where he had many friends among hotel staff. Instead, he found himself on Ibiza and reacted violently, storming out of the hotel and into an unseasonable dark and rainy night.

The search was called off after three days and his skeleton was found by hill walkers a year later, 2km above the hotel where he had been staying with his parents. The skull bore fractures which could have occurred in a fall, but could equally have been caused by a blow from an attacker wielding a large rock. How a man with the mental age of eight could climb a steep, rocky hill in pitch darkness was never discussed.

His father Derek told me, 'Jeffrey was totally uncoordinated in his hands and feet. When I took him to football to see his favourite team Stockport County, I always had to help him up the tiers.' The verdict was accidental death.

Against the newspaper group's publishing policy, which always sought to avoid reports of doom and gloom, I had followed some of these tragic stories to their conclusions, interviewing relatives and witnesses and always seeking a response from the expatriate community. I've worked with Paul Kenyon – of the BBC's *Kenyon Confronts* – bearding property fraudsters and dodgy real estate agents in their homes and offices, and I've slunk around Benidorm with Yorkshire Television filming an undercover exposé on crooked money exchangers for a *Package Holiday – Undercover* documentary. My reports have exposed timeshare conmen and dodgy builders and I've awoken in the early hours of the morning to listen to the shattering of glass as yet another frustrated villain takes out his revenge on my car's rear window.

Often in confrontation with my employers, I saw the journalist's role in Spain as a unique conduit through which information could flow to the investigators, unhampered by problems either of language or the foreigner's dislike for the police, who still carried the taint of Franco's rigid regime.

Without doubt, the Spanish Old Bill themselves are responsible for this attitude. As I've stressed earlier, they don't want to know. Certainly, my efforts to pass on information, as in the case of one particularly complicated murder, were met with petulance. Who was my informant? How dare I refuse to reveal my source? Did I know I myself could be arrested?

One example of my efforts, coupled with the local police response, perhaps illustrates this point most clearly. A letter was sent to me from Portugal as a result of my report on the discovery of a battered body found in Santa Pola. From the letter, I was able to identify the body, but the ensuing investigation was eventually buried five years later with the victim never being officially named. Yet I had at some risk supplied the Guardia Civil with the name of the victim, the alleged killer, and the man behind the killing, a cuckolded husband living in Estepona, who had ordered the contract.

The police accepted my identification of the body – I even had photographs of the victim when alive – but it would have meant extending enquiries to the UK, since all the parties involved were English. That would have meant the bureaucratic and time consuming process of going through Interpol, since that's the way collaboration by international police forces has to work. The case is still officially unsolved and the deceased's family has never been informed.

With all this in mind, perhaps at this point it would be appropriate to explain the differences between the branches of the Spanish constabulary. Towns and cities with populations of 20,000 and over are the domains of the National Police Force. Smaller towns and villages have their own local municipal police force under the control of the mayor, and this is responsible for traffic control and the enforcement of local ordinances.

The Guardia Civil is a rural paramilitary force responsible for civil order and enforcing the law beyond city boundaries. The force has barracks in all small communities. Much feared during the reign of Franco, whose 36-year dictatorial regime they enforced rigidly, the *civiles* have toned down their act, although the sight of a brace of armed *guardias* at a roadside checkpoint is still enough to make brave men sit up and concentrate on the road ahead. It was men from this force, led by Lieutenant-Colonel Antonio Tejero Molina, who stormed the Madrid

Spanish Parliament in February of 1981, demanding an end to the fledgling democracy that had followed Franco's death six years earlier.

In the case of Anthony and Linda O'Malley, the official opinion of Benidorm National Police, the force immediately responsible for an inquiry, was that the missing couple had gone off elsewhere on a whim and neglected to inform their family. They would eventually come to their senses and ring home or they would be found some months later sitting on a beach in Málaga sipping margueritas and watching the sunset. Wasn't that always the way of foreigners in Spain?

Insistence that the missing couple were sensible middle-aged parents and responsible adults who wouldn't miss their homebound flight and fail to return an overdue hired car without a very good reason fell on deaf ears among the Spanish constabulary.

Back in the UK, it was a different story. A worried family member had contacted the North Wales Police. The couple had failed to turn up at Málaga airport for their charter flight home on 13 September. Anthony's credit card had been used to make some 'uncharacteristic purchases' and had been blocked by the Yorkshire Bank until a telephone call from Anthony himself had explained they were 'fitting out' their new home.

Of even more concern was that the ever-conscientious Linda had failed to turn up for her work as manager at the Ellesmere Port discount retail store of TJ Hughes, where colleagues expressed their disbelief that she would leave them in the lurch without a word. A fellow worker was even more adamant when interviewed: 'That's not Linda,' she told me. 'Wild horses wouldn't keep her away from the job she loved. I've hardly ever known her take a day off sick, let alone overstay a holiday.'

A missing persons' inquiry was eventually launched and the UK press picked up the story. Eventually, word reached me at my news desk in Finestrat through a colleague on a UK daily. Anthony's brother Bernard and Linda's elder married daughter by a previous marriage would be arriving in Benidorm accompanied by two North Wales family liaison officers and could we feed back copy?

From the news desk, we arranged a press conference at Hotel Meliá, probably the first ever held in southern Spain dealing with missing Brits, courtesy of Benidorm Town Hall. It was heavily attended by both Spanish and UK press, including the BBC. We even supplied an interpreter in the form of a *CBN* reporter, Jaime Garrigós Parkes. The Spanish police failed to appear, later claiming that they hadn't been informed.

Bernard O'Malley and Linda's daughter, Nicola Welch, had been painfully unprepared for a press conference. They could only tell the assembled journalists that Anthony and Linda had flown overnight to Spain from Manchester on 30 August, hoping to bid at auction for a villa they had seen in an advertising circular. The last call home had been at 8.30pm on 4 September.

I asked if they had a photograph of the missing couple. They had three but no extra copies had been printed for the press. Later, I moved closer to Nicola and made to slip her my card. My move was blocked by DS Steve Lloyd, one of the accompanying Welsh detectives, who would become a mainstay of the investigation. But his move to block me had not been foolproof; I'd learned a few tricks of my own. My card disappeared into Nicola's pocket.

Nonetheless, the family were warned off and she never contacted me.

It seemed at that time that the blanket of silence encouraged by the Spanish police had already been taken up by the Welsh contingent, whose members were obviously anxious not to upset the host force. However, in the case of the missing O'Malleys, it went even deeper.

During occasional visits to the Costa Blanca to further their missing persons' inquiry, Welsh police were unable to convince their Spanish colleagues of the suspicious circumstances involved in the disappearance. The result was that no Spanish police officer was involved in the investigation until February 2003, when the UK Police Intelligence Unit traced the kidnappers to Valencia.

With the Welsh inquiry based in Wrexham and Colwyn Bay, no local information was available to the expatriate press, which, after all, had the ear of the foreign community among which the missing O'Malleys had undoubtedly moved.

This unfortunate lack of contact with the press would later delay the arrests of Anthony and Linda's killers by months, although it couldn't delay the victims' fates. The date of the press conference was 2 October, and the trail was already cold. Linda and Anthony O'Malley had been dead for at least a fortnight.

6

A MAJOR INCIDENT

DS Steve Lloyd and WPS Sharon McCairn, the family liaison officers who had accompanied the two family members to Benidorm, flew back to Wales on Tuesday, 8 September, leaving DI Nick Crabtree and DC Dave James as replacements to continue with their failed attempt to stir the Benidorm National Police into action.

Back in Wrexham, they found that an MIR – a police abbreviation for a Major Incident Room – had been set up at the headquarters and enquiries were now proceeding regarding the missing couple's bank accounts, spending and telephone calls, as well as any other relevant pieces of information.

Later, Welsh police would discover that Anthony made three mobile telephone calls from Málaga Airport soon after the couple's arrival. It is interesting to note that no calls were previously made from the couple's UK landline to any of those numbers. To my mind, this proves beyond doubt that Anthony O'Malley first became aware of the existence of those numbers after his flight had landed in Spain.

Here we must acknowledge the existence of someone at the airport who passed on the numbers to the new arrivals. I would later place a man I shall call Hal Edwards at the scene, a known hustler, whose wife would later be seen by a female informant driving the O'Malley's hired Fiat Stilo in La Nucía near Benidorm on 1 September.

Apart from a background check to unearth any reason why Linda and Anthony O'Malley should decide to defect from their home and family, Welsh police now had to consider the possibility that the couple had come to harm in Spain. DNA samples were taken from Bernard O'Malley and Linda's daughters Jenny and Nicola.

Such is the time when family liaison officers come into their own; for the family of a missing person, a request for DNA is potentially the prelude to the most serious of incidents, and the possible death of loved ones. Steve Lloyd needed all his training and diplomacy to explain the need to the donors.

Dental records for Anthony O'Malley were also obtained and all the collected data was forwarded via Interpol to Spain for inclusion in the international database which stores information and makes it readily available to police forces seeking a match for an unidentified body.

Eerily, although it could not have occurred to those involved in the case at the time, the Spanish international database is called 'Fenix', a name whose English counterpart of 'Phoenix' would herald a longed-for breakthrough when all hope of finding the couple had faded.

Help was also being sought from the media both in

Spain and the UK. Reports of the couple's disappearance had appeared briefly in the Spanish press but, just as the nationality of the missing couple stirred interest in the provincial English-language newspapers, it equally fostered disinterest among Spanish editors, who believed they had regional and national stories of far more interest to their readers.

Even at *Costa Blanca News* I had difficulty convincing my executive editor that the story should hold the front page for more than one edition. Barring my own conclusions, which had been influenced by my conversation with Anthony's brother and Linda's daughter at the press conference, the general consensus of opinion around the news desk was that Anthony O'Malley was probably somewhere in France with a much younger lover and his wife's body was at the bottom of a ravine off the motorway to the French border. Oddly, no one accused Linda of murdering Anthony, which I suppose must say something about the expectations of our society.

Sightings were being reported to my office from all points of mainland Spain and the Continent, identifying the missing couple as a pair spotted drinking coffee in Marbella or boarding the Baleares ferry in Denia or Barcelona. The Welsh officers manning the Major Incident Room in Wrexham were also ever mindful of the old coppers' adage that a crime not solved in 48 hours will probably never result in the file being closed. But hope was briefly stirred by the possible sighting of the O'Malleys' hire car near Málaga.

A BBC *Crimewatch* programme broadcast on 24 October featured DI Nick Crabtree, Bernard O'Malley and Linda's younger daughter, Jenny Stewart. At the end of the programme, a beaming DI Crabtree reported the sighting of a blue car among trees at the side of the N-340, the highway that the O'Malleys would have taken to return to Málaga on 13 September. It was a brief flash of hope in what seemed an increasingly impossible case, but it was short lived. A local police patrol was dispatched to the area but the car, if it were ever there, had disappeared from sight.

But cruel fate had not finished with the despairing family waiting for news in Widnes. Just before a dismal Christmas approached, Anthony's surviving brother and sister, Bernard and Christine, suffered the tragic loss of their mother, Josephine O'Malley, a sweet, elderly lady worried into her grave by the disappearance of her son and daughter-in-law in a foreign land.

Josephine O'Malley was buried on 10 December 2002 at the local Catholic church. It was another bitter blow to the family and a sad event that made the Welsh detectives at Wrexham even more determined to unravel the mystery facing them.

Det Supt Alan Jones was now convinced that the inquiry in Wales had run its course and that the focus of the investigation now needed to be shifted to Spain.

Determined to convince the Spaniards of the need for their co-operation in the search for the O'Malleys, Alan Jones and Steve Lloyd flew to Spain from Manchester Airport on 2 February 2003, passing over Valencia, unaware that the puzzle was about to unravel before them because of the actions of a man who was considering his next option in a southern suburb of the city 35,000 feet below.

7

STEPPING ON A GRAVE

A week after the couple's arrival in Benidorm, Anthony
O'Malley sat with his wife in the hot morning sun
in the café-lined Calle Ibiza in Benidorm, the town to
which they had returned to rent a small self-catering
apartment after checking out of the Altaya Hotel in Altea
on 4 September. Money wasn't an immediate problem but
their house-hunting budget would be called upon to lodge
Anthony in the area until 23 September, the day he
planned to attend the Villajoyosa auction with SPA
representative Joanne Miles and secure their longed for
retirement property.

They had seen Joanne Miles the day before, sitting with
clients on the terrace of the Meliá Hotel when they came
out of the Plus supermarket opposite with their self-
catering purchases. Anthony had waited with the bags by
the car while Linda had crossed the road to tell Joanne they
would meet up with her on the following Tuesday to pick

up their NIF (Fiscal Identity Number) documentation from the National Police Foreigners' Office in Calle Apolo XI.

It was an appointment they were not to keep.

Anthony opened the Friday copy of *Costa Blanca News* that he'd just bought from a nearby newsstand and, out of habit, turned to the small ads property section. Opposite him at the shaky wrought-iron table, Linda tried to avoid her coffee slopping on to her breakfast croissant as her husband suddenly changed the position of his elbows and straightened in his chair.

'Hey, look at this, Lin... ' He turned the newspaper around and, with his thumb, indicated an advertisement in the centre of the page. 'Bloody hell... this looks good. 4,000 square metres, two bedrooms, pine trees and mains water and electricity. It's got a mobile number. Shall we give it a call?'

Linda read the advertisement to herself then shrugged. 'Where's Bocayrent?'

Anthony shrugged in turn and picked up his mobile from the table. 'Only one way to find out,' he said.

There was a mild disappointment. The man who answered the call and gave his name as David regretted that an appointment had already been made for that morning with another person anxious to view the villa. Could he call them back later that afternoon?

Anthony gave him his mobile number and closed the phone. 'You never know, love,' he patted Linda's hand, 'we might be in luck and it'd save all this fooling about with an auction.'

Anthony O'Malley had felt despondent when an escorted trip inland to a decrepit farm property in the rural flatlands behind Villajoyosa had not proved worth their time. The farm buildings, whose rusting iron frames had been scattered on a rise of land leading to a dusty row of vines, had been in dire need of repair. The promised swimming pool had turned out to be a cement-lined box sunk into the ground and no more than 3m long. Water to serve the household was collected in a rain depository or had to be brought in by container lorry. Now he seemed reanimated by the thought of finding a viable property.

Linda smiled in response to her husband's sudden lift of spirit. 'But we've been warned about private sales – we should go through an agent or a solicitor.'

'Ay, you're right,' her husband agreed, 'but it'll do no harm to look, will it?'

'No, love,' Linda smiled at his eager expression, 'it'll do us no harm at all.'

★ ★ ★

The call from David came just after 1.30pm. He hadn't liked the first would-be buyer and would be happy for them to drive over that afternoon. The villa wasn't exactly in 'Bocayrent' but nearer to Alcoy. He would meet them in front of the stationers at the foot of the Fernando Reig cable bridge in the middle of Alcoy.

Anthony scribbled down directions from David and took the car to a Benidorm service station to top up the tank. Bank records would show that the card transaction for ?30 worth of petrol took place at 1.55pm. They would make the 100km drive to Alcoy after lunch. Avoiding the more direct but mountainous route over the rugged *sierras*, the journey would take a little more than an hour.

Meanwhile, in number 7 of the tree-lined Calle Roure on the Baradello Gelat urbanisation, David and Matthew had already put their sinister plan into action. The former had contrived to have a fierce argument with his wife and brother-in-law that had ended with the bemused woman leaving the villa. Acting out his pretended anger, David in turn had gathered up his three daughters and mother-in-law and driven them to the rented apartment in Valencia, which the entire family had occupied before moving into the villa in Alcoy in the previous month.

By the time that Linda and Anthony O'Malley met up with the man who introduced himself as David Velázquez at the Fernando Reig Bridge in Alcoy, the house had, in any event, been cleared of any potential witnesses, including the children. Even the property behind number 7 that shared a communal drive with the villa was empty. The owner was to comment later to me in an interview that he and his family had been absent 'throughout the tragedy'.

Anthony's smile as he brought the Fiat to a stop outside the villa must have been beatific. The white-walled, box-like property was fronted by a raised veranda, hidden from the road that passed by the rear of the villa.

The pine trees and occasional Holm Oaks were scattered in clumps across the lot's 4,000 square metres and the business-minded Anthony may even have sized up the surplus land for the building of an eventual garage workshop for the repair and restoration of his beloved vintage cars.

A dark-blue metal plaque screwed to the perimeter wall announced the address as Carrer Roure 7. 'Carrer Roure' in the regional Valencian dialect means 'Street of Oaks', referring to the evergreen holm oaks indigenous to the area.

Linda, too, would have been enthusiastic. 'So much room for the dogs to run,' she may well have happily pointed out to Anthony.

'Ay, and so many trees as well,' one can imagine him adding with an impish grin.

It can certainly be assumed by a conversation that I later had with the earlier house-hunter that Matthew wasn't introduced at that first meeting. Douglas Eames, the first caller, recalled, 'When I pulled up outside the property, a younger man was working near the pool with a hosepipe. The man who guided me from Alcoy said he was the gardener. In any event, the villa wasn't what I was looking for, so I thanked him and drove off.'

Mr Eames, who would later make a statement to Benidorm police after his wife telephoned me following a newspaper article I wrote on the murders, has never understood what prompted him to drive away without even exiting his vehicle. He realises it was probably the luckiest day of his life.

Ushered inside, the prospective buyers would have made an inspection tour of the property, encouraged by the solicitous David, and enjoyed a celebratory glass of wine with their future captor before agreeing to take up his offer to return early the next morning after 'sleeping on the idea of signing a contract'.

At Linda's certain insistence, David would have agreed that everything would go through a lawyer, whom they would all visit in Alcoy on the Monday. Meanwhile, would they not accept his offer for them to move in the next day with their luggage and get the feel of their new home since he and his family were now living in Valencia? It would, David would have assured them both, save all those tiresome return journeys between Alcoy and Benidorm, plus their accommodation bills in Benidorm since the villa was now unoccupied.

This seems to be the only possible explanation why the victims' suitcases were found by police at the Valencia apartment, stored, to his own eventual downfall, by the magpie-like David. As investigators would realise, one hardly carried luggage when viewing a property.

One wonders if, as the couple returned to their car that warm September evening, they didn't feel an involuntary shiver. Just as if they had walked over their own graves.

★ ★ ★

Nine days later, alarmed by the lack of contact – Linda's last telephone call to her family was at 8.30pm on 4 September – Linda's married sister, Barbara Murphy, reported to North Wales Police that the couple had failed to return from a two-week holiday in Spain. The date was 16 September. The last reported sighting of Anthony and Linda had been by Joanne Miles in Benidorm on 6 September.

8

SETTING THE SCENE

It may come as a surprise to those reading this account that there is little liaison between the investigating authorities and the press in Spain. Sadly, in general, the police don't want to know.

It's the same attitude seen with police in other European nations, including Britain, when a citizen takes, to coin a phrase, 'the law into his own hands'. They are the experts, after all, aren't they? They don't take kindly to the public 'taking the law into their own hands'. Ask Tony Martin.

In Spain, the press are regarded as pariahs by the law-and-order boys. It's all part of the Spanish psyche, of which the most important ingredient is *pundonor*, a macho Spanish concept meaning 'a matter of honour' or pride.

Among ordinary Spaniards, a favour is highly prized – provided it goes without saying that it wasn't really needed. No man is so poor that he needs your loan, but thank you, he will accept it in order not to offend you. And the favour must be returned tenfold.

Such a concept doesn't occur in the philosophy of the Spanish police, be they Guardia Civil, national or local constabulary. To the guardians of law and order in Spain, *pundonor* means they're perfectly capable of solving the case without outside help.

This attitude even extends to poor collaboration between provinces. It is not unknown for a criminal to abscond while on bail, but such is the reluctance of magistrates to imprison offenders on remand that even those with no fixed abode are given non-conditional bail. The result is that few present themselves for trial and, instead, move to another province where, thanks to the absence of a central information system, they are not the subject of an arrest warrant. Thus criminals, especially immigrants, are free to move around Spain from town to city, always one step ahead of the law.

With regard to liaison with the public, once a case is handed over, it becomes police property. It may be your wife who's been murdered, but you've lost her. You'll be kept at a distance until the investigators hand their findings to the Public Prosecutor, when the police withdraw their involvement. Meanwhile, no press conferences will be called, no descriptions released, no family liaison officer appointed, no public appeal launched.

In Spain, the role of family liaison officer, one which figures greatly in this story of the North Wales Police's close contact with the relatives of Linda and Anthony throughout, is virtually unknown. Under Spanish law, a policeman will not even reveal his name to you and is not allowed to comment on a case without the express permission of his superior officer, who will equally refuse to release information without the permission of his boss... and so it goes on.

Names of criminals and their victims appear in the Spanish press identified only by their initials. 'M de M has been charged with the murder of JV' doesn't make for gripping reading.

The most frustrating aspect of this refusal to communicate with the public, which is immediately apparent to visitors to Spain, is that few police stations provide a translator service. While it may be true that foreigners in Spain should learn the language, most of them don't. And it's even worse for residents, where reporting a crime can be a dire experience for expatriates who find it much easier to confide in an English-speaking reporter. While it's true you won't find many Spanish speakers among police in a nick in Wigan, Spain should take into account that its main industry is tourism, with British holidaymakers its biggest customers.

I once wrote to the Alicante Commander of the Guardia Civil, pointing out that, as a local newspaper news editor, I had personally helped their officers in a number of cases, including the identification of two cadavers, by passing them information supplied by the expatriate public. I asked him why our Spanish-owned English language newspaper wasn't even on his mailing list?

I eventually began to receive a fairly regular and irrelevant flow from the Commandancia of arrests made and weekly crime statistics. M de M was still murdering JV in various scenarios. No help in an inquiry was ever sought, no photo of a missing person ever released to my office.

Unfortunately, this error of judgement was compounded by the prevailing attitudes and working practices of the English-language press in southern Spain. It may also have been true in the north for all I know, but it was on Spain's southern Mediterranean seaboard that I saw it at its most dire.

There, any mention of investigative reporting was met with a quizzically raised eyebrow and a knowledgeable smirk by the proprietors. The truth is that many senior editorial staff were untrained expatriates who had drifted through newspaper staff advertisements into a form of pseudo journalism from previous employment in offices, shops or waiting on tables. It was a classic case of the chronically myopic ineptly leading the congenitally short-sighted.

The advertisement-hungry proprietors added to the myth by presuming that the sole role of journalists was to write on the back of advertisements. Wire services were often seen as too expensive and shunned. Instead, reports were lifted and copied from publications of the underpaid Spanish press such as *Información* and *El Mundo* and translated into English copy by deskbound translators whose total experience of investigative journalism may have been a telephone call to confirm the description of a lost dog. The news was not always accurate, because the Spanish attitude to journalism also denied investigative reporting. Spanish journalists printed what the authorities let them see and that's what ended up in the local English-language press.

A running joke among the industry's few professionals was the one about 'DRAINS IN DENIA', a coastal resort up the coast from Benidorm that is constantly upgrading its waste water drainage system. 'DRAINS IN DENIA' was always a big story that could fill a front page and required little thought to string together.

Were there more interesting stories to follow? Of course there were – expatriates who murdered their partners, both male and female; young men who disappeared on holiday; private old people's homes run on a shoestring by exploitive owners; drugs and prostitution; and misappropriation of NGO charity funds.

Such stories emanated from the foreign communities and, as such, were seen by the Spanish press as of little interest to its readers and given only a grudging few column inches. Only occasionally were they picked up by the UK national red-tops through an observant local stringer, in which case the local English-language publications were stirred into copying week-old English text instead of translating it from the Spanish.

This is not a direct criticism of the English-language press in Spain. In a non-conformist sort of way, I earn a living from it and I'm grateful. As we move deeper into the 21st century, attitudes are changing. For example, in 2006, *Costa Blanca News* and its associate newspapers were bought by an international media group and have since seen vigorous and welcome changes in editorial management and staff training. All I'm doing here is setting the scene of the 2002–03 O'Malley investigation in context.

But it is a fact that those who printed expatriate newspapers in Spain saw themselves as solely providing a much-needed service by bridging the language gap with regard to local events, the weather, and clinically sterilised petty crime reports…and, lest we forget, drains in Denia.

Yet in September 2002, into this long-established culture of cards held tight to the chest, poor institutional motivation and inter-departmental rivalries, North Wales' police officers were about to launch their own missing persons' inquiry.

9

THE CELLAR

It had been a pleasant morning. They had arrived early and had now left David in the villa to walk together among the trees. Matthew the gardener had waved and smiled at them and they had nodded in response.

Linda had plans for a garden; she missed her flowers and plants left behind when they had sold the property in the picturesque Horseshoe Pass above Llangollen to move to the smaller end-terrace in the town. Now she could imagine blazes of colour from the iridescent blue Jacaranda trees and the purple and yellow bougainvillaea, although she doubted whether either would grow at the higher altitudes of Alcoy.

Never mind, there would be something available, perhaps roses and daffodils to remind them both of their adopted homeland of Wales. David had told her they could expect snow in the winter. Just imagine – white Christmases in sunny Spain! Who'd have thought it?

On the drive over from Benidorm that morning, she grudgingly admitted to herself that David had been right about them staying in Alcoy. Even after Wales, the road between the coast and Alcoy was a rugged switchback of sharp bends and narrow passes. There was a more direct route north across the Sierra de Carrasqueta, but the man at the service station yesterday had waggled his hand and blown on his fingers. *'Para las cabras,'* he had said – 'for the goats'.

Yesterday evening, David had seemed in a hurry, explaining that he had to drive back to Valencia that night, but today he seemed content to tell them stories of Alcoy, how beautiful the snow was in winter and of the magnificent Moors and Christians Fiesta held each April. How the family would enjoy that!

They had planned to go into town for lunch, but David and Matthew had insisted on preparing a barbecue for them on the veranda. They had also talked at length about how they should pay for the villa, which David had assured them was theirs for immediate possession, explaining that he and his family used it merely as a *casa del campo*, a summer retreat. He had questioned her husband at length on their finances and, after a few glasses of David's potent *sangría* over the meal, Anthony had been happy to convince him that sufficient funds for the total cash payment were residing in the English bank and could be transferred within 24 hours.

David had seemed very content on hearing that and had asked them about their home in Llangollen. Yes, they'd sell that later, Anthony had explained, to give them an added retirement nest egg. Linda had felt uncomfortable at Anthony's frankness regarding their finances. Surely it was enough to tell David they could pay for the villa with no problem? Anthony, she decided, was getting a bit too garrulous with the wine. She'd tell him when they were alone in the bedroom that afternoon.

She had had a slight headache before lunch and decided to stay at the villa and sort out their suitcases rather than accompany Anthony and David in her husband's plans to become acquainted with the neighbourhood. Before lunch, she thought, she would ring home and tell the girls the good news.

She had left the mobile with her handbag and their cases in the bedroom but now it had gone. Anthony had his own so surely he wouldn't have taken it. The villa didn't have a telephone. David had assured them there would be no delay in getting a line in but, as a marketing consultant, he preferred not to be disturbed when spending leisure time with his family. She decided to wait until Anthony returned.

She could tell by Anthony's flushed face that he had been drinking. He smiled at her with that big characteristic grin she knew so well and swept her into his arms.

'It's all settled, my love,' he told her. 'We're speaking to the lawyers tomorrow.'

David beamed and nodded behind him. 'Wonderful, isn't it? I think this calls for a special drink.'

During the meal, she began to feel tired and light-headed. Anthony visibly dozed once or twice and she had to shake him awake. She had drunk only one glass of the *sangría*, a red wine and lemonade mixture with fruit juice and a liberal dash of spirits mixed by David in the kitchen as Matthew the gardener, now introduced as David's brother-in-law, had fired up the charcoal barbecue and laid out the meal. She noticed the other men hadn't touched the *sangría* and decided she'd had enough herself. Anthony had dropped off to sleep opposite her.

She was surprised when David stood up and shook him roughly by the shoulder. 'Come on, Anthony, it's time to see the cellar.'

Anthony opened one eye and waved David away. 'T'morrow,' he said.

'No, I said now,' said David roughly and pulled him to his feet. Anthony swayed on his feet and Matthew took his other arm. Suddenly, Anthony waved his arms and shrugged himself loose.

'What's going on?' he demanded. His eyes widened at the sight of the pistol that had appeared in David's podgy hand.

David waved the gun at Linda. 'You first, Linda dear, around to the side of the house and down the steps... we'll bring your husband along, never fear.'

'Why the cellar?' she said fearfully, but she already knew. She had told Anthony of her doubts and mistrust of the men on the journey over, but he had insisted she was wrong. They'd had one of their very rare arguments about it, and he had told her it was a chance in a lifetime to get the home they wanted. She had acquiesced. But now?

She was pushed down the stairs as the two men fought with the still struggling Anthony and then David barged her aside to push open the cellar door. He switched on a dim light at an outside switch near the door and she saw they were in a confined space of barely 6ft across and 6ft high, forming a narrow corridor under the veranda. A small barred and netted window was above to her right, level with the ground outside. Two iron-framed single beds stood nose to tail along the length of the cellar. Each bore a mattress and a single blanket.

Anthony was bundled past her and thrown on to the furthest bed and she stood frozen to the spot as David snapped a handcuff on to her husband's wrist. She knew she should run – but to where? Before she could force her legs to move, she was dragged on to the second bed and she felt the cold steel snap shut around her left wrist.

Anthony was attempting to rise, dragging the bed frame with him as he struggled to get at their captors. He was screaming and shouting unintelligibly in a terrible rage, but David lifted what looked like a stick from a corner and poked at him. Anthony screamed and collapsed to the floor, the bed frame scraping across the rough cement floor as his knees buckled.

David then turned to her and touched her with the stick. A bolt of lightning seemed to shoot through her body and she felt the most incredible pain. She was aware of Matthew's grinning face in the light of the dim bulb. She thought her heart would stop its wild beating there and then.

'So,' said David, spitting out his words, 'the party's over and you'll both fucking behave or you'll get more of this.' He waved the cattle prod at them. Anthony swore and attempted to lunge forward again, but this time David turned the cattle prod on Linda. She screamed and writhed with the agony of it.

David's fleshy face was like stone. 'You see, Anthony, you foolish English cunt? If you don't behave, your wife gets the cattle prod. Do you understand, you stupid bastard? Now, you're both going to stay here and make no noise. Any trouble and I'll kill one of you.' He waved both the prod and the pistol for emphasis, then continued harshly, 'All we want is your money. Think about it. We'll be down to have a chat about that in the morning. Meanwhile, we'll have the PIN numbers of your cards.'

Anthony again swore viciously and David swung the cattle prod once more in Linda's direction. She cried out and recoiled across the mattress but Anthony was already shouting a series of numbers at the fat Venezuelan. David turned and pointed to the door, which Matthew opened and exited.

Anthony raised himself from the floor and stood watching the fat man. Defiance had gone; he wanted no more harm to come to Linda. 'Let her go and you can have the lot,' he offered.

'Get me all the money and you can both go,' David sneered back at him. 'But until then, you stay here... get the message?'

He followed Matthew through the door and they both heard the lock snap closed and a key turned. The light went out.

'Oh, God... Anthony,' whispered Linda, 'what have we got ourselves into?'

'Don't worry, love. They just want the money,' he told her. 'How could I have been so bloody stupid?' He rattled the handcuff against the bed frame in anger.

'We'll be all right, Anthony. It's not your fault, don't blame yourself, love, we'll get out of this somehow,' she whispered into the darkness.

Anthony didn't reply and she felt her own adrenalin fade throughout her system as sleep and the drugged wine overtook them both. They lay handcuffed in the cellar of the house that had fleetingly been their dream but was now their worst nightmare.

They heard footsteps overhead and then a car started up in the drive. If Anthony O'Malley had bothered, his acute professional ear would have identified the engine tone of their hired Fiat.

At 3.55pm on 8 September 2002, the first of five withdrawals was made on the O'Malley's credit cards. The haul that day was €720, all made in Finestrat, as far away from Alcoy as possible as David avoided any possible link to the area. These withdrawals would sound the second alarm.

10

INQUIRIES IN SPAIN

On their arrival in Benidorm, Alan Jones and Steve Lloyd booked into the Meliá Hotel on Calle Doctor Severo Ochoa. Centrally located and just a short walk from the central strip of the Avenida del Mediterráneo, the four-star hotel was ideally placed and had Internet broadband connections in each room to allow messages and images to be sent or received by means of a laptop computer.

The first priority of the two detectives was a meeting with Spanish police and to present the professionally translated summaries of the enquiries undertaken. Both noted that the Spanish police still appeared to show 'very little interest' in the case.

Much to the discomfort of the Spanish, Det Supt Alan Jones pulled rank as a senior visiting British police officer and insisted on visiting every retail outlet in Benidorm, Alicante and Valencia where the O'Malley credit cards had been used. His request was met without enthusiasm, although one detective was grudgingly assigned to accompany the Welsh officers. At that time, both Jones and Lloyd were under the misapprehension that these outlets had already been visited by the Spanish police. They were to discover, as I had myself, that the majority of shops had no recollection of a previous visit by police, despite promises that had been made back in September.

The first stop was the Hotel Playa Ambassador on Calle Gerona, within walking distance of the Meliá. Although five months had passed, the Welsh detectives had no problem in obtaining a receipt for €81.74, generated by the couple's Yorkshire Bank credit card on 31 August 2002. The O'Malleys had paid in advance for a double room for one night, arriving at 1.31pm.

The next visit was to a Benidorm pizzeria, where, on 3 September at 10.59pm, Anthony and Linda had paid €34.07 for two pizzas and a bottle of wine.

Jones and Lloyd followed the trail to the Hotel Altaya on the beach road in Altea where the missing couple had booked in on 1 September, the day they left the Ambassador, for just three nights, paying €297.83 on booking out at 9.34am on 4 September – an early hour to leave a hotel carrying luggage unless somebody had somewhere specific to go.

Although never resolved by the police of either force, I believe Anthony and Linda O'Malley returned to Benidorm as a base for their search for property in the surrounding areas. Elsewhere are described the efforts of reporter Tom Cain and myself to trace their location by talking to apartment porters, but Benidorm is a large town and there are literally thousands of apartments for rent.

The location in the town is not important, although it would more likely have been the hotel area around Calle Ibiza, a street close to the pizzeria where the O'Malleys had eaten on 3 September. What is important is that the *second* telephone contact with their abductors' mobile after the initial calls to the number from Málaga on the night of 30 August took place on 7 September, and the newspaper in which they saw the Alcoy villa advertisement did not hit the streets until the Friday – 6 September.

Staff at a Chinese restaurant where the couple had eaten on Thursday, 5 September, vaguely remembered the couple but one wonders if all Europeans look alike to the Chinese. The last card transaction made by the O'Malleys was the modest €30 spent on petrol on Saturday afternoon, made a few minutes after Anthony received a call from a mobile phone later traced to the killers.

During all of these visits to the hotels and restaurants, Alan Jones obtained receipts signed by Anthony O'Malley. Others collected from shops after 7 September would show marked differences in the signature that were plain to the trained eye. All receipts were submitted to the Forensic Science Services in the UK for handwriting analysis and supporting evidence was obtained to prove that the signatures were clumsy forgeries.

In itself, the fact that a card thief can pass off a stolen credit card as his or her own doesn't come as a surprise, for few shop assistants bother to check a signature, often returning the card before offering the receipt to be signed. However, in Spain, some proof of identity would have been asked for and we can only assume that the forging skills of David allowed him to make up an identity card sufficiently convincing to enable him to pass himself off as Anthony O'Malley.

Another important task of the Welsh police was the recovery of the overlooked CCTV tapes that would have recorded the images of customers at the stores where the illicit purchases had taken place. I myself had already picked up an image of David buying sportswear to fit his large frame at Footwear in the Gran Via shopping mall. Unfortunately, shop CCTVs are of notoriously poor quality, with the tapes recorded over repeatedly until objects and people appear as not much more than indistinct blurs. I had fared better, but my identification of David as the 'kiter' – criminal slang for anyone working a credit card scam – was made with the benefit of hindsight after his arrest. No such factor was open to the Welsh police.

Whether any positive identification was made from the CCTV tapes bought by Alan Jones from the security office of El Corte Inglés in Valencia is doubtful. Certainly, a report circulated in the Spanish press to the effect that a man had been identified was denied by Spanish police, but then it would have been, considering they knew nothing about the tape purchases or of their removal for examination to Wales. As Steve Lloyd would report, 'The Spanish detective allocated to us hardly lasted a day before he got bored and disappeared.'

On 8 February, Det Supt Jones and DS Lloyd returned to the UK to prepare a final report of all enquiries undertaken by North Wales Police in the UK and Spain which would show, without the shadow of a doubt, that Anthony and Linda O'Malley had become victims of crime in Spain. An answer to the mystery of their disappearance was still not forthcoming; the only crime apparently committed against them was the fraudulent use of their credit cards.

Neither officer was aware at that disappointing point in time that, within three weeks, an answer would be provided that would bring the case to its final and tragic conclusion.

11

THE CREDIT CARD TRAIL

Three weeks after the press conference, I watched the *Crimewatch* video that a colleague had sent me from England and marvelled at DI Nick Crabtree's tie. Nonetheless, the man was doing a credible job of presenting the case of the missing 'Welsh' homebuyers, as the O'Malleys would come to be erroneously described in the English press.

DI Crabtree and DC David James were later to replace DS Lloyd and WPS McCairn in the role of liaison with the Spanish police, who seemed determined to ignore their presence. DS Lloyd would later ask me if I was 'having a laugh' when I enquired how collaboration had been between the two forces. He insisted, 'Liaison with the Spanish police was minimal during the investigation and non-existent after they [the kidnappers] were formally charged. To be honest, when we came over for the trial the [Spanish] cops were so surprised to see us that they interrogated us with regard to why we were there... '

The trial would be attended by DS Lloyd and DC James in their roles as family liaison officers. Det Supt Alan Jones would also fly in to attend the final few days.

Throughout the six months of their missing persons' inquiry, the Welsh police fielded a formidable team of officers to Spain. It was these men and women who would follow the trail of the missing couple, double-checking credit card purchases, obtaining CCTV footage and, where possible and with the grudging help of a bored Spanish detective, interviewing possible witnesses.

The results of my own enquiries were regularly passed to Wrexham where Det Supt Alan Jones was heading the inquiry. Vastly experienced and a dogged adversary in the war against crime in his native Wales, he was determined to see the investigation through to its conclusion, whatever that took. His assisting officer, DS Steve Lloyd, a veteran detective with 25 years' service and father to a teenage daughter, was no stranger to the traumatic events that a September could bring and still carried painful memories of his experiences in New York the previous autumn in the aftermath of 9/11.

During the last month of the O'Malley investigation, to be known as the 'Phoenix phase', DC Dave James and DI Sue Harrop would keep a watching brief with Interpol in Madrid, and Dave James would later travel to the east coast to liaise with the alerted Valencia National Police once the trail had become warm again. Det Supt Alan Jones would also be a regular visitor, making his last visit to Benidorm in February and flying home to supervise the investigation from North Wales as the case neared its dramatic climax in Valencia.

It should be stressed at this point that all evidence presented at the trial, with the exception of any confession, was collected and handed to the Spanish authorities by the North Wales team over the six months' course of its unassisted investigation.

Meanwhile, in late September of 2002, the case had certainly attracted attention in the expatriate and UK press, with a photograph of the decidedly tubby O'Malleys embracing and smiling at the camera during what looked like a night on the town. In reality, at the time of their disappearance they had both slimmed down considerably. At 5ft 10in and around 160lbs, Anthony had a spare yet powerful physique. Linda was 5ft 4in and fashionably slim for her height at 122lbs. However, although it would make the couple less recognisable in the flesh, the holiday snap did no harm in portraying a happy, slightly over-indulged middle-aged couple on holiday. It would attract peer sympathy among holidaymakers who might be able to help with sightings, which are notorious in any missing persons' search, when the subjects are often seen and even spoken to by eager informants as far apart as Alaska and the Cairngorms. Very few sightings ever turn out to be genuine but, in theory at least, each one must be painstakingly investigated by the police involved in the hunt. In my own investigations in the past, I can remember many a cold and uncomfortable early-morning stakeout because a suspect or missing person had reportedly been seen in the area.

The BBC's *Crimewatch*, although broadcast in the UK

and only available to a Spanish audience through satellite, turned up a possible sighting by a resident expatriate of a blue Fiat Stilo apparently abandoned among some trees at the side of the N-340 near Málaga. Although the location made sense, the sighting was never confirmed and no car was later found at the location. However, the N-340, which stretches the entire length of the Costa del Sol from Cádiz through Andalucía and Murcia and into Valencia Province to Alicante, is a rugged and often mountainous highway with the Málaga to Alicante section notorious as a 550km continuous black spot.

Although I now knew from the Spanish Property Auctions rep Joanne Miles, who was the last person to speak to Linda O'Malley in a chance meeting outside the Meliá Hotel in Benidorm on 6 September, that only Linda planned to fly home on 13 September and Anthony planned to stay for the house auction on 23 September, the hire car was due to be returned to Crown Car Hire at Málaga Airport on 13 September.

There was also a good chance – again ignored by a cynical Spanish police department – that the Fiat could have been involved in an accident. It was a thought, incidentally, that would occur to darker minds as the search dragged into months. Alternatively, the car could even have left the road and become lodged in a ravine from where it would be invisible to motorists from above. Stranger things have happened.

It was just an idea, but I was puzzled as to why a police helicopter hadn't over-flown the route. The answer, of course, was that the Spanish police were still dragging their heels and assuming that the O'Malleys would eventually come to their senses and phone home. It would take the North Wales Police to get any action from the national force but that was still months ahead.

I contacted a flying pal, Keith Preston, at Muchamiel private airfield just north of Alicante city. Would he spread the word among fellow pilots that an overview of the N-340 south would be much appreciated? Of course he would, and the part-time hobby pilots from Muchamiel began a search of the ravines at the side of the N-340 as far as Málaga. It would prove fruitless, although I believe it turned up some missing wrecks and solved a few mysteries, but nothing related to the search for the O'Malleys' vehicle.

Still, it was a start and helped ease the frustration of seeing little being done locally to find the couple. But a method that would prove more useful to investigators, namely a follow-up of outlets linked to the credit card purchases, had been requested of the Spanish police, without success, at the first hint of the O'Malleys' disappearance in September, soon after Linda's sister in Liverpool had reported the couple missing.

Suspicions had been aroused by the uncharacteristic spending pattern of the couple's Yorkshire Bank Gold Mastercard. Up to 7 September, the card had been used sparingly to pay for hotels, meals and petrol but, from the following day, the pattern had gone haywire. Between 3.55pm and 5.04pm on 8 September, four withdrawals of cash totalling €720 had been made on the UK Mastercard, with one withdrawal of an extra €300 denied at 4.14pm by a wrongly inserted PIN number.

Three of these withdrawals had been made with the Yorkshire Bank card at a Finestrat cashpoint close to Benidorm, with the last withdrawal at the Carrefour hypermarket ATM using the recently issued CAM bank card, credited with the deposit used by Anthony to open the CAM Bank account in Benidorm on 2 September, assisted by Joanne Miles. Ominously, cash withdrawals were also being made on the couple's household Barclaycard account.

On the following day of wild withdrawals, 9 September saw the purchase of general goods, an expensive video game and men's sportswear – at XL, far too big for Anthony's slimmed down frame – bought at various outlets in Alicante city, followed by cash withdrawals in the same area totalling over €700, plus a Valencia District road toll for €2.18 that would later sound alarm bells.

It was interesting to note that the goods and clothing were now being purchased using the Yorkshire Bank card and avoiding the swiftly depleted CAM Bank account that could result in a challenge. The 'kiter' obviously wanted to keep his or her head down. But it was already too late for that.

Although the stores' CCTV surveillance tapes would not be studied until the official arrival of the North Wales unit, I was following an intermittent trail of card movements given to me by a helpful CAM Bank manager who was equally puzzled at the lack of Spanish police enquiries.

My trail led me to descriptions of a 'wide' man accompanied by two women and two female children who had been recorded making the purchases. The Spanish police could have had their man but didn't know it.

12

A SLIP IN TIME

Spanish Property Auctions representative Joanne Miles met the O'Malleys in Benidorm on 2 September, their third day in the Costa Blanca resort. Joanne Miles had been alerted by her UK-based employer to meet the couple and arrange the non-resident bank account and identity documents that would be necessary to enter the house auction as bona fide bidders.

They met at the resort's Meliá Hotel, where Ms Miles chose to meet her clients on the spacious terrace of the hotel cafeteria. Once the introductions had been made, the necessities were explained. Before a bidder could enter any property auction that involved a state-sanctioned sale, they would need a *Número de Identidad Fiscal*. Translated as a 'Fiscal Identity Number', or NIF, this would register the O'Malleys for any financial dealing in Spain. It would also allow them to make tax returns should they reside in Spain for the qualifying period of 187 days each year.

This fiscal number is also issued as a *Número de Identitad de Extranjeros*, an NIE, or Foreigners' Identification Number, for expatriate residents and non-residents with financial affairs in Spain.

Application would have to be made at Benidorm National Police Headquarters in person. Joanne Miles provided the necessary forms and Linda and Anthony carefully filled in their applications that were filed that day but never collected.

The next step was to open a Spanish bank account armed with the notice of NIF application, for which a number is automatically granted pending the process of documents. The granting of a number while the application is still pending is typical of Spain as it still struggles to develop fully into a bureaucratic democracy. The days of settling one's affairs at the Town Hall by presenting the official with a chicken went out with the death of Franco in 1975. Nowadays, everything depends on the computer.

Since no one is ever refused an NIF or NIE, there logically seems no reason to delay the issue, although formality insists that the due process must take effect and that a sufficient number of civil servants view the application and stamp the form. I've always said there's an awful lot of Irish in the Spanish, a disarmingly logical nation.

The account was opened in the Caja de Ahorros de Mediterráneo (CAM) branch in the Rincon de Loix area of Benidorm at Calle L'Ametlla del Mar with a deposit of €300. Also issued were two credit cards, a Mastercard and a Red 600 card that could be used to pay road tolls on the Spanish motorway network. It was the careless use of a

Yorkshire Bank card by one of the O'Malleys' abductors in paying at the Valencia South exit that, among other clues, later led investigators to decide that the focus of the search should be moved to the Valencia suburb of El Saler.

Joanne Miles arranged to see the O'Malleys a week later and concentrated during the intervening days on finding the exact location of the property for auction, a location that wouldn't be discovered until I contacted the new owners weeks after the auction that Anthony O'Malley failed to attend.

Her next sighting of Anthony and Linda was less than a week later, although she would get the date horribly wrong, with disastrous results.

On Friday, 6 September, the day that the fateful advertisement was to appear in the small ads property section of *Costa Blanca News*, Joanne Miles looked up from the terrace table at Hotel Meliá where she sat discussing a sale with clients and saw Linda O'Malley waving and smiling as she crossed the road towards her. Anthony remained across the road outside the Plus supermarket where the couple had apparently been shopping. Anthony held two carrier bags as he waited for his wife to return.

Linda asked Joanne Miles if there had been any luck locating the property, since both she and her husband were anxious to view before the auction. Linda also remarked that the search elsewhere for suitable property had come to nothing and that Anthony would be staying on for the auction to be held on 23 September in the courthouse of Villajoyosa, just a few kilometres away. An arrangement was made to meet on the following Tuesday.

But Joanne Miles would confuse her dates and had

already told an interviewer conducting a live GMTV broadcast from the Meliá Hotel on 1 October that she had spoken to Linda O'Malley on Friday, 13 September, an ominous date and almost certainly the day on which Linda and Anthony died.

The time slip of one week caused consternation among those studying the trail of cash withdrawals and purchases on the missing couple's credit cards. For if the O'Malleys were at large in Benidorm on 13 September, it would mean that the 'uncharacteristic purchases' that had so alarmed their family back in the UK and caused the Chester-based bank to block the card had been made by the couple themselves.

Why, we wondered, would Anthony suddenly realise the need for a Dictaphone, a wireless video camera and a burglar alarm – and for whom were the shoes and schoolbooks, news of which had filtered through to the press?

I finally spoke to Joanne and asked her to check her dates carefully. She eventually checked with the clients with whom she'd been sitting when Linda approached and found they had flown back to the UK within that same week. Joanne Miles had met Linda O'Malley on 6 September and suddenly it all fell back into place. The second appointment arranged for the following Tuesday was for 10 September, not 17.

Unfortunately, the experience of Alan Jones had told him that such vacillation from a vital witness boded no good for the investigation and there were even doubts in my journalistic mind whether Mrs Miles had deliberately put the investigation on the wrong footing.

That wasn't true and it was accepted that a genuine

mistake had been made. Nevertheless, Joanne Miles was branded an unreliable witness. It was a case of a witness eager to help the police to resolve the tragedy of a loving couple who had disappeared abroad and getting her dates confused.

Who can blame her, for how many times has that happened to each and every one of us? The difference here, though, was that two people were still missing, and any incorrect recollections would make it that much harder to locate them, and discover what had happened.

13

THE SPIDER AND
THE FLY

On 30 September 2002, the overnight JMC 10 flight from Manchester to Málaga's Pablo Picasso Airport descended over the moonlit brown-and-yellow patchwork of the fields beyond the city. Anthony and Linda O'Malley would have craned to look out of the aircraft window at the unravelling landscape. They both knew Spain well, although they were most familiar with the Costa Blanca resort of Benidorm where they had spent many enjoyable holidays. But this trip was special.

Linda contributed to a news-sheet distributed by a Leeds-based company that specialised in Spanish properties for auction and there the couple had seen the brief description of a retirement property of their dreams, a villa with land situated on the Partida Moratella Chica, an area close to the renamed AP-7 *autovía* near Villajoyosa.

The couple would have been looking forward to their arranged meeting with Joanne Miles in Benidorm on 2

September to discuss the process of buying at auction. This is a very lengthy procedure in Spain, where property auctions, especially those dealing with embargoed properties, are conducted through a court. It is necessary for foreign bidders to have at least a non-residential bank account, which would require the allocation of the previously mentioned NIF tax identification number. Bidders must deposit at least a third of the property's reserve price – in the O'Malleys' case this was €40,000. Joanne Miles would be available to assist with all the bureaucratic red tape but there were still pitfalls.

Although they were unaware of all the pitfalls surrounding property auctions on their arrival in Spain, Linda and Anthony O'Malley would soon become disillusioned by an acquaintance they would make in the Arrivals hall of the airport. My investigation was to prove that there, around the timeshare stands, hovered the character I have previously identified as Hal Edwards, my assumed name for this known hustler on the lookout for 'marks' such as the O'Malleys.

Hal would start the chain of events that would eventually lead to death in a cold, clammy cellar in Alcoy, but his part in the drama would be summarily dismissed by the Spanish prosecutor despite a burning question that was never answered at the trial of the killers.

Simply, who initiated the first contact between Anthony O'Malley and his murderer? In an e-mail dated 13 March 2006, Det Supt S Alan Jones confirmed to me, '... Anthony received a mobile telephone call from [the suspect] on 07/09 shortly before the petrol purchase and I can link the telephone that called Anthony's mobile to *a mobile telephone that Anthony called upon arrival at*

Málaga on 30/08. Unfortunately, I have no idea how much of the real story will be given at the hearing?' The italics are mine.

Much would be made of an advertisement placed by the killers in *Costa Blanca News* on 6 September, yet North Wales Police were aware that Anthony O'Malley telephoned not one but two mobile numbers belonging to his convicted murderers from Málaga in the early hours of 31 August. How did he come by those fateful numbers? There is no doubt they came from hustler Hal.

Hal was an expert at spotting his marks. He made a fair living out of fleecing gullible foreigners as his wife would later boast to an informant. The scams were simple enough. Hal would either pass on the mark for a commission from the scam-master, as I believe happened in the case of the O'Malleys, at the same time wheedling an 'introductory fee' from the victims.

Alternatively, he might offer to act as a representative and take cash for services he had no intention of fulfilling. In any event, he would have made contact and heard the O'Malleys' story, perhaps told in that euphoria of arrival that the couple would have felt. Hal would have tried to dissuade Anthony and Linda from the auction and impress on them, perhaps with a knowledgeable wink, the amount of desirable properties available on the Costas, all to be easily found with the 'right contacts'.

Evidence of Hal's involvement also solves the mystery of how the O'Malleys' hire car was seen being driven by a woman in La Nucía on the morning after their arrival in Benidorm. The couple had driven the 550km from Málaga overnight, stopping with the dawn to look at likely areas around Murcia and arriving in Benidorm around 1.00pm.

Records show that they booked into the town's Ambassador Playa Hotel at 1.31pm, paying €81.74 in advance for one night's board.

The next morning, 1 September, after a good night's sleep, they would most likely have visited Hal and his wife at their home in La Nucía, impressed by Hal's willingness to help two fellow Brits find their dream home in Spain. It was on that occasion that, flushed with the largesse of gratitude, Anthony probably allowed Hal's wife to use the car for her business appointment when she would be seen by a young woman who would later pass that information to me.

Again, persuaded by Hal's apparent connections in the real estate business and wishing to keep in close contact, on 1 September the O'Malleys booked into the more convenient Altaya Hotel on nearby Altea's beachfront just north of Benidorm and stayed three nights until 4 September.

Their date with destiny would take place three days later in a town 45km beyond the rugged peaks of the Sierra Aitana visible from their hotel window.

Fate was moving Linda and Anthony O'Malley inexorably closer to their appointment with death. On the following day, two men entered the first-floor reception area of the *Costa Blanca News* head office on the La Marina industrial estate of Finestrat on the southern border of Benidorm, and placed an advertisement for a two-bedroom house in a 4,000 square metre lot in Bocairent, a small township south-west of Alcoy.

In order for an advertisement to be placed in the newspaper, I had introduced a scheme whereby the advertiser had to identify him or herself by a passport or identity card. The reason was to avoid the sale of stolen goods through the newspaper's small ads section.

The man who placed the advertisement identified himself as Matthew Don but was unable to produce identification. His companion then showed the receptionist a Venezuelan identity card in the name of David Velázquez. Both names thus appear on the booking form. The NIF number given by the man calling himself David was false.

Following the arrests, I asked Jasmin Rokadia, the receptionist who had accepted the advertisement, if she remembered anything about the men, but almost seven months had passed. The only thing that had stuck in her mind was the confusion over identity cards.

The advertisement promised pine trees, water, electricity, and warned off agencies. The price quoted was €30,000, and a mobile number was given. For what it was worth, Bocairent had been spelt wrongly and wasn't the true location of the villa, one supposes because the fraudsters wouldn't want the advertised property recognised by its true owner, but that wouldn't have mattered to the O'Malleys, who, we must assume, read the advertisement with excitement when the newspaper hit the stands on Friday, 6 September.

Here was a property with enough square metres to exercise their cosseted dogs to their hearts' content, and all for a price almost equivalent to the 30 per cent deposit they would have had to put down at auction.

In an ITN interview for the *Tonight* programme hosted by Sir Trevor McDonald on 12 May 2003, I would remark on camera to presenter Fiona Foster that the €30,000 would have looked like a typographical error to the experienced eye. Adjacent advertisements for similar properties gave prices ranging from €128,000–€260,000.

But to Anthony and Linda O'Malley, it looked like heaven had answered their prayers. They called the number and an arranged meeting place in Alcoy was established. There was, however, a slight hiccup in that another client had rung and would be viewing the property the next morning. Would they be kind enough to await a call on Saturday afternoon? Of course they would, and why not? To the excited couple, it looked too good to be true.

It was.

Following the press conference a month later, the following story of the missing couple and the family members' appeal for help appeared under my byline as a front-page lead on 4 October:

HUNT FOR MISSING BRITS
FEARS GROW FOR SAFETY OF WELSH COUPLE ON THE COSTA
by News Editor Danny Collins

FEARS ARE GROWING FOR THE SAFETY OF ANTHONY AND LINDA O'MALLEY, A MARRIED COUPLE FROM LLANGOLLEN, NORTH WALES, WHO DISAPPEARED ON A HOUSE HUNTING TRIP TO SOUTHERN SPAIN.

Mr and Mrs O'Malley were last seen by Joanne Miles, a representative of UK-based Spanish Property Auctions on 13 September when they met in Benidorm to discuss the possible purchase of a default mortgage property in Partida Moratella near

Villajoyosa. The couple failed to attend a further meeting planned for 17 September.

Mrs Miles told Costa Blanca News, *'They were scheduled to fly home on the 13th, but Mr O'Malley was prepared to stay on for the auction on 23 September. They would also have needed an NIE number and a BBVA bank account number to enter the auction, which they applied for but never collected.'*

A blue Fiat Stylo, registration 8588 BPT, hired by the couple from Málaga Airport on their arrival on 30 August, is also missing.

Speculation surrounds the possibility that the couple may have been lured inland to look at a fictitious property as a result of a casual meeting in a bar and robbed of a substantial amount of cash transferred from their UK account to a Benidorm bank on 11 September.

UK POLICE JOIN THE HUNT

Two officers from North Wales Police flew into Alicante on Wednesday and are liaising with Spanish police in the search. Meanwhile, Detective Superintendent Alan Jones and DI Nick Crabtree of Wrexham CID are leading the UK inquiry. DI Crabtree told CBN, *'We are very concerned for this couple's safety. Anyone with information on their whereabouts is asked to contact Benidorm National Police or call our UK Incident Room on 00 44 845 607 1002.'*

A RESPONSIBLE COUPLE

At a press conference arranged by Benidorm Town Hall Press Office yesterday, which was heavily attended by both Spanish and UK media, Bernard O'Malley, brother of Anthony, and the couple's daughter Nicola, told reporters, 'Our last contact was by telephone on 4 September, when they called to send birthday greetings to members of the family and told us they would fly home on 13 September. They are a very responsible couple who would not disappear on their own accord.'

Since their disappearance, purchases and cash withdrawals described as 'extravagant and out-of-character' have been made in various coastal towns using the couple's joint credit card.

Mr O'Malley is 42, height 1.75m, with a moustache and receding greying hair. Mrs O'Malley is 55, height 1.62m, with shoulder-length brown hair worn in a bob. Those wishing for confidentiality can contact the Costa Blanca Newsdesk on 96 585 52 86 extension 213. All relevant information received by CBN will be immediately passed to investigating officers, but the informant's identity will be protected.

Below the text was a photograph of a Fiat 'Stylo' (sic) of the same model as the missing car.

Not all of the information was correct but it was all that was available at the time of going to press. The model of the car was actually spelt Stilo, not 'Stylo', and a letter was incorrect in the car registration suffix. Also, as already mentioned, Joanne Miles reported wrongly that she last saw the O'Malleys on 13 September. On prompting, she checked her records and realised the encounter had been a week earlier on 6 September.

Consequently, the meeting that the O'Malleys never attended was scheduled a week earlier for 10 September. This involuntary bout of misinformation led to Miles being branded an unreliable witness by the Welsh police, to my mind an unfortunate but no doubt practical professional judgement by those far more experienced in the art of investigation than I.

I had hardly driven home from the office when the call reached me. Staff told me that a hysterical young woman was trying to contact me, claiming she was in fear of her life. I left my dinner uneaten and called the number I was given.

Because of what I know today and because of the people concerned, I cannot reveal the young woman's name and I am aware that even the circumstances in which she came by the information could point the finger in her direction.

Her story sounded like a huge breakthrough in the O'Malley investigation. She had spoken to a woman driving a blue Fiat Stilo, of exactly the description down to a vague remembrance of the number plate figures that I had given in my report. The woman had told her that the car was rented by recently arrived friends who were staying in the area for a few days and had allowed her to use the car that morning.

On reading the newspaper, she had panicked because the woman driving, who was the wife of a heavy local villain known for pulling off property scams on gullible English tourists, had called her and asked her to call at the house for no apparent reason. The husband had recently returned from Málaga, where the O'Malleys had landed on arrival. Who else was it but Hal?

It sounded very credible to me. I got the frightened girl

to a safe house location and called the UK police liaison officer who had tried to stop Anthony's stepdaughter from taking my business card.

Eventually, my informant was interviewed by the North Wales detectives and the information passed to the Spanish police, but with no result. Her anxiety that Hal or his wife might realise that she could identify the missing car was put down to paranoia. No one bothered to check out the address she had given as the location where she saw the hire car, except me. But the trail was cold. The car, if it had ever been there, was now gone. It came as no surprise to me that had Hal disappeared as well, along with his wife.

Why should I have believed the distressed young woman who came to me with the information? I believed her because her story added up. She said the car was 'an unusual blue'. Some of the new Fiats of 2002 were painted an eye-catching, vibrant blue. The driver's husband was known to me as a conman and trickster who often boasted to his pals of ripping off tourists. His wife had placed him in Málaga on the date of the O'Malleys' arrival. The same man would go from seeking loans from friends to sudden affluence and would return to the UK within a month. But there was an even more damning clue that wouldn't emerge until months later. It was another example of withheld information that would have rung alarm bells.

Anthony had received a call from a mobile shortly before his petrol purchase on 7 September and North Wales Police linked the telephone that called Anthony's mobile to one of the mobile telephone numbers that Anthony had called upon arrival at Málaga in the early hours of 31 August. The original contact had been made in Málaga. It had to have been by Hal.

I can't help thinking that if the Spanish police had taken my distressed informant as seriously as I had, then the focus on Hal would have turned up the culprits in early October; too late to save Anthony and Linda, but soon enough to avoid their family's agony of not knowing their fate for five more months of anguish.

14

A VITAL MISSED CLUE

The nature of credit card purchases had taken a surprising turn on 10 September, when computer equipment worth €394.90 was bought using Anthony's Yorkshire Bank card from Benidorm technical retailers Cima.

Less than two hours later, in Alicante, the card user purchased a state-of-the-art Dictaphone, a wireless micro camera and a burglar alarm, the two latter items for use in the surveillance of the victims through a cold-blooded computer link to the apartment in Valencia. The day continued with the purchases of shoes, both ladies' size 40 and gents' size 43, three withdrawals totalling €700 in cash and, again, the all-important Valencia District toll on the Yorkshire Bank card, this time €2.53, which should have given an indication to any alert detective of the base to which the perpetrator was returning each day.

Even more important were the computer purchases listed below:

O'MALLEY DEBIT CARD PURCHASES
AT CIMA C/ALMANSA 32, BENIDORM 10.38am,
10 September 2002

5126 Powermind MS910 7C + PAX266DI
1348 Ventilator P4 84789 2.4 GHZ Ball OEM
1524 Microprocessor Intel P4 - 2.0GHZ 512KB (478)
1538 Tower ATX P4 SEMI - T +F A 300 Watt
Esmeral Serie: 278/FC03002544
1153 DD 60GB IDE Seagate ST360020A U100 5K -
Serie: 6EX05M7R
986 DD 40GB ST343016A U100 7K -
Serie: 3H57AV4K
1074 DVD Reader - ROM IDE 16XLG Caja + Soft -
Serie: 23ZG090910

This type of equipment, when coupled with the wireless micro camera, sounds the alarm bells for cash point card fraud, but the purchases were never revealed to the press and only became public at the trial. Any streetwise operator worth his salt would have recognised the obvious link and tightened the theoretical area of the search. Valencia plus credit card fraudster should have upped the ante. It wouldn't until North Wales Police were on their third frustrated visit to Spain six months later and called into my office at the *Costa Blanca News* building.

Det Supt Alan Jones and DS Steve Lloyd admitted they were getting nowhere in their liaison with the Spanish police. Alan Jones admitted to me, 'We always need a local officer to accompany us since we have no jurisdiction in Spain, but whoever we get treats us as if we're on a fool's errand and is forever looking at his wristwatch and wondering whether it's time for lunch.'

DS Lloyd added to the tale of frustration and woe. 'We'd like to make four enquiries a day but we're lucky if we get to any, let alone one.' There was, they admitted, no more they could do.

It was at that meeting that they took my point that the press could do little to help if they were kept in the dark and Det Supt Jones made the decision to reveal to me and reporter Tom Cain the list of computer purchases.

Tom Cain and I studied the list at length and then gave them the good news that could have been announced six months before but would nonetheless eventually resurrect the trail. The man or men they were looking for were experienced credit card fraudsters who had a base in the Valencia area.

The clues were obvious if one knew the way these scallywags worked. A tiny wireless camera would be placed under the sunshade of the cash-point machine and would record the card owner's hand movements as he or she punched in their secret PIN number. It would also pick up the card details as the card was placed in the slot to be easily lifted off later in freeze frame.

Basically, that is all the fraudster wants. He or she will be nearby in a car with a laptop plugged into a receiver tuned to the camera. With that information in hand and with the right equipment, card cloning is a piece of cake and the account will be stripped within a few hours.

The ultimate beauty of the scheme is that the cardholder has no idea of the theft since the card has never been out of their sight and they have never told a soul their PIN number. The banks are aware of this type of fraud, just as they know that a modified card reader of the type used in restaurants and shops can deliver all card information right down to the PIN number to a dodgy operator.

It is not in the banks' interests to admit it since it could lead to massive compensation claims from defrauded account holders. But take it from one whose profession it is to be aware of these things – they know, and they make sure it's your loss, not theirs.

Det Supt Jones and DS Lloyd seemed happy with our information and said they would pass it on to Valencia detectives who seemed more on the ball. What neither they nor I knew at the time was that a masterfully conducted breakthrough of their own was about to lead to them to the men they sought.

But that was in February 2003, months away from the day of the original purchases. In October 2002, the Valencia clues had been there but no one was looking.

Meanwhile, in September, the card jamboree had continued. More computer equipment including a hi-tech scanner was bought on 11 September, along with an attempt to buy a €1,900 laptop from an Alicante supplier.

Unfortunately for the kiter, the spending spree had come to a temporary end. Perturbed at the 'uncharacteristic' spending pattern and, at the urging of the distressed family in Wales, Yorkshire Bank had blocked the card.

Between 3.27pm and 5.01pm on the following day, four separate attempts were made to draw cash on the blocked card. One can only imagine the fury of the thwarted robbers and the punishment inflicted on both Linda and Anthony before the latter was made to put in a second appearance at CAM Bank in Benidorm and request the urgent transfer of the entire Yorkshire Bank balance to the recently opened CAM account.

In a written note faxed with the document to the UK bank manager, Anthony asked the bank to deal with the transfer as a matter of extreme urgency, explaining that the money was needed for a deposit on a house that the couple had decided to buy and that the cash must be paid before their scheduled return to Wales the next day.

Hella Henneberke, manager of the CAM Bank international office in Benidorm, told me that Anthony O'Malley had seemed 'normal' and 'just anxious to get the transfer arranged' before he and Linda flew home. She also said that the man who identified himself as Anthony O'Malley on that afternoon and who returned to collect the cash the next day, 13 September, appeared calm and in control even when told he would have to attend a nearby branch to collect the money since the Avenida L'Ametlla branch didn't have enough cash in the vaults to pay the €25,000 that had been requested in small denominations.

It is unlikely that an impostor could have played Anthony's part in the bank that day, since it was only ten days since the O'Malleys, accompanied by Joanne Miles, had sat across the desk from Hella Henneberke and opened a bank account. The transfer request, which was to be faxed to Yorkshire, also carried the scribbled note from Anthony asking the bank manager, who was a known acquaintance, to act with all speed.

Again, it's doubtful that even the most accomplished

fraudster could have pulled that off. The only thing that Ms Henneberke thought strange was Anthony's refusal to have the transfer request faxed there and then from the CAM Bank facility. Instead, he insisted that he would fax the documents later, which seemed odd given his plea for urgency.

It is obvious with hindsight that Anthony was under orders to return to his captors to allow them to examine the documents and make sure they carried no hidden message. The papers were faxed an hour later from a Mailbox outlet on the other side of town. I later spoke with the Mailbox franchise manager and his staff to seek a description of the sender but too much time had passed. Alarmingly, they told me that no enquiries had been made at the franchise by Spanish police who would have been told of the location by Welsh police within days of the fax transaction.

Answering Anthony's call for urgency, the cash was transferred to Spain that same afternoon. Henneberke also thought it odd that she hadn't been visited by the Spanish police and, as stated earlier, it prompted her to give me details of the few card movements that had gone through CAM Bank. This may well appear to be a departure from bank procedure but nothing was being done by the book in this inquiry.

So one question must inevitably be asked – why didn't Anthony, alone in the director's office and under no surveillance, pass Hella Henneberke or her assistant a note explaining his and Linda's plight and asking for the police to be called?

The answer, I think, is because Anthony O'Malley believed that 13 September was to be his and Linda's last day of captivity. He had almost certainly been promised that when the money from the UK had been paid to his captors, he and his wife would be released or at least left in captivity at the villa until a phone call giving their location was made to the Spanish police.

It should be remembered that Linda was still a hostage and threats to murder her if Anthony gave the alarm had almost certainly been made. It's also likely that any directions that Anthony could have given the police would have been vague.

Even if he remembered the wording of the advertisement after five days of captivity and torture, he may well have imagined the house was in Bocairent.

As the practical and shrewd thinker the man was known to be, Anthony O'Malley would have shrugged off the thought of losing the money and acted out his last imagined chance to get both himself and Linda out of their predicament alive.

Unfortunately, through a bitter twist of fate due to Linda's undiagnosed and aggravated heart condition, his brave logic was to fail utterly and result in both their deaths 24 hours later.

It was arranged that Anthony would return the next morning to withdraw €25,000 of the transferred cash that, in total, amounted to €28,186.20. It was all the money that the O'Malleys had saved during years of hard work to pay for their dream retirement home in the sun. Now it was, Anthony believed, the cash that would buy back their lives.

15

THE CASH TRAIL ENDS

The trail of purchases and cash withdrawals would last for six more days following the major withdrawal on 13 September. That had left just over €3,000 in the CAM account but it was not to be overlooked by the kidnappers. The list of purchases would now include expensive Burberry shirts, more gents' shoes, this time in size 45, which pointed to a second male involved, plus children's schoolbooks. After 13 September, all the purchases and cash withdrawals were made in and around Valencia city.

What would have become glaringly obvious to the Spanish police should they have cared to look was that their prey, now confirmed as a family man and not a loner, lived in an area adjacent to the regional capital of Valencia. It would certainly be obvious to anyone who saw the full list of purchases but, by then, the defendants were in the dock in Alicante. In February, I had seen only the list of computer purchases.

But why hadn't experienced Spanish officers, relying on documents and evidence gathered by the dogged North Wales Police, not realised where their inquiry should be focused? The answer to that is easy. There was no Spanish police inquiry, nor had there ever been. Despite the requests passed through London via Paris to Interpol in Madrid and on to Benidorm, the national police in that town still regarded the O'Malley's disappearance as a common occurrence not worth the effort of its stretched manpower.

Even the evidence of card fraud wasn't regarded as important enough to launch an investigation. The whole weight of the inquiry into the fate of the missing O'Malleys rested on the shoulders of Det Supt Alan Jones and his assisting officers, DS Steve Lloyd and DC Dave James. Fortunately for the investigation, these men had the tenacity of Welsh terriers.

For Alan Jones, it would be his last major case before retirement, which must have given rise to sighs of relief among Welsh criminals. For this unassuming, courteous and elegant Welshman has the look of one who would pursue a villain to the end. If ever the phrase 'no hiding place' could be turned into human form, it would be that of Alan Jones.

His sergeant and detective constable, Steve Lloyd and Dave James, are men one would describe as copper's coppers, a much abused and hackneyed phrase that brings to my mind a tireless dedication to the job in hand. In Wrexham, Steve Lloyd is attached to a unit dealing with the physical, sexual and emotional abuse of children and young persons. As a family liaison officer, or FLO, along with Dave James, he also fills a role that was developed at a national level following a recommendation in the Macpherson Report on the murder of black teenager Stephen Lawrence.

Of average height, with prematurely grey hair worn in a military style brush cut, Steve was to accompany Alan Jones through periods of frustration in Spain, providing the willing ear needed in such circumstances. I would get the impression over the months that he also kept them both sane and avoided a few blow-ups from his more volatile 'guv'nor', who often seethed with visible impatience at the lackadaisical attitude of the Spanish police.

Dave James is younger, married with two teenage children and gives off a glow of energy. It would fall upon this dark-haired and quietly spoken bespectacled detective, who at the time of the inquiry had completed 16 years in the force, to make a second visit to Spain when he travelled to Madrid with DI Sue Harrop to liaise with the hard-bitten officers of the National Kidnap and Extortion Unit as the net closed around the suspects in Valencia.

★ ★ ★

The early records of movements in the O'Malley accounts at the Yorkshire Bank, CAM Bank and Barclays show that the last withdrawal from the cards took place during the afternoon of 19 September, when €140 were withdrawn, leaving just €12 in place of the thousands removed by the unidentified kiters.

But even with no contact from the couple and the three bank accounts stripped of cash, the Welsh police could not convince their Spanish counterparts that a crime had been committed. In DS Lloyd's summary to the Welsh coroner, the frustration is obvious: 'It is now believed that

Anthony himself, probably at gunpoint, had attended the CAM bank in Benidorm on Friday, 13 September 2002 to withdraw €25,000 in cash. The matter was reported to the Spanish national police in Benidorm via Interpol but the Spaniards seemed incredibly disinterested, despite North Wales Police best efforts to convince them that Anthony and Linda had been [the] subject of serious crime, and despite North Wales police officers having visited Benidorm on three separate occasions to meet with their Spanish colleagues *absolutely nothing had been progressed by the Spanish police.'* (My italics.)

In short, what DS Lloyd was revealing was that despite the suspicions that led to a request to Spanish national police in October 2002 to launch a criminal investigation into the O'Malleys' disappearance, that request, although given lip service, was ignored.

Again, it's necessary to point out that all evidence used by prosecutors at the trial, other than that recovered at the time of the arrests, was collected by North Wales police officers conducting their missing persons' inquiry on the Costa Blanca. These included bank records, fax duplicates, statements from witnesses where possible without a translator and even CCTV tapes, which were duly gathered and taken back to Wales for examination rather than being handed over to the Spanish police who, in the words of a more voluble member of the Welsh team, 'would have done bugger all about it.'

The first visit of the North Wales officers had been in the role of family liaison, a duty that is peculiar to UK forces in the case of kidnap, murder, or a suspicion of either or both. The officers assigned to the victims' families, DS Steve Lloyd and DC Dave James, would be there to offer advice and counsel, to defend their charges from an always intrusive press and, in a worst-case scenario, tell them gently of the discovery of a body or bodies, and that their worst fears had been realised.

The first of the O'Malley family to follow Anthony and Linda's route to the Costa Blanca were Anthony's elder brother Bernard and Linda's daughter Nicola Welch.

Bernard O'Malley, a big, broad man with the challenging, truculent tilt of the jaw seen in some photographs of Anthony, was softly spoken, the Liverpudlian twang uttered in a low, rumbling register and in a tone that registered hurt and disbelief. I believe this amiable and likeable moustachioed Northener had already guessed what I and my colleagues in the UK press feared from experience... that Linda and Anthony were already dead.

At the press conference, Nicola, an extremely self-contained young woman, married with children of her own, had given off an aura of efficiency, laying out photographs of her missing parent and stepfather and speaking in a strong, clear voice through reporter Jaime Garrigós, the *CBN* interpreter.

But as interest in the case grew and the 'honey bees', as the free-spending TV media are called in the trade, moved in with their offers of free air travel and five-star accommodation, I would meet and get to know Linda's youngest daughter Jenny Stewart, who bears such a resemblance to her mother as a young woman that she must even now cause others to blanche with a recall of grief each time they look at her.

I would also meet Anthony's sister Christine Spruce, a small woman who wore a constant expression of stoic bewilderment and who would attend the trial three years later with her husband. On that occasion, the family were guests of the BBC while being represented as aggrieved parties in the *Acusación Particular*, a Spanish process of law by which relatives and dependants of the victims can claim compensation for their loss as well as seek a heavier penalty for the accused through their counsel.

In Spain, family, or private prosecutions, are conducted in parallel with that of the State. In the UK and USA, such a civil trial is conducted separately, usually after an unpopular verdict, and has, unlike in Spain, no legal power of imprisonment.

Since the Welsh police were frustrated and the Spanish police were doing nothing, it often fell to me to speak to the family and discuss various theories to be either followed through or discounted. Much of their time was spent being chauffeured around by the BBC or ITV television crews and giving soft-lens interviews against a backdrop of a sandy beach and palm trees. In no way do I mean that as a criticism of a loving and grieving family suddenly thrown into the spotlight. It is simply a phenomenon always present in high-profile cases.

The TV companies want their nine o'clock news footage and are always willing to push victim's relatives through a hoop to get it. It's the dark, hidden side of journalism that often impedes those involved in the investigation but is regrettably all too prevalent in the business. It is certainly largely responsible for the ubiquitous counsel from TV producers that their charges should never to talk to the rival press.

As far as I was concerned, that wasn't the kind of media I wanted to talk to, although I was often interviewed by both major UK TV companies eager for any snippet of news during the deadlocked investigation. But as far as pushing the story along, they needed no encouragement from me.

16

THE LAST
WITHDRAWAL

Anthony O'Malley sat slumped on the rear seat of the Fiat Stilo driven by Matthew as the car crossed the cable bridge in the centre of Alcoy. He had been well drilled in the part he must play at the bank in Benidorm by David, who sat next to him.

Today was 13 September, the day he and Linda should have been driving south along the motorway to return the hire car at Málaga Airport and catch their evening flight back to Manchester where Jenny would be waiting.

Yesterday he had gone into the bank alone and asked for the transfer of all their cash in the Yorkshire Bank in Chester to the account at the CAM Bank. He couldn't remember just how much that would be since he knew David had been drawing money daily but he guessed it was around £18,000 or £20,000. More importantly, David had promised him that he and Linda would go free today once the money was in the kidnappers' pockets.

Anthony vaguely toyed with what he would tell the police once they were released, although David had threatened him that he and Matthew had 'powerful friends' who wouldn't hesitate to settle the score should he give too much information. Even in his wretched mental state, Anthony allowed himself a wry grin. He wouldn't hesitate to tell the police every small detail to see these bastards behind bars, just as he and Linda had been so cruelly confined this last week. Just as Linda was now.

She had been locked in the cellar alone while he made this last journey in captivity. David had warned him that others would be watching the bank operation in Benidorm. David had even told him they had a teller in the bank who would sound the alarm should Anthony try to alert the bank staff. Linda would die unless a certain person received a telephone call that all was well.

Anthony didn't doubt it. All he had to do was stay calm and get them their money. Get them his and Linda's money, then it would soon be over.

His mind wandered back to the foolish mistakes he had made by being too loose-mouthed about their finances after a few glasses of David's heady sangría. Linda had put a warning hand on his arm at one point and he knew he had gone too far.

Then there was his headstrong acceptance of moving into the villa without telling a soul. Of course, they had planned to ring the girls and surprise them with the news once they were established in their new home but it had never happened; never could happen now. Alone, he knew he might have taken a chance in physically tackling either of the men. But whereas David was overweight and seemed to get out of breath easily Matthew seemed strong and might have been a problem. Together, they were his equal and more. Besides, he had Linda to think about.

Her screams when the sadistic David had used the cattle prod on her had ripped right through Anthony. Once free, he would make them pay. Until then, he must dance to their tune.

They eventually reached Benidorm and Matthew found an unusually empty parking space a few doors down from the bank. David exited the car's rear door and ushered Anthony out on to the pavement. Then the fat man repeated his instructions in a low voice, to avoid being overheard by the English-speaking tourists and holiday-makers bustling by.

Anthony was to enter the bank and go to the room on his left, where arrangements would be made for him to receive the money. He was to withdraw €25,000.

Matthew would stay in the car and David would be watching the bank from the cafetería opposite. Any false moves, any sight of uniforms converging on the bank and Linda would die. Anthony nodded and moved towards the bank. As he walked away, he was aware of the car pulling away past him. Matthew would circle the block until signalled to pull over and pick them up.

Inside the bank, Anthony was greeted by the young assistant of Hella Henneberke, the director of the international office. There was a problem. The money had arrived promptly on the afternoon of the previous day but the bank had not had time to amass the funds. Could he return tomorrow?

Anthony was swept by a wave of panic. Today was to be their day of freedom. He must leave with the money. Finally, after a few telephone calls, the matter was resolved. The nearest adjacent CAM branch in Calle Gerona, just a short walk away, could help with the low denomination notes that Anthony had been instructed to request.

He took the letter of introduction from Ms Henneberke's assistant and exited the bank, waving across the road to David and pointing to his right. David crossed the busy road at an angle, waddling between the traffic, his face a mixture of inquiry and trepidation.

Anthony explained the problem and David waited until Matthew appeared with the car then flagged him down and explained the change of plan. Matthew drove off towards the Calle Gerona branch while David and Anthony followed on foot.

No one will ever know how many times Anthony would have considered pushing the fat man under the wheels of a passing truck were it not for the threats against Linda.

Eventually, they reached the bank and David growled his final warning. Thirty minutes later, Anthony reappeared clutching a large brown envelope which David snatched greedily.

The journey home was made without conversation. Matthew carefully negotiated the mountain road once they had turned off the N-340 at Villena towards Alcoy.

On the journey down the main highway that morning, Anthony had noticed large walled institutional buildings behind wire link fencing on his left. Now, as they loomed to his right, he squinted his sore eyes in an effort to read the name on the board as they passed.

David saw his movement and smiled knowingly, 'That's Fontcalent Prison, Anthony. Where people less intelligent than I serve their sentence when they're caught.' If

Anthony O'Malley prayed at that time that his captors would one day see the inside of the cells, his prayers would be answered.

David would spend three years on remand behind those grim walls and would enter there to serve his half-century sentence after the trial. Matthew, meanwhile, would languish 30km away in Villena. Justice would indeed be served one day.

Finally, as they turned into the development of Baradello Gelat, Anthony forced himself to speak to the man he abhorred. 'So, now you've got your money, are we off then?'

David nodded. 'Of course. As soon as we're a decent distance away I'll phone the police and tell them where to find you. I keep my promises, Anthony... you'll see if I don't.'

But then, as Matthew turned the car into the drive and David snapped the handcuffs on to his wrist, Anthony heard Linda's desperate scream. 'Help! Help! Please God help us!'

'That fucking woman!' David exploded from the car and half-waddled, half-ran towards the cellar leaving Matthew to close the final cuff onto his own wrist.

A dark cloud of foreboding descended over Anthony as David disappeared around the far rear corner of the villa. He could hear the fat man's vicious oaths drowning out Linda's desperate screams.

17

A PLACE IN THE COUNTRY

As speculation grew about the O'Malley's possible fate, a photograph appeared in the UK *Daily Mirror* of a rustic property known as La Caseta. The tumbledown building was located in an area known as Els Parrals – 'the vineyards' in the local Valencian dialect. It was assumed by all to be the property that had first lured Anthony and Linda to the Costa auction and the general assumption was that the photograph had come from Spanish Property Auctions.

The white stucco, red-roofed building and outhouses were set back from the dirt road behind a pierced masonry wall on the right hand side of a Y-junction leading across vineyards and scrubland.

Strangely for an auction property, it was also seen on a placard in a Villajoyosa estate agent's window by a member of *CBN*'s advertising staff for a price of €126,000, which put it just within the O'Malleys' price range and definitely worth a look.

Again, I took Tom Cain – a recent addition to the news desk staff and a veteran of the second Gulf War who had recently retired as a Warrant Officer of the Royal Tank Regiment – to accompany me. Tom had opted for a post-retirement career in journalism after moving to San Juan de Alicante with his pretty Mexican wife Rose and their six-year-old daughter Paige.

Tom, a grizzled and experienced campaigner, still bearing the remnants of his WO2's de rigueur bushy moustache that would have been much too severe for civilian life and prone to wear old army khaki drill calf-length shorts to the office in summer, readily accepted the offer to accompany me on a trip that was really an exploitation of his tank-driving skills in the bumpy, rut-ridden landscape.

We took off with a map to look for the building. The rural Spanish countryside is not *A-Z* territory but we eventually located the property, which was unoccupied and in an obvious state of disrepair. I noticed the extent of the surrounding vineyards, around 3,000–4,000 square metres to my inexperienced eye, and a small empty concrete box of a swimming pool set to the right of the building.

The house was built on two levels due to the sloping ground, with steps leading down to a lower extension with a locked up-and-over door.

Tom and I explored around the rear of the building and uncovered a stone hatchway into a large cement water depository. Water is a precious commodity in the drought-ridden south of Spain and most rural properties have no piped mains supply. Instead, rainwater is collected by a series of gullies, or *acequias*, that channel the flow into a tank that, in turn, serves the house.

In times of severe drought – some parts of the area haven't seen a decent rainfall for 15 years – supplies are bolstered by deliveries made by a water bowser.

We levered the hatch off the dank depository and, reminded of the corpse of a missing Swiss woman that I'd been led to in a garden soak-away a year previously, I used a handily abandoned long wooden pole to probe the cloudy depths.

We then used the mountain rescue method familiar to both of us of searching for bodies by probing the soft earth of the vineyards in a grid pattern with long sticks and pausing to smell the ends for signs of decay. In retrospect, it was probably overkill but no one else was doing anything.

At that time, we were unaware of the extent of the credit card and money trail, relying on what we were told by Bernard and Nicola at the press conference and what I'd heard from Hella Henneberke at CAM Bank. This was still barely a month after the disappearance had been reported and the couple might just be alive. If Anthony and Linda were being held anywhere, it should be in the house or one of the locked outbuildings.

Unable to gain entrance without leaving sign, we drove back to the office and I called Joanne Miles, who confirmed to me that the house in Els Parrals wasn't the auction property. She had no idea how it had got into the newspaper. Did she have the location of the auction property? She could only give me the address I had already near Chica Moratella, a low hill whose silhouette could be seen 5km distant from the house among the vineyards.

I knew at that stage that the auction that had taken place on 23 September had seen the house that was advertised in the Spanish Property Auctions news sheet sold to an Alicante property company. I would need to contact the company for directions.

But that still left us with the mysterious property in Els Parrals. Although I couldn't imagine even a squatter falling in love with this pile of bricks and rubble, who had identified it as the house the O'Malleys had set their heart on?

Although the main players who would appear linked to the location have never to this day been formally identified, I believe I know who they were. I was yet to discover in risky circumstances that Linda and Anthony had actually viewed this house in the company of a Spaniard and an Englishman, the latter possibly the man later to be named by the defendants as the main protagonist in the kidnap, robbery and murders of the O'Malleys. The mystery was no nearer being unravelled and was getting more complicated by the minute.

The harbinger of my impending brush with violence was a presumptuous journalist who was already on an easyJet flight bound for Alicante. I have no wish to name this idiot in print; suffice to say that he eventually received a severe tongue-lashing from Det Supt Alan Jones for his selfish actions in impeding an inquiry when the facts were reported to the Welsh police. At that point, we could have been very near to picking up the warm trail of the O'Malleys, but for this man's clumsy approach in alienating a vital witness.

18

PLAYING WITH FIRE

A BBC Wales team arrived in my office for yet another interview but I declined on the grounds that I had nothing more to say. Any information I gathered was being sent to the North Wales Police HQ at Colwyn Bay, and I was learning my own lesson of never talking to the commercial press.

It may seem an odd arrangement where an investigative journalist used his own time to pursue enquiries on behalf of an estranged police force 1,000 miles away, but perhaps not that odd in the circumstances. Neither their officers nor I had any authority or jurisdiction in Spain. And where the Welsh police were concerned, with their lack of the language and Spanish street savvy, compounded by no help from the Spanish law enforcers, they were further down the food chain than I was.

Meanwhile, my thoughts were on La Caseta in Els Parrals. I planned to visit the estate agency that had advertised La Caseta, the house featured in the *Daily Mirror*, posing as a prospective buyer and to gain access to the property. If Linda and Anthony had been there I would possibly come across some sign.

At this point in time, I had a theory that the O'Malleys had spoken to some scallywags in Benidorm of their plans to buy in the rural area and had been taken to the house to set them up for the scam.

I was aware of a story going the rounds, possibly apocryphal, that this had been the fate of an earlier couple who had met a local English villain in a bar and spoken of buying a property. The local bandit had charmed the marks with the story of a little farm going for a song, provided it was a cash buy. He would negotiate with the senile owner and get them a bargain for no more than the pleasure of helping out fellow Brits.

As the story goes, the delighted couple turned up for a rendezvous the next morning carrying a carrier bag stuffed with cash, the amount of which varies with the teller, and were promptly taken up into the mountains by their Good Samaritan, and there robbed, shot and buried.

It was a gruesome tale with some possible merit since the villain, a scallywag of fearsome reputation and limited mental aptitude on the Costa, was named, having likely spread the tale himself. True enough, who would look for a couple who'd sold up and moved to Spain, unless they had left a family behind to worry about them? After all, people disappeared all the time, didn't they?

I called the Villajoyosa estate agent and set up a meet at the house with the owners for the following Friday, the only day available in a busy schedule since the newspaper went to press on Thursday night.

Still intrigued by the vineyard house and with Tom anxious to check out some nearby locations mentioned by his sister Liz, a London medium, we set out on the Saturday morning prior to making my appointment with the owners and cruised around the area. Liz Cain's involvement in the case, and that of other more 'unconventional' methods of detection, will be addressed more fully a little later. With us was Tom's adult son Jonathan, who speaks fluent Spanish, as do all the family from the influence of their Mexican wife and mother.

Liz Cain had given us some interesting clues. In particular, one was the figure of a stone bird, which she told Tom would be found very near a site connected with the missing couple. Nearing the site, I nudged Tom and pointed over his shoulder. There was a large stone bird forming part of the gable end of a nearby house.

After touring the area for an hour or so, we made to pass back by the house to take some photographs when we noticed two cars parked outside off-road. Standing on the veranda was Anthony's brother, Bernard O'Malley, with a female producer and, to one side, in front of the lower extension and on camera, stood a journalist speaking to two very decidedly angry Spanish farmers.

The rural couple, who looked like father and son, were gesticulating angrily and looking very miffed indeed.

Meanwhile, Tom and I took the opportunity to slip through the open upper doorway and view the bleak interior. A corridor and internal door led down some steps into the extension which appeared to be used as a tool shed, housing a clutter of rusty ironware and an old ploughshare.

On exiting, I took Bernard O'Malley aside and asked

him what was going on. He told me the presenter had arranged to meet the owners and had taken Bernard along for colour. It was all so pointless.

A situation that could have given up information that might have been useful to the North Wales Police had been breached for the sake of a few minutes of TV footage and I watched my potential witnesses drive off in a cloud of dust in their old farm vehicle.

It was then, as I prepared to tell both the presenter and producer where to put their film, that Tom's son Jonathan dropped the bombshell. He had overheard the older farmer admit to recognising the O'Malleys from a photograph and adding that the couple had been accompanied by two men.

I looked at Tom. The choice between giving the presenter the edge of my tongue or of following a potentially vital witness wasn't a hard decision to make. All three of us dashed for the car.

The exit from Els Parrals and the direction in which the farmers were heading meant crossing under the AP-7 eastern toll road by way of a concrete tunnel shaped like a large water pipe. The farming duo must have seen us take off after them but obviously were in no mood to talk. Whoever was driving the ancient old pick-up took it through the tunnel at a high rate of knots and swung right on to a dirt track paralleling the highway. A cloud of dust boiled up from the vehicle's wheels and we were hard pressed to follow the road which had great gouges hacked out of its surface edges by the recent autumn rains.

Tom managed to keep us on the road and I blessed his past experiences in handling lumbering tanks over dunes and along wadis in Iraq. Ahead, we were running into our own sandstorm as the farmers' truck cut left into a hollow between two hills and accelerated away in the direction of Villajoyosa.

The dirt road gave way to a single-lane blacktop winding through orange groves and Tom stepped up the pace so as not to lose our reluctant quarry. Within a few more hairy kilometres, we were bumper to tailgate, so much so that we didn't realise the next sharp right turn had taken us into the churned courtyard of an old farm building and the son was exiting the pick-up accompanied by bull-like roars, that I realised were coming from the man himself.

He seized what looked like a family-sized sapling from its roots and came hurtling down the yard to where we had stopped. The sapling turned out to be a mattock, a formidable axe-like implement, its wide, flat blade gleaming in the sunlight as he raised it above his head with the obvious intention of bring it down though Tom's windscreen.

I was out of the car and waving my press card as he arrived. The sight of the card, which is not dissimilar to a police warrant card, brought him up short but I didn't plan to mislead him. I gabbled off who we were and why I needed to speak to him.

I think he was sulking at not having put the mattock through the windscreen. He was certainly unimpressed and snorted something about reporters playing at policemen. I bit back on a retort that if I were playing at being a Spanish policeman, I'd be sitting on my backside ignoring a murder inquiry – the Spanish aren't big on cynicism – and, keeping a wary eye on the still raised mattock, addressed the father who had sidled up behind his son and stood there doing a fair impression of the elder Steptoe.

With crafty sidelong glances at his son, he told me the

Buyer Beware: The Alcoy villa offered for €30,000 by the killers. Steps to the cellar are at the extreme right of the photograph. The window of the cellar where the victims were murdered and their bodies buried can be seen in the foreground.

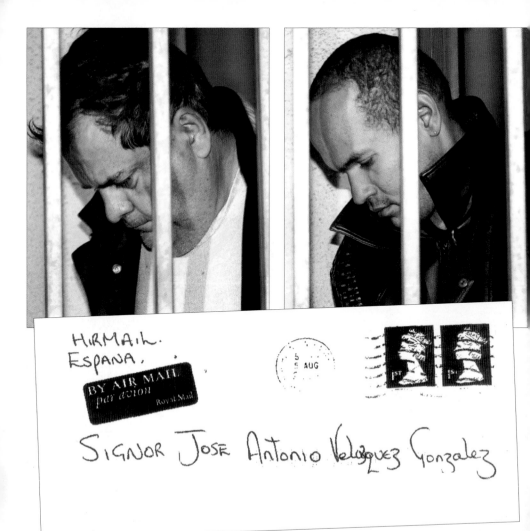

Top: Jorge Real Sierra (*left*) and José Antonio Velázquez (*right*) immediately following their arrests in Valencia.

© *National Police Archives*

Centre: Velázquez's name features above the address of an envelope sent to the Venezuelan while on remand by mystery man 'Bradley'.

Bottom: Real Sierra covers his face from photographers as he arrives by prison van for the trial in Alicante in 2006.

© *Shropshire Star*

Top: The victims, Anthony and Linda O'Malley.

Bottom: The River Dee and the picturesque North Wales town of Llangollen, home of Anthony and Linda O'Malley.

© *Dave James*

Above: DS Steve Lloyd and DC Dave James. The Welsh detectives visited Benidorm three times during their missing persons' inquiry. Their requests for assistance were ignored by the Spanish until the calls from 'Phoenix' were traced to Valencia.

© *North Wales CID*

Right: Detective Superintendent Alan Jones, the supercop who led the hunt for the O'Malleys. It was the senior detective's decision to follow up messages from mystery caller 'Phoenix' that led to the arrests in Valencia in 2003.

© *Crimewatch*

Top: DI Nick Crabtree with Bernard O'Malley and Linda's daughter Jenny Stewart at the first Wrexham press conference in September 2002.   © *Shropshire Star*

Bottom: The author discusses the case with BBC *Tonight* presenter Fiona Foster.   © *BBC*

Top: The press conference arranged by Benidorm Town Hall at the Meliá Hotel in October 2002. The Spanish police did not attend.

Bottom: Anthony's brother and sister, Bernard O'Malley and Christine Spruce, with Linda's daughters Nicola and Jenny at the Hotel Meliá, Benidorm, during the early stages of the missing persons' inquiry.

Top: Eileen Proctor, the Derbyshire medium who gave an accurate description of the murdered couple's grave 'in a white house among many trees'.

Bottom: Jijona, where the author and reporter Tom Cain were directed by Tom's sister, medium Liz Cain, in search of the victims' burial site. The white angel apparition, actually an illusion created by vegetation against a white stone wall, can be seen in the bottom left-hand corner of the photograph.

The scan sent by 'Phoenix' to the O'Malley family that was intercepted by the North Wales Police. It shows Anthony's passport and Visa card, and Linda's wedding ring.

© *North Wales Police*

reason for their joint anger and why they had departed so quickly from the house in the vineyards. They had gone there that morning expecting to make a sale and a man had pulled them in front of the camera and accused them of murdering an Englishman and his wife.

I asked why they hadn't hit *him* with the mattock, and that brought a smile from the elderly gentleman.

The old man was contrite although his son was still on a low simmer, so I addressed myself to Dad. I asked him if the house had ever been up for auction and he shook his head, 'Never, *señor*. I built it for my family with my own hands 35 years ago.' He held out his calloused, leathery palms for my inspection but I was still watching the mattock. He went on, 'I owe no man cash nor favours. My house and land are mine to sell or to do with as I wish.' I was beginning to like Dad, so I broached the sore subject of the O'Malleys.

Yes, he did remember the couple and half-recognised the Spanish man who was with them. He'd seen him around in Benidorm and Villajoyosa. The other man was English, he was sure. Certainly, he had spoken very bad Spanish with an atrocious accent. He thought he might have seen the Englishman in a bar in a certain location of Benidorm.

This brought to mind a Benidorm expatriate scallywag who well known as an exponent of the property fraud game. His bar was famed for selling massive English breakfasts *al fresco* while the wheeling and dealing took place. The bar was in an area popular with holidaymakers and I could imagine Anthony and Linda dropping by for breakfast and mentioning their search for property.

I asked the old farmer to elaborate but his son looked at him as if it wouldn't take much for Dad to get his share of the mattock. I asked if I could call back with photographs and I thanked them as I backed into the car and Tom put it into gear for our reverse retreat. If I went back there it would be in an armoured car and with a platoon of the Guardia Civil.

I gave a sidewise glance at Tom, who was grinning broadly. 'I hope you had my welfare in mind,' I told him.

'No problem, boss,' he grinned back. 'If he'd have nobbled you, all you had to do was bleed and hang on to the bumper. I'd have dragged you out short time.'

'An uplifting thought,' I assured him as we swung back on to the road to Villajoyosa and sanity. I bet he scared the djellabahs off them in Basra.

19

ROCK BOTTOM

Throughout November 2002 and in the run-up to Christmas, I had tried to keep the O'Malley case in the spotlight but it was difficult. Interest had waned among the Spanish press and the radio stations kept their silence.

While journalists appreciate stories that have 'legs' – something that will run and run – the story of the missing house-hunters was not sustainable. Perhaps the general public agreed with the Spanish police that Linda and Anthony were sunning themselves on a beach or sitting down to a plate of grilled lobster and a glass of Rioja in a restaurant somewhere further south.

The rumours that always follow a disappearance began to crawl from the woodwork. Anthony had a younger lover and had dumped Linda, who was now distraught in a Moroccan doss house and unable to pay her bill. Worse, a woman claiming to be a psychic claimed Anthony was in France and that Linda's body was in a ravine near Valencia.

I admit even I'd toyed with the idea that Anthony's involvement in the second-hand car trade had led him into contacts with the imported stolen car market in southern Spain. It was true that some local English villains, including a mate of Hal of Málaga Airport fame, were engaged in a profitable steal-to-order business.

The idea was that anyone could order a particular model of car, say a Jeep Cherokee or a sporty late model Porsche, and pay an upfront deposit. The gang would then arrange for their British-based colleagues to steal the car in the UK and arrange shipping papers to import it into Spain semi-legally on false number plates.

In fact, Anthony's forte was restoring vintage cars and selling them on to collectors, but I was unaware of his history at the time. In other circumstances, it might have been a path worth pursuing.

However, one call I got from the UK which impressed me many months later was from a Derby-based medium who had given me some strong leads in the past.

Eileen Proctor had once directed me to the body of a missing woman that was finally discovered in a soak-away; I had passed this information on to the Spanish police. Again, they had been slow to respond and I had to rely on the pressure from German police who were holding the victim's boyfriend in Duisberg on charges of using the missing woman's credit cards. They asked the Spanish authorities to open the soak-away I had identified, and the shocked officers found the body, which had mummified after a year immersed in soapy waste water. They still cross themselves and make the sign against the evil eye when I walk by.

I'm not a religious person. I've seen too much in my job

to believe men's fates are ruled by a caring creator. But neither am I blinkered. If I see it, I believe it, but I'm not gullible. My views on the spirit world are certainly unorthodox and would make many mediums disown me but, believe me, I've seen it work.

How? I really don't know, but as an evacuated child in Yorkshire during the Second World War, I saw cups move and saucers fly when I was lodged in the home of a very disturbed medium in a village called Moorends. Besides, the investigation was going nowhere else at that stage.

Mention mediums to the average UK copper and he'll roll his eyes and look through you. His average Spanish counterpart will make a sign to ward off the evil eye. In a country that still remembers the Inquisition, spirits are demons and those through whom they speak are witches and wizards. I don't have much of an opinion either way.

Mrs Proctor told me she had spoken to Linda, who had described a large suspension bridge with red cables and a white house surrounded by pine trees. I filed the information and forgot about it. Later on, it would fit in uncannily with the town and the property where the O'Malley's bodies were found.

But I was seeking hard facts, not visions. If the murdered dead can speak, why don't they tell us where they are instead of the Ted Roger's type old Dusty Bin clues we're supposed to unravel?

Someone in the case of the O'Malleys once phoned to tell me the bodies were hidden within sight of a church with a blue-tiled, domed roof. Anybody who's ever been to Spain will know that would cut the possible locations down to a minimum of around half a million.

The truth is, we were at an impasse. The Welsh police

were due to return home and take up their missing person enquiries from Wrexham; the Spanish police weren't talking and apparently weren't doing anything either; and the public didn't seem to have a clue.

Anthony and Linda O'Malley had settled their bill of €297.83 at the Hotel Altaya in Altea on 4 September, telephoned daughter Jenny at 8.30pm and then disappeared for two days until being seen by Joanne Mills in Benidorm around lunchtime on 6 September.

I knew they had used their Yorkshire Bank credit card for what DS Lloyd described as 'two lawful purchases' of €25 for dinner at a Chinese restaurant in Benidorm on 6 September and €30 for filling up their hired Fiat at a Benidorm petrol station on the following day.

The question was – where on earth had they gone after that?

One possibility for their disappearance from the radar might have been their desire to economise until the auction, and they may have been put in touch with someone willing to put them up or hire out an apartment for a short while. There's a lot of black economy under the surface among expatriates on the Spanish Costas. Many couples find an extra income in letting out their apartment when they go back to the UK to escape the searing summer heat. The lets are usually managed by the apartment concierges or *porteros*, who pocket a commission on the fee. There are also those who have bought a second apartment as an investment and let it out through postcards pinned on a supermarket notice board or advertisements in the local freebie news sheet.

It was reasonable to assume that Anthony and Linda had decided to seek out a cheap, self-catering apartment where

Anthony could stay while awaiting the auction on 23 September, hence checking out of the Altaya Hotel on 4 September. At the impromptu meeting with Joanne Miles on 6 September, Linda had told her that they hadn't found anything to date so that would rule out an earlier meeting with David and Matthew, which the friendly Linda would have been sure to mention.

If they had rented somewhere casually, it would mean unclaimed suitcases in an apartment, since my conclusion was, whatever had happened to them, they wouldn't have taken their suitcases to a fatal rendezvous. Somewhere, a nervous apartment owner would be fussing about what he or she had read in the newspaper and was wondering how they could tell the police without becoming involved with the tax office for undeclared income.

I wrote a short piece in *Costa Blanca News* inviting the apartment holder to come forward and promising complete confidentiality. Meanwhile, Tom Cain and I hit the streets to enquire at likely apartment blocks and cheaper *pensiones*, the Spanish equivalent of B&Bs.

I didn't know at the time but, months later, I was to discover that their suitcases had indeed travelled with the O'Malleys on the invitation of their prospective kidnappers to move in and get the feel of the dream home that was to become their prison and eventual death cell. But that hadn't occurred until the morning of 8 September. In any event, no one took up my offer to come forward, and the mystery deepened.

20

THE WHITE ANGEL
OF JIJONA

By January of 2003, the investigation had died. The visiting Welsh officers had flown back to the UK, convinced that there was nowhere left to go with the inquiry. The O'Malleys had vanished off the face of the earth and the trail of clues, such as there had ever been, had run out.

This was around the time of the disclosure to me by Alan Jones of the computer purchases. With that receipt lay the only possibility of a breakthrough.

Tom Cain's sister, the London medium, had recently sent Tom a dowsed map (holding a pendulum or other free-hanging object over a map of the area) that pointed to a location inland between Alcoy and Jijona, the *turrón* capital of Spain. Turrón is an almond-based confection similar to nougat, whose local recipe is guarded as fiercely as the French protect that of their champagne. However, it wasn't sweetmeats that were on my mind when I looked at the location on the map.

It was, by now, a logical conclusion to me that Anthony and Linda had gone inland in their search for their dream home. Benidorm teems with holidaymakers during the summer, but anyone staying on through the winter months would stand out like a sore thumb, yet there had been no report of a sighting. Even the kooks, those odd conspiracy theorists who always write to newspapers, had gone quiet.

It was on a crisp morning in January that Tom Cain and I set off for Jijona. The area indicated by Tom's sister Liz was on the outskirts of the town close to vineyards and overlooking the road up from the coast as it cut through the foothills of the *sierras*.

I was using a Spanish army map that showed old footpaths cutting through the dowsed area, which seemed to be located on the other side of a dirt escarpment and some old water depositories.

There was also an abandoned stone building that yielded nothing more than some rotting sheep carcasses. Tom drove down the escarpment in his best tank- invasion style while I leaned away from the edge and pretended to study the map.

Eventually, we left the estate car and walked the paths on foot. Whatever the cynics may say, the fact was that, on that day, we were nearer to the O'Malleys than anyone involved in the investigation had been since the couple's disappearance. Mediums Eileen Proctor and Liz Cain were more successful in locating the area of Linda and Anthony's disappearance than two national police forces with the latest technology at their fingertips. That surely must make the cynics think twice.

Again, let me stress that this was only an experiment when all else was at a standstill, but the fact is it brought tangible results that unfortunately only fitted the pattern in hindsight. Other than that, it was back to sifting apparently unconnected and random clues and pieces of evidence.

The central mark of the dowsing rested on a shallow canyon surrounded by overgrown mossy banks. These banks turned out to contain underground, cave-like cavities, with open vents to the sky. I didn't notice them until I'd narrowly escaped falling into one. These underground caverns were obviously works of nature adapted for living by man and had probably been inhabited up to the last century. Now they appeared to be used by itinerants and drug abusers. Syringes littered the floor, along with animal bones and the remnants of wood fires. A few old mattresses lay torn and reeking of stale urine.

If our journey was to achieve any result, they all had to be searched, but it was not a pleasant job and we were both glad when it was over.

I looked again at Liz's map and saw another ringed area further towards the west of Alcoy, which lay some 25km to the north. But it had been a long and dirty search and I decided to head back to Alicante. Before we left, I stood at the top of the escarpment and took some photographs for the file.

Costa Blanca News did not have a photo desk and reporters using the office Nikon had to wait for film to be developed at a nearby franchise on the commercial estate. It wasn't until Monday afternoon that I received the photographs. One in particular made me pause and look again. It was a view from the escarpment that took in a marshy field below and the tumbledown stone corral where we had found the dead sheep. But down in the left-hand corner of the photograph was the unmistakable form of a figure dressed in white.

I scanned the photograph on to my computer and enlarged it but there seemed to be no doubt. The hair stood up on the nape of my neck, for looking up at me from between a line of three trees was a white angel. Unsympathetic staff in the office thought it looked like a goat.

I began to wonder if this talk of communing with the dead wasn't causing me a little temporary insanity. Of course, there have been famous psychics who have worked successfully with police in criminal investigations, such as Dorothy Allison, the American psychic whose rather redundant speciality was tracing the remains of murdered children, or the Dutch psychometrist Gerard Crosiet, and I'd come across it myself in the case of the missing Swiss woman Dina Prietzel; but I drew the line at white angels.

Tom Cain was curious enough to drive back to Jijona the next weekend to check the site out, but no trace of the figure was found. Was there something in Liz Cain's map after all? The mystery was solved a week later when we both returned to the location. The White Angel of Jijona that had so mystified us and our colleagues turned out to be a pattern formed by undergrowth on a white rock; the sort that, in days gone by, had Tom and I been small devout peasant girls, would have launched pilgrimages of invalids and miracle recoveries. I wasn't impressed by the discovery.

The fact is that much of what I would hear from both

Eileen Proctor in Derbyshire and Liz Cain in London tied in with various facets of the investigation, including place names and site descriptions; however, apart from the journey to Jijona and the further indications of Alcoy as a burial site from Eileen Proctor, none of this material would ever give a direct lead to the resolution of the mystery. In the case of the O'Malleys, there would be only token help from the esoteric side of the triangle.

21

A WEEK IN HELL

The handcuffs had been changed for leather straps but this was no mercy move on the part of the kidnappers. The constant chafing of the metal handcuffs had bitten into the man and woman's wrists and David feared an infection that might kill his captives before the money ran out. He had splashed their wrists with crude, neat disinfectant and ignored the moans of pain. They would moan much more if they denied him the information he wanted.

Linda and Anthony had been locked in the cellar since the previous evening and today David planned to wring out full details of the couple's actual cash worth. He had arrived at the Alcoy villa around 8.00am, having left Valencia where he had slept with his family an hour earlier and taken the N-340 south through Játiva. The hire car had run well and he had no fear of being stopped. The Fiat wasn't due for return to Málaga airport until 13 September, the end of the week, and he had already used the computer and scanner in the Valencia apartment to make himself a credible ID in the name of Anthony O'Malley.

He ate a buttered roll with marmalade and drank a coffee with Matthew before taking the cattle prod from the hall cupboard and walking out on to the veranda. There, he stamped his foot on the marble tiles to let his captives below know that he was up and about. Let them look up to the concrete ceiling and wonder what he had in store for them that would soften their minds. They had both already tasted the prod the evening before and would remember the searing shock of pain that would barely register on a reluctant, lumbering cow, but could reduce a human being to the incalculable agony of convulsing muscles.

Matthew followed him down the narrow steps at the end of the veranda that led to the metal cellar door. David unlocked the door and pushed it inwards, aware of a shuffling within the dim morning light from the solitary window.

'Good morning,' he said, 'I trust you both slept well.'

He listened impatiently to the woman's sobs and her husband's threats of retribution and justice and told them both to hold their tongues. 'This is simply a business transaction,' he told them. 'You will remain here until you've paid for your release.' They told him they had no money and he sneered in their faces.

'I think a different story from yesterday, my friends, when you told me you had cash to pay for this house. However, I'm sure you can be persuaded to change your minds.' He switched on the prod and stabbed it briefly at

Linda's ankle. She shrieked and struggled away from him, held by the thin leather straps tied to the metal frame.

Her husband's bed frame groaned as he struggled against the restraints. 'Leave her alone, David, you bastard. She doesn't know anything. Have you no shame? She's a grandmother, for God's sake.'

David pressed the prod into Linda's stomach and her scream was greeted by a snort of laughter from Matthew. Anthony's roar of rage shook the cellar and he fought his bonds like an angry bear. 'If I get loose, I'll fucking kill you both. Leave her alone!' His last shout broke in his throat as he began to hyperventilate in his terrible anger, but his captors remained impassive. Once again, the cattle prod was extended and Linda screamed her agony to the ceiling. She turned her head towards her husband and sobbed through her pain. 'Don't tell them, love. They'll have to let us go soon.'

'Oh no, madam,' David spat back at her, 'you'll either tell me what I want to know or you'll die here. Are you thirsty? You will be when the sun starts beating through that window. And there's not a soul around for kilometres, even the neighbours have been kind enough to take a holiday. What do you say to that, *señora*?' He attempted to jam the cattle prod into her again and she fought him off with her legs, but still the jolt ran through her.

She felt herself fighting against the darkness that suddenly closed in on her and she was violently sick. As she collapsed back on to the mattress in exhaustion, she faintly heard Anthony's voice once again reciting the numbers to David. She felt the prod touch her again but all she could do was moan. The fight had gone from her.

The O'Malleys were to remain entombed in the cramped cellar for another four days, when Anthony O'Malley was ordered to wash, shave and dress before being driven on two occasions to the CAM bank in Benidorm first to request and then return to withdraw that sum of €25,000 that he believed would buy his and his wife's freedom on that last day.

During almost a week of hell, they were fed a minimum of prepared food, probably rice, almost certainly brought over from Valencia by David on his daily visits.

For the first few days, Matthew was left to guard the couple, sometimes, if we are to believe his brother-in-law's evidence, actually bringing women to the villa to assist him. Again, there is also the emerging spectre of 'Bradley', the third man who would be named by both defendants at their trial, who could marginally have been involved in the plot from the start. This man, who is currently in the UK, is aware of the accusations levelled at him in court but has neither replied to or acknowledged my very direct attempts to communicate with him.

There was no doubt in the minds of the investigators when they disinterred the remains of Anthony and Linda O'Malley from their shallow grave that both Linda and Anthony had been tortured at length over the five days of their captivity.

Linda had also been beaten violently on more than one occasion. Forensic pathologist Salvador Giner of the Institute of Legal Medicine in Alicante told the court that liquid formed in the decomposition of the male corpse had soaked into the body buried underneath, meaning that the tissues and skin of the lower corpse were preserved in a hydrated condition, allowing pre-mortem wounds and contusions to be identified. Giner's examination detailed bruising to the neck and face of Linda O'Malley and scorch marks on the skin of the arms and lower legs.

There was also a large subdural haematoma measuring 5.5cm in diameter to the upper right area of the back of the head, consistent with either a blow with a blunt object or a fall against a hard surface.

Death, in Dr Giner's opinion, was caused by heart failure brought on by stress. When questioned by the prosecution with regard to this conclusion, the Spanish pathologist pointed out that there was no sign of a frothing residue in the lungs characteristically present in cases of asphyxiation.

It would have been the aim of the killers to strip the bank account of their victims until nothing remained. Although equipment exists in the computer market to read information from cards even to the extent of recovering the PIN number – a fact always denied by banks – such sophistication might well have been beyond David, despite his obvious familiarity with computer technology.

Far easier, then, to retrieve the information from the victims, with no problem involved for an immoral mind devoid of human ethics. Having heard him in court, it is my opinion that the man would have burnt babies to get the information he required.

While his fellow conspirator sat slumped in his seat between two prison guards, the man calling himself David constantly leafed through notes throughout the hearing, and exchanged meaningful looks with his defence attorney. Two men sat before the Alicante court, rightly accused of the illegal detention, robbery and murder of

Anthony and Linda O'Malley. But one wonders if the Spanish police were more anxious for a conviction than for bringing all guilty parties to justice.

My own investigations would eventually beg the question – were there unfilled places for at least two others on that hard-backed prisoners' pew?

22

A RAG, A BONE,
A HANK OF HAIR

In late November came two reports of bodies found in the Benidorm area. The first was discovered high on the Sierra Helada, a mountain range that rises from the cliffs at the northern end of the town and follows the coast as far as Altea. Although quickly discounted as that of Anthony O'Malley due to the bizarre circumstances in which it was found, this male skeleton evoked some interest as the possible remains of 23-year-old Derek Cross, who had disappeared in November 1996.

The cadaver was found at the top of the sierra in an area frequented by homosexuals, which Mr Cross certainly was not, but the only clothing found on the skeleton was a pair of tattered and sun-bleached jockey shorts bearing a UK department store logo.

Eventually, DNA testing proved the victim not to be Derek Cross, but even that provided a poignant point. Someone else, possibly a British subject, had died in that lonely spot and lain undiscovered for long enough for gulls and crows to strip the flesh from the bones, now scattered and bleached by the sun. Another lonely soul with no family to raise the alarm or mourn his passing had died on a mountain ridge overlooking the glitter and false gaiety of the Costa Blanca's most popular resort. An investigation into the identity was never pursued.

The second cadaver was much more interesting. A mechanical scythe cutting the undergrowth bordering the AP-7 toll road to the Costa del Sol, the route the O'Malleys would have taken to catch their flight home on 13 September, threw up a desiccated skeleton, the huge blades shattering the brittle, sun-dried bones as they were dislodged by the rotor. More importantly, the body had been found on the southbound side of the carriageway, in the direction of Málaga. It was time to consider a possible hijack and murder.

The area where the corpse was found was just north of the La Marina services, a toll road stop notorious as a base for setting up violent attacks on motorists and their passengers. Here, the normal *modus operandi* is to pierce a tyre of the target vehicle, which would probably have suitcases and travelling bags on show on the rear seats, while the driver and his or her passengers were using the service's facilities.

The restaurant and washroom area at La Marina services is reached from the southbound side of the carriageway by a footbridge, effectively leaving a parked vehicle unguarded and out of sight of its owner for long minutes, crucial to the hijackers.

When the intended victims drove away from the service stop, the hijackers' vehicle would follow until the puncture took effect, causing the victim to stop on the hard shoulder of the road, ripe for robbery as the hijackers played Good Samaritans and stopped behind with an offer of help.

The usual protagonists in this type of robbery, familiar to all regular users of European motorways, are South American criminal immigrants.

It was possible that this ruse or one similar had been perpetrated on the O'Malleys, with at least one of the couple, more likely Anthony who would have put up a defence, pulled from the car and slaughtered at the roadside.

Tom Cain and I drove to the site. The traffic police who had been called to the scene, in this case the local Guardia Civil, were unhelpful. The remains were taken away in a blanket with no opportunity offered for a photograph. Once again, the law-and-order boys saw the incident as their exclusive territory and certainly not something for public discussion or consumption.

One of the officers at the scene even refused to reveal the sex of the corpse. It was, he insisted, 'impossible to tell', a remark that caused guffaws from the assembled pressmen since the pelvic bones of a skeleton are always a giveaway, the female's being wider and shaped quite differently to assist childbirth. A veteran journalist from *Información* asked whether the *civil* in question had led a sheltered life?

Nonetheless, as is the custom in Spain, we were kept behind a hastily erected barrier while the Guardia strode up and down peering into the long grass in search of they knew not what. Knowing we'd get nothing from the pitiful heap of bones now being loaded into the back of an ambulance, a vehicle far removed from the needs of its present occupant, we drove up past the service area and took the next exit out to Villajoyosa and back to the office in Finestrat.

The next day was a Saturday. Tom Cain lived some distance away in San Juan de Alicante, so I planned to drive out alone the next morning and find the scythe operator.

That proved to be no problem. At 10.00am the next morning, I stopped on the motorway bridge south of La Marina services and saw the swathes cut into the underbrush by the machine. The high pampas grass grows rapidly along the toll road borders, despite the arid climate and, if not hacked back regularly, it encroaches into the hard shoulder.

It's a dangerous occupation for the rotating scythe driver, since all manner of rubbish is thrown from cars over the months. Shattered bottles erupt like howitzers, and are hurled forwards or backwards, ricocheting on to the cab by the clockwise motion of the horizontal blades. It must have been a shock to see a scarecrow of bones appear to leap up from the long grass before splintering in all directions.

I drove back down to the toll entrance, picked up the southbound carriageway and overtook the scythe, parking on the hard shoulder some distance in front of it to avoid the whirling detritus being thrown out.

The operator flapped his arms as I walked back towards him and shouted a warning. A large lump of metal, possibly a discarded silencer, thumped on to the tarmac some metres in front of me and I threw up my arm to shield my face.

The operator relented and switched off the blades,

preparing to berate me as I approached – another crazy foreigner seeking directions.

I waved my wallet at him without flapping it open to show an ID; I figured if he then assumed I was from the police, that was down to him. As soon as I mentioned the cadaver, he looked embarrassed and slightly shifty.

'*Sí, jefe,*' he said, recalling that he had told the *civiles* from *tráfico* there had been a sudden whirling of dust and a strange taste in his throat.

'*¿Como canela, verdad?*' 'Like cinnamon, right?' I suggested.

He nodded and looked surprised, and I felt a twinge of disappointment. While a two-month-old corpse left in the open will still harbour the nauseating smell of corruption, a dried old specimen takes on the distinctive, sweet and dusty tang of cinnamon, as if Nature realises she has to do something about her deodorant after a respectable period of corruption has passed. The timescale was wrong for it to be a corpse of either of the missing Brits.

The scythe driver sealed it for me by describing the other rubbish that had turned up in the same upheaval. There had been a tattered coat of some description and very definitely a backpack that the Guardia had taken away with the bones. The Guardia hadn't been very thorough, so there was probably more around the site which he'd be honoured to point out if I cared to look? I didn't.

So there it was. An itinerant or possibly a hitchhiker had been mowed down and flung into the undergrowth at the side of the road. Had he or she been missed at a planned rendezvous? Had the driver felt the bump and wondered later at the crumpled nearside wing?

What was sure was that no one had reported anything of

the incident. A forensic pathologist would later report the body had lain in the roadside grass for at least seven months. Another unclaimed body on the Costa Blanca.

Someone hadn't been walking facing the traffic and had paid the price. But that didn't help me. Where on earth were my absent home-seekers?

23

CAUGHT ON CAMERA

Christmas 2002 came and went with no further news of the O'Malleys, other than the sad report that Anthony's elderly mother, no doubt stressed at the mystery of her son and daughter-in-law's disappearance, had died on 2 December. Another tragic blow for the O'Malley clan, now consigned to spending Christmas without three of their beloved family members.

On a chance, I dialled Anthony's mobile number and got the message box. I left a message asking him to call me and that I had some important news regarding his family. I was to discover later that the kidnappers, with a magpie's sense of hoarding, had kept both Linda and Anthony's mobiles. They may have smirked when they finally heard my message. But their magpie refusal to abandon even the smallest of their spoils would eventually prove to be their undoing.

It's a fact that most kiters are caught by CCTV

surveillance. It's also a fact that after a flurry of the new broom syndrome, these are usually switched off or left without tapes. Luck, however, was on my side when I followed the CAM Bank director's lead and visited the huge department store chain of El Corte Inglés in Alicante.

In the course of their inquiry, the Welsh police would literally have to buy CCTV tapes from the stores in Valencia when following the credit card trail on their last visit in February 2003. Alan Jones later told me he'd had to pay the equivalent of over £150 for surveillance tapes that could and should have been seized by Spanish national police who had neglected to check out the stores as requested by Colwyn Bay HQ through Interpol in Madrid.

But in the run-up to Christmas, I was way ahead. I drove to Alicante and parked beneath the store in Avenida Maisonnave. I had no luck in the Menswear department until a recalled reference to computer purchases in Benidorm led me to try Electricals in the basement.

There, a very nervous young guy who mistook me for a foreign policeman (don't ask) remembered a large man in his fifties whose English bank card bore the name O'Malley buying a burglar alarm in September. He remembered this distinctly because he had stayed with a family of that name during an English language summer course in Dublin and wondered if this O'Malley could be a relative. But the man's Spanish had been perfect and his accent had been South American.

Did he remember anything else? Yes, there had been two women, one quite old, and a couple of kids. Could he describe the man to me? No problem, a little under my height – I'm 5ft 10in – but bigger, more corpulent, with thick, dark wavy hair. The man had worn frameless spectacles and he'd been carrying something in a Footlocker carrier bag. Footlocker is a US franchise selling sportswear and athletic shoes with an outlet in the Gran Via Commercial Centre in Alicante.

Once there, I was in even greater luck. They still had a copy of the CCTV tape in question when I gave them the dates I was interested in.

Oddly, the purchase of outsize men's sportswear had been made on 9 September on the Yorkshire Bank cash card, a day earlier than the burglar alarm in El Corte Inglés. I only had the CAM Bank movements but one piece of information had led to another. So perhaps our kiter had been using the Footlocker bag for his lunch the next day? I was beginning to get the feeling that I wasn't dealing with the brain of Kiters Anonymous, and that this particular kiter wasn't the sharpest tool in the box.

Still, happy to let shop staff believe that I was a reincarnation of Slipper of the Yard – in my profession, you take your luck where you find it – I watched the tape in the security office. There was my fat South American ransacking the racks, sans family.

CCTV tapes are notoriously bad in reproduction so this guy wavered in and out of focus but the podgy face and thick, dark hair were clear enough, as were the frameless spectacles. The hair, I noticed, was parted on the right, usually a sign of a left-handed person.

I thanked the shop manager and left; I now had a description of the kiter as a portly South American. The large size of clothes purchased on that day had me guessing his weight at around 250lbs. Added to that, I now knew he was probably married to one of the women he'd been seen with in El Corte Inglés; the assistant had described them as a 'family' and I had a pretty good picture of the man.

If I had then managed a look at the complete credit card purchase list that I wouldn't see until after the arrests, I could have added he was probably living in Valencia and had a child or children of around eight-years-old, according to the grade of schoolbooks purchased. But I didn't have that information. If the Spanish police, far more aware of investigation techniques than me, had bothered to do the rounds, they would have had the full story. Indeed, an inquiring mind might have instigated a search among Valencian schools' second-graders for a seven or eight-year-old with South American parents.

The kiter was certainly leaving enough clues behind. Months later, when our man was finally arrested, I would find that this description fitted him like a glove.

Why hadn't the Spanish police come to the same conclusion? Because they hadn't been there to find out.

24

A HOUSE FOR AUCTION

I was still determined to present the old farmer of Els Parrals with photographs of some local villains, including Hal, preferably when his son wasn't around. But there still remained the mystery of the property at Moratella Chica.

A few phone calls to the court records office had shown that the property had been sold at the 23 September auction to a developer called Alicante Naves SL. I took down the details and contacted the company, where an obliging employee offered to fax me a contour map of the area with the property marked on it. When I received this, I was able to match the contours to a Spanish army ordinance map that gave me an overall picture of the area with exit and entry roads.

It was little wonder Joanne Miles of the Spanish Property Auctions team couldn't locate it; this was in bona fide bandit country. I doubted if Anthony and Linda had ever set eyes on it, but it was still a detail that had to be attended to.

Again, I recruited Tom Cain and his station wagon to ride out the bumps. The road led us back under the AP-7 and past La Caseta, the house among the vineyards mysteriously visited by the O'Malleys in early September of the previous year. We were now into January 2003.

We followed a tarmac road and eventually turned south to cross the AP-7 again, this time by way of a narrow overhead road bridge. A large water tank was sunk into the earth to our right and a track too narrow for the car led down to tiered olive groves.

We parked the station wagon and followed the path down. The first house we saw was perched on a wide ledge above olive terraces. There was an old, rusting Seat in the yard but no one appeared to be home. Because of the steepness of the hillside, we were actually looking down on to the roof of the main dwelling. The whole set-up looked shabby.

Keeping on the main path to the right, Tom and I arrived at high walls set with a pair of ornamental iron gates. Inside, across a cobbled courtyard, was a well-kept looking villa. I pressed the bell set into the wall and the courtyard erupted with dogs – big dogs, small dogs and intermediate-sized dogs, all snapping and snarling and barking through the gates.

I backed off from a vicious-looking Alsatian, who was rolling the whites of its eyes at me and looked like it was measuring me up for an *al fresco* snack. I felt relieved when an old man appeared, walking through the seething pack of dogs like St Francis of Assisi. I flashed my press card and asked about the house up the hill. He didn't know the occupants but understood the *pobres* (unfortunate people) had suffered money troubles with the bank. The house had been seized for auction by the bank, a phrase that reminded me of the American Depression and put me in mind of Faye Dunaway and Warren Beatty as Bonnie and Clyde, taking pot shots at the For Sale sign on an embargoed property.

In this case, with a touch of Spanish romanticism, the new owners were letting the impoverished ex-owners rent the property. A happy enough story, but I wondered if Anthony and Linda had seen the terrain whether they would have still harboured thoughts of the house as their dream home? Not unless their dogs could abseil, that was for sure. The property was literally built on the side of a steep hillside with the descending olive tables no more that 2m wide. Or perhaps they had seen it and had discarded the idea of bidding on 23 September. Had that led them to ask around or check estate agency windows in Villajoyosa where the Els Parrals house was advertised?

From there, perhaps they'd asked for help and spoken in the wrong bar? I couldn't help feeling that their escorts to the earlier property had eventually passed them on to some villains further up the criminal food chain.

The Els Parrals property had been up for sale at €126,000, according to the old farmer, still within their price range. I never found out what the hillside property bought at auction, but it wouldn't have been much. Certainly more of a bargain for the O'Malleys than wherever they were now. I took some photographs and decided to call it a day. Perhaps it was time to get some head-and-shoulders shots to my old pals Steptoe and son in Els Parrals

Tom and I had a chat and decided that the old farmer's description matched the local scallywag who ran a bar. We had once staked a nearby market at 5.30am following a tip-off that Ibiza victim Jeffrey Hodgson had been seen helping to unload a van there and we got some funny looks from the stallholders who must have mistaken us for the law and were anxiously trying to hide their hooky merchandise.

Once the market is in full swing, pickpockets roam in groups among the crowds. In a surveillance video that I'd once been given to pass on to the national police, they were all there. Women pickpockets operated with overcoats draped over their shoulders and false arms in their pockets while their real hands were busy dipping into handbags. Brazen groups of four or five gypsy women closed in on tourists carrying 'steal me' backpacks and boldly unzipped and rifled the pockets as victim and pickpocket strolled along virtually side by side. A woman had been filmed here wandering along with her empty handbag trailing like an un-strapped concertina over her shoulder, recently robbed by a band of gypsies that had moved on to other victims. The pickpockets, or *carteristas*, are almost invariably women, probably because there's less chance of them being challenged, although their male minders are never far away.

Our goal was a nearby bar, owned by the man we suspected of taking the O'Malleys to the Els Parrals property. Later, the bar proprietor would be declared 'out of the frame' by North Wales Police and an informant

Top: The tiled plaque at the entrance to the housing development of Baradello Gelat.

Bottom: Calle Roure 7. Note the proximity of the neighbouring property on the right, which faces the window of the cellar where the victims were held for five days before their murders. Fatefully, the owners of the chalet were absent throughout the whole of September.

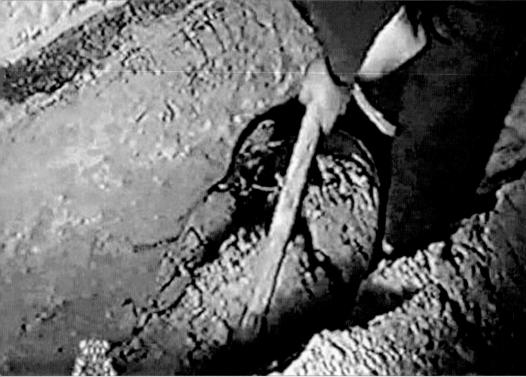

Top: A police officer is seen through the wire of the window of the cellar preparing to break through the cement floor into the O'Malleys' grave. © *Spanish National Police*

Bottom: Exhuming the remains of Anthony O'Malley. © *Spanish National Police*

Top: The door to the cellar reached by a flight of steps from ground level, down which the O'Malleys were dragged into captivity.

Bottom: A view through the grille of the cellar door. On the floor to the left is a pair of gloves left by a forensic officer. Between the bars, the broken cement floor marks the burial site.

The side view of the murder villa. The entrance to the cellar can be seen at the bottom right-hand corner of the building.

Top: The chalet in Els Parrals, mistakenly identified as the auction property sought by the O'Malleys. Nevertheless, it was visited by the victims in September 2002 accompanied by a mysterious Englishman and a Spaniard.

Bottom: The actual auction property never seen by Anthony and Linda, who might have found it inappropriate because of the steeply sloping terraces.

Top: The CAM bank office in Benidorm where Anthony was taken to withdraw €25,000, which he had been told would buy his and Linda's freedom, on the day the couple died.

Bottom: Plus supermarket opposite Hotel Meliá in Benidorm, where Joanna Miles last saw the couple alive on 6 September 2002.

Above: Items recovered during the search of the Valencian apartment included the registration plate of the stolen Fiat, the O'Malleys' passports and credit cards, two pistols, a Dictaphone (lower right) and an electric cattle prod (top left).

© *North Wales Police*

Left: The El Saler apartment block where the killers were arrested after Welsh police traced the signal of the mobile telephone used by 'Phoenix' to Valencia. © *Steve Lloyd*

Alicante Palace of Justice where the trial was held in 2006. The bottom left-hand arch of the main building marks the entrance to Court number one. On the extreme right is the alley along which prisoners enter the court building.

would pass on to me the name of another bar owner whose name would also be brought up at the trial.

To avoid confusion, let me make it clear that, at that time, nobody knew Linda and Anthony's fate. Whoever had taken them into the back country to view the old farm would very likely have had another property in mind when the couple baulked at the €126,000 price tag or, more likely, at the state of the property.

The idea of kidnap wasn't top of my list because it had never happened in these circumstances in Spain to my knowledge. There had been no ransom demand, so everybody involved in the investigation assumed they had been robbed of their credit cards and treated in such a way that they were unable to contact their family. Let's be frank, it seemed likely they were both dead.

That was the biggest problem facing the North Wales Police. Any homicide investigator knows that the chance of solving a murder fades rapidly if no progress has been made in the first 24–48-hour period. At that time, the O'Malleys had been missing for nearly six months.

The scam that I was considering the most likely was the carrier bag of money and a hurried burial in the countryside. If that were so, then the bar owner was probably our man. The man in question was also known as a confidence trickster well versed in property scams. In fact, he was soon to disappear as completely as the O'Malleys when the real owner of the bar, a man of fearsome build, discovered that his tenant was negotiating the sale of the bar right under his nose to an unsuspecting buyer fresh off the plane.

Photographing local villains on the Costa del Crime is not a hobby with a future. You can't stick your camera in the man's face, but you can include him in the shot with a bit of subterfuge. I've often worked with TV companies filming documentaries about the Costa's Mr Bigs or the timeshare barons. I've gone among the touts wired up and acted the gullible holidaymaker ripe for picking and we've always got our shots.

Most scallywags on the Costa will object to having a stranger take their photograph. The toothy, tanned smiles lighting up above clanking kilos of gold neck-chain are reserved for family gatherings. Anyone else sneaking around with a camera could be the Old Bill on holiday.

The way to do it here was to pose in front of the target then move slightly aside just before the shutter clicked. Every holiday snapshot has figures in the background, right?

We wandered into the bar around mid-morning and ordered a couple of beers, then I pretended to consult the large calendar behind the bar while I actually checked out the details of the bar's framed opening licence. I leaned back across the bar and smiled like a loon while Tom focused on our man and zeroed in on him behind me. Once developed, those photographs would be shown to my mate Steptoe but, before that could happen, I had word from the UK.

Out of courtesy to the North Wales Police, now back in the UK after exhausting all avenues of investigation in Spain, I had e-mailed Det Supt Jones in Wales and told him of my intentions. The message I received back was dated 12 March and read: 'Thanks for the e-mail. Do nothing. I will be in touch. Alan.'

Not one to impede a police operation, I halted any further investigation. It seemed like the Welsh police were suddenly on the trail again. I was later to learn that Alan Jones and Steve Lloyd had already flown to Madrid and, within two weeks, I was to witness the chilling disinterment in Alcoy. I was also to learn of the dramatic arrests in Valencia following the sinister rising of Phoenix on the Ethernet.

25

ENTER THE FAT ONE

It was about this time that two particularly nasty murders occurred on the same night, in Alfaz del Pi and Villajoyosa. In both occurrences, the two male victims had been tied to chairs and hacked to death by persons unknown – except that I'd received a letter naming a nasty piece of work from Bulgaria, an ex-policeman in his native land, who was acting with a criminal band as enforcer for a cigarette smuggling ring. These guys brought the cigarettes in from Bulgaria in containers and shipped them to the UK via Spain, with dodgy Customs personnel at each end smoothing the trip. It was even a form of local enterprise, with expatriates offered the chance in bars to buy a 'key' comprising 2,000 cigarettes for €200 and eventually to sell them on at a profit or smoke themselves to an early grave before the next consignment.

The two murder victims turned out to be collectors for the smugglers and had been sent to their own early graves for omitting to hand the money over.

What I needed was a word with my mate Glasgow John, an informant *par excellence*, who confided the most reliable information to whoever he trusted not to reveal him as the source. The *nom de plume* suited him admirably. I'd known John for most of my years on the newspaper, having been introduced into the freemasonry of 'grasses' by the late and deeply lamented Nigel Bowden, known to newsmen from John O'Groats to Gibraltar as the inestimable Slippery of the Costas.

The only problem with Glasgow John was that his information came highly priced. Once contacted, he would name one of several bars in his itinerary and get there at least two hours before the appointed time, during which he would run up a tab of the most expensive malt whisky on the shelf in his benefactor's name. It always paid to be early at the rendezvous.

On this occasion, he'd had enough to start his rant about life in the Gorbals of Glasgow as a young man with all the old tales of kippers nailed to the back door for a wipe with a slice of bread. Nonetheless, he had what I wanted, which was the story on the street behind the collectors' murders.

Knowing that it had already cost me in fine Highland malt, I also broached the subject of the O'Malleys. Had he heard anything?

'Aye,' his rheumy eyes sparkled, 'I have the word.' He eyed the whisky bottle that the arm-weary barman hadn't bothered to return to the shelf, having decided it was a waste of effort. I twiddled a finger at the barman to refill John's glass and asked for the tab. It was up with IBM shares.

'Well, what've you got?' I asked him.

'D'you ken El Gordo?' After a few tots of the finest, Glasgow John always spoke like he was at the Highland Games. But the only El Gordo I knew was the Spanish State lottery draw, literally translated as 'the Fat One', which takes place each year just before Christmas.

My informant looked surprised at my ignorance. 'Aye, him of the passports.'

I must have still looked baffled, so John went on to describe a document forger who supplied passports, ID documents and driving licences to order. This El Gordo was putting around a name involved in the O'Malley's disappearance, which seemed to have become a top talking point among the local scallywags.

Glasgow John gave me the name of an Englishman that meant nothing to me, but something else did interest me – El Gordo was apparently South American and lived in Valencia.

26

THE THIRD MAN

I didn't immediately pass the name given to me on to the Welsh Police; there was no point, since any inquiry would have to be made by the Spanish who weren't bothering at that stage. It would, though, crop up three years later at the Alicante trial, when the 'third man' would be named in open court as 'Bradley', the name given to me by Glasgow John, identified as an English acquaintance of José Antonio Velázquez, who, according to the defendants, acted alone in the murders of Anthony and Linda O'Malley.

At the trial, David – in reality, arch-villain Jorge Real Sierra – would deny all knowledge of the O'Malleys. José Antonio Velázquez – aka Matthew – would admit to planning the scam with the mysterious Bradley, but insist to the prosecution that he then went to Valencia and left the Englishman at the villa with the victims.

Later, I would come across the information revealed in a

letter, of which I'd acquired a copy (again, don't ask), written by Real Sierra to an associate, that the Englishman had 'owned a possibly gay bar in Benidorm called Oliver's'.

Based on my assumption that an old trickster like Real Sierra would know that, for a story to be credible, it would need a truthful foundation, after the trial closed I followed the trail of 'Bradley' around Benidorm. Certainly, the man had existed. My enquiries would also lead me to an Alfaz del Pi hangout for local gangsters where the name would be recognised and lead to threatening phone calls warning me to drop the search.

Eventually, the female owner of a Benidorm bar put me on the right track. Jackie Wainwright has run her own very cosy and respectable bar, Oliver's, for nearly 30 years in Benidorm Old Town, and she'd never heard of Bradley by that name or any of his possible aliases that I had, by then, turned up.

She did, however, seem to recognise a photograph that I had acquired during a related inquiry, the details of which, for legal reasons, cannot be mentioned here. She told me, 'Yes, I vaguely recognise this man, but not his friend. He may have put money into a Spanish bar. But it soon ran into money troubles and closed down.' The friend she referred to was José Antonio Velázquez in a photograph that had been taken soon after his arrest.

Much would be made of the 'third man theory' by the lower end of the local English language press, ever anxious to score a scoop over its more conservative opposition. An English-language Alicante radio station even broadcast an hour-long debate on the possibility. The fact remains that if it were a fabrication on the part of the killers it had, like all good fabrications, a foundation of truth.

There is no doubt that José Antonio Velázquez González knew the third man, whom I shall from now on refer to as 'Bradley', the name given in court by both of the accused and the name I had heard from my informant, Glasgow John. I have in my possession the photocopy of a letter written by Bradley in the south of England and addressed to José Antonio Velázquez while he was awaiting trial in prison in Spain for the O'Malley murders. The content of the letter makes it clear that it was written in 2005, two years after the arrests. Strangely, it thanks Velázquez, while turning down an offer of money, although the reason for the offer is not made clear. Does this mean there is a hidden hoard that the courts do not know about, in itself interesting, since both conspirators have pleaded insolvency in the face of indemnities to the relatives of the victims ordered by the court? It would also appear from the timeline that Bradley returned to the UK either late in 2002 or early in 2003, and that Velázquez was aware of some problem in the UK, since Bradley's letter thanked him for but refused his offer of financial help.

A check with the licensing department of Benidorm Town Hall confirmed the demise of the bar pointed out to me by Jackie Wainwright. The business had folded, given Spanish records, either late in 2002 or very early in 2003, about the time of the O'Malleys' disappearance.

In a letter to an associate at the time of the trial, Real Sierra wrote, 'José Antonio met Bradley in the Scrub's bar of Benidorm [sic]. Seems like Bradley owned a bar... I believe Bradley and J Antonio were lovers....' He goes on to name other 'associates' of his brother-in-law, including a Galician named Antonio and 'Matthew Don', of whom he writes, 'However, I am not sure, for JA says that Bradley and Matthew Don are the same person'.

It should be noted that the third man defence did not appear in either of the accuseds' first statements to police following the arrests, neither was it mentioned during the months of the *juicio oral* (oral proceedings) in Alcoy before the examining judge. As such, it was not admissible in evidence at the Alicante trial and was discarded by the three judges in the sentence summary of 12 April.

Velázquez had also changed his evidence to include the mysterious Bradley, whom he claimed sometimes went under the alias of Matthew Bradley.

Velázquez told the court that he had hatched the plot to rob the O'Malleys with Bradley, whom he left in charge of the villa after following Real Sierra and the family to Valencia on the evening of 7 September, after which he claimed no contact until told the plan 'had gone well' by Bradley, who then sold him the O'Malleys' hired Fiat Stilo for €2,000.

Velázquez' defence, conducted by counsel José Córdoba, assisted by José Soler Martín, claimed that a subpoena had been sworn to bring Bradley, aka Matthew Bradley, to court, but he had never been traced.

To the pressmen sitting on the wooden benches, it smacked of a flimsy story cobbled together by desperate defendants. But there was too much other proof that linked both of the accused to the villa and the placing of the advertisement, which is explained elsewhere in this book.

According to Real Sierra (aka David), a family argument led to him taking his mother-in-law and children to the apartment in El Saler, Valencia; thus he was absent when the O'Malleys viewed the property and agreed to stay until the purchase went through, unaware of the horrendous conditions planned for them.

Real Sierra further claims that, apart from being aware that some sort of scam was in progress in Alcoy – he admits using the O'Malley's bank cards to draw cash and make purchases for himself and Velázquez – he was unaware of the nature of the scam until informed of the disastrous outcome by Velázquez, who claims it was Bradley who committed the murders.

The story has all the makings of a bad plot but it should, in my opinion, have warranted further investigation.

Velázquez would further claim that Bradley sold him the O'Malleys' hire car for €2,000. None of the above, however, would be known to me until after the trial. The investigation still had a long way to go.

27

THE MEDIUMS

Frustrated by the lack of movement in the investigation, I had an esoteric moment and, out of curiosity, e-mailed Eileen Proctor, the Midlands medium who had previously contacted me about a large bridge spanning a gorge with a description of a white villa set among trees. This time, back came a description of a slim and attractive woman in despair. There were three men involved. The woman had argued with her husband because she didn't trust them. Her name was Linda.

Anthony, according to Eileen, would not come through. He was very angry at being deceived and she sensed a problem surrounding his religion. Anthony O'Malley, like most Liverpudlians of Irish stock, was Roman Catholic. Eileen told me that both were dead and she gave a description of the grave as described by Linda.

'There are red bricks at the side. The top slopes inwards. There's stone on top. There are steps out and a door.'

Considering that the victims could have been buried anywhere, it was an accurate description of the site. The cellar had been partitioned by a wall of red bricks, leaving a space no more than six feet across where the O'Malleys had been imprisoned and eventually buried. The grave had been dug through a concrete floor and then enlarged outwards, hence the sloping sides. And the floor had been re-laid with cement. A door in the cellar end wall led to a flight of exterior stairs up to the garden.

Other messages followed of a ring containing a red stone seal that Linda had left at home in Wales and she complained that her wedding ring had been taken. All this would prove to be true, but where were the bodies buried?

It must be said that Eileen had been spot on the ball in the past and was highly enough thought of by Manchester police to have been called in to help in the hunt for the body of Keith Bennett, a victim of folie à deux serial killers Ian Brady and Myra Hindley, and whose body is buried somewhere on Saddleworth Moor.

As I mentioned earlier, Eileen Proctor had been instrumental in bringing a killer to justice when she contacted me from Derby in 2000 to ask for my help in tracing missing Swiss expatriate Dina Prietzel whose 'spirit' was contacting a local UK spiritualist group. Here is not the place to tell that story other than to say that I did find the body, hidden in a soak-away that Eileen Proctor directed me to in the garden of the victim's house in La Nucía. She also named the murderer, although nobody was ever convicted of this. The only conviction was of a boyfriend who is now serving a prison sentence in Germany for fraudulently using the dead woman's credit cards.

Proctor had also warned me of wild dogs during the

Prietzel investigation, and my wife and I, while searching to locate the murder site from the medium's directions, narrowly escaped an attack by a pack of feral dogs on a mountain road by bundling ourselves into the car and locking the doors as the pack slathered at the windows.

Are there wild dogs in Spain? Yes, there are, courtesy of the cavalier temporary expatriates who buy a puppy when they move into a Spanish villa and abandon the animal to fend for itself when they decide to return to the UK. My wife and I have never forgotten the sight of those hungry dogs showing their teeth and salivating at the thought of us as two ready-to-eat English takeaways.

Tom Cain's sister Liz also began to 'communicate' around that time, sitting in a small summerhouse in her London garden and linking up with Linda, who was 'always anxious to talk'. As with Eileen Proctor, Anthony didn't want to say a word.

At one point, Liz would send Tom and me inland as far as Jijona using a map she had dowsed. At that time, we had been nearer to the bodies than anyone else involved in the hunt for the couple. Jijona is just half-an-hour's drive from Alcoy. It should be stressed that neither of these psychics knew the other, neither were they aware of the other's existence in the inquiry.

In the future it would be Eileen Proctor who put me almost on the doorstep. Eileen had previously mentioned a long red 'suspension' bridge and a stand of pine trees with a white house. The only suspension bridge of any note that I knew of locally was the massive Fernando Reig red cable-stayed bridge erected in 1987 across the deep Serpis river gorge that divides the town of Alcoy; houses among pine trees spoke of urbanisations. Linda and

Anthony O'Malley were found buried in the stone cellar of a white house standing among 4,000 square metres of Mediterranean pines and holm oaks.

As January 2003 slipped away with no other leads to follow, I drove around the outskirts of Alcoy on my own for a while, crossing the vertiginous bridge many times and showing Anthony and Linda's photograph to strangers. I also took photographs for my files with my pocket-sized Kodak digital.

Looking back through those files, I see a road junction lined with pines and, just in the hazy distance to the right, I can see the glimmer of sunlight on a polished tiled wall. It is the entrance to Baradello Gelat, the urbanización where Anthony and Linda died.

Although nothing I received from the UK mediums during the investigation physically helped to locate the O'Malleys, it can't be denied that, with hindsight, some of their indications were spot on.

While on the controversial subject of mediums, it's fair to say that, although they'd probably cut their wrists rather than admit it, UK police have used mediums in their inquiries into some of Britain's most notorious cases.

Apart from the self-acclaimed 'psychics' who telephoned me to tell me Anthony O'Malley had murdered his wife and dumped her body in a ravine before going on the run – an illogical conclusion since he was joint owner of the Welsh property that he would supposedly never see again nor profit from – I saw no harm in listening to anyone who had a theory on the missing couple.

Even then, hard-nosed newshound that I was, I had checked with Anthony's brother on the possibility of Mr O'Malley having a young lover hidden away who had perhaps joined him in Spain after Linda had been disposed of. Bernard O'Malley didn't even raise his eyebrows at what could have been seen as an impertinent question. He simply shook his head. Anthony was devoted to Linda and, wherever they were in whatever sort of trouble, they were together and supporting each other.

As for the use of mediums, there will always be debate, but it's my belief not to knock what you don't understand. January 2003 was a desperate month for all of us. No one would have guessed it was all soon to be brought to an end by the deadliest of all deadly sins – unadulterated greed.

28

A WORD FROM
THE WISE

When Glasgow John had been bankrupting me between tots at our meet in Benidorm, he'd mentioned that the mysterious third man whose name was being sent out around Valencia was a regular of Scrubs, an infamous little bar on the Alfaz del Pi Estrada that had been named after the old lags' abbreviation for HMP Wormwood Scrubs in West London.

Needless to say, many of the regulars all looked like they were waiting to sign up for a voyage with Captain Hook and it wasn't the place you took your wife unless she was a black belt in judo or a crack shot with a pistol, always providing you had one.

The Estrada is a long line of shops and bars lining a service road at the Alfaz del Pi junction with the N-332 and is famous for its tatty nightclubs known as *puti bars* after the Spanish word for prostitutes, who reputedly use the bars to pick up their clients. It was also the site where an unidentified customer had picked up a cab, later to leave the driver robbed and bleeding to death from stab wounds on the beachfront of Albir.

Scrubs had also notoriously been the scene of a recent shooting where the bullet had passed through the cheeks of the victim at such close range that smoke was still billowing from the wounded man's mouth as he shouted curses at his fleeing attacker. As I said, not a place you'd take the wife.

On a whim, I dropped by one afternoon after I'd left the office and took a drink at the bar, ignoring the eyes that had followed me in from the door. Some of the clientele would have recognised me from my byline photograph and, in particular, from a story I'd once filed involving Yuri Slivinsky, a young television engineer who'd been stabbed to death on the orders of his drug-dealing, one-armed employer whose repair shop had stood almost next door.

As is usual in such establishments, the stares eventually turned to open curiosity and I was approached by an evil-looking character who leaned tattooed arms the size of prize marrows on the bar beside me and asked what the fucking hell I was doing there. I asked him if he'd missed the sign outside that said 'bar', and lifted my glass to show him I was drinking.

He stared at me, trying to work that one out, and then laughed anyway as if it was beyond him. I bought him a drink and we eventually got talking about local crime. He seemed anxious to get his name in newsprint, pointing out that he'd done hard time in the UK and knew just about every villain I'd ever heard of, including the Krays. But then, every scoundrel who's ever been south of Watford

Junction lays claim to have drunk with the Krays or the Richardsons at some time.

The mention of the Krays brought me to 'Bradley', the name given to me by Glasgow John, since my Scots informant had also mentioned a connection with Reggie Kray. For the reasons above, I hadn't paid much attention at the time, since it was par for the course of these monologues that if the person telling the tale hadn't been in the Blind Beggar in Whitechapel Road when the paranoid schizophrenic Ronnie Kray gunned down George Cornell for calling him 'a fat poof', then he was cousin to the young homosexual found in bed with Ronnie when the police raided the Krays' East London home. Such is gang life. Everyone has drunk with the Richardsons and faced off Frankie Fraser. Everyone tells lies too.

I mentioned the name and my new pal nodded his head. I felt this one would have admitted knowing Bonnie Parker and Clyde Barrow if I'd bothered to ask him, but he did appear to know my man, describing him with details that fitted with the descriptions I'd gathered from elsewhere. He also mentioned a Spanish man that the named man was often in company with and gave me an odd, knowing wink and a nudge that nearly floored me.

By this time, other clientele had drifted in and decided I was the diversion of the day. A few gathered around, nodding wisely as my brawny companion spoke. They also knew the named man, an armed robber who'd done time with Reggie. A good-looking Flash Harry, very sure of himself... well in with a Spanish man and in some sort of business partnership with a Gallego (a native of Galicia, on Spain's north-western seaboard) called Antonio. Could this be the partner in the failed bar? But what I really needed to hear was a connection with the O'Malleys.

My luck was in with a man who was introduced to me as Little Dave. Dave told me he knew my man as 'Lee'. It was a simple shortening of the Christian name I'd been given by Glasgow John. Little Dave confirmed that Lee had apparently had a financial interest in a Benidorm beachfront bar near the Old Town that had closed with money problems at the end of 2002. There had been other problems, apparently – something had also gone down about that time that had kept Lee away from Scrubs for some weeks. Dave thought a job had gone wrong. The Spaniard whom Lee had seemed close to had also disappeared about the same time.

The dates matched up with the O'Malleys' disappearance but all I had was El Gordo's recommendation via Glasgow John that I should speak to an ex-armed robber who had probably left Spain. Not a lot to go on and nothing physically to tie the mysterious Lee, aka Bradley, to the O'Malleys.

It may seem surprising that so many 'hard men' were prepared to discuss a fellow ex-con with a newspaper journalist, but there's a wide gap between talking to the police and talking to the press. This wasn't grassing; this was seen more as an exercise in publicity for the calling.

I also knew these gatherings could turn as nasty as a pack of wolves that had stumbled on a lame rabbit when alcohol started to take effect. I'd turned down offers of drinks throughout the afternoon, waving my car keys at the donor in explanation, but now I thought it was time to leave. I'd established that Glasgow John had been talking about a real person.

Then Little Dave clinched it. 'I saw Lee in town just before last Christmas,' he told me, referring to Benidorm. 'He was with his Spanish mate and an English couple outside a bar by the Rincón. He told me they were Scousers over looking for a house. He winked when he said it.'

The Rincón de Loix is an area at the northern end of Benidorm's Levante Beach, heavily populated with English cafés and bars that have earned it the sobriquet of 'Bacon and Egg Alley'. Could Little Dave describe the couple? No he couldn't. My sudden interest had brought the shutters down. Dave had gone into the age-old 'I wasn't there... I didn't see it, and I wouldn't know him again anyway... ' mode.

But I now had my man in the frame. Despite the dubbing of Anthony and Linda O'Malley by the UK and Spanish press as Welsh at the time of their disappearance, both by their accents were Liverpudlians or 'Scousers'. Little Dave's reference to before Christmas could be stretched to take in the months of autumn, so Bradley had probably met the O'Malleys around the time of their disappearance. This was information that the police should know about.

I would later call Benidorm national police and speak to a *judicial* who claimed to be an inspector in Homicide but wouldn't tell me his name. Should I come in to make a statement? He took my number and said he'd call back. I never heard another word.

By now, the atmosphere in Scrubs was beginning to get fraught. Little Dave had wandered over to a group of drinkers and was telling them about our conversation. Heads were popping up like fighting cocks and staring in my direction. I could imagine myself in for a bit of rough and tumble before I made it out of the door.

Some of the older customers were obviously trying to cool down the hotheads who were more into playing the role of hard men. One of the elders looked at me and tilted his head towards the door. I'd been asking questions and I wasn't welcome. I nodded in return and made a line for the exit.

I saw a movement to my right as someone moved to block me off. There was a scuffle as a path was made for me and then I was outside and in my car. As I've said before, not a place to take the wife.

The telephone rang on my desk the very next morning. A rough voice told me the speaker 'knew what I was about' and 'where I lived' and to 'forget the fucking O'Malleys'. The man I'd discussed in Scrubs bar 'had friends'. It was made clear the speaker also knew who my wife was. That worried me.

As shocked as I was, I didn't believe for a moment that the threat was actually connected to the name I had enquired about in the Scrubs bar. Among that sort of community there are always sad characters born into the wrong century. They've missed the opportunity to be Billy the Kid or Al Capone, so confine their activity to a bit of strut and swagger. These scallywags like nothing better than to threaten anonymously from the other end of a telephone, but it would be an unwise man who didn't consider all possibilities. Perhaps someone thought I was getting too close to another event, like the story of the couple who'd been shot, robbed and buried in the foothills, according to the local gossips.

As for physical warnings, in my line of work these were

common. A report on timeshare touts had once seen me head to head with an enraged 'off-site consultant' who had come storming into the office one morning and the rear window of my parked car had been mysteriously shattered that same night.

I hung up on my caller and decided the investigation was now taking on a sombre note. This was more serious. Someone out there knew something and wasn't keen on me sharing the information.

29

THE RISE AND FALL
OF PHOENIX

By early February 2003, Operation Nevada had run out of ideas. In the words of Alan Jones, 'We had nowhere left to go.' In Spain, shaken if not stirred by the credit card withdrawals and the transfer of cash from the UK, national police were now a little more convinced that all was not well with the missing O'Malleys.

Alan Jones and DS Steve Lloyd had returned to Spain and were now in contact with detectives in Valencia, prompted by the payment of motorway tolls at booths to the south of the regional capital that figured on the credit card receipts. During their visit, the Welsh officers continued checking the retail outlets where the cards had been used, following much of my earlier trail in tracking down the kiter. Having no authority in Spain, Alan Jones was prepared to buy the CCTV footage from the shops in order to identify the card user – he was to purchase 28 video tapes and take them back to Wales for investigation.

During some of these visits to the shops and department stores on the list, the Welsh detectives were accompanied by a plain-clothes national policeman, who was soon to become increasingly absent.

It is interesting to note that the Spanish did not extend their enquiries to studying CCTV footage and it was left to the officers from North Wales to take this obvious approach to the investigation. Later, the Spanish would excuse themselves by insisting that the image quality of the CCTV footage was too poor to be worth the bother.

It was around this time that the Welsh detectives visited me at the newspaper and revealed the list of the purchase of computer components that allowed Tom Cain and me to point them towards credit card fraudsters as a possible link in the investigation.

Indeed, Real Sierra and Velázquez were possibly under police surveillance following this revelation when the missing hire car was spotted near the apartment in El Saler and the investigation intensified.

Meanwhile, a breakthrough occurred in the UK. On 28 February, almost three weeks after Alan Jones and Steve Lloyd had flown to the UK to write up the final case report, DC Dave James received a call from the UK National Missing Persons Bureau. An e-mail message had been sent from Portugal to the NMPB charity asking to be put in contact with the O'Malley family in the UK.

The sender had introduced himself as a private investigator who claimed he had tracked down the whereabouts of Linda and Anthony O'Malley. The couple, he would tell the family, were being held for ransom near Málaga. The price for their release was £50,000 but he would act as negotiator and bring the sum down. For this, he wanted a modest £8,000 in advance. The caller identified himself by the codename of Phoenix.

A fact not known to the mysterious Phoenix was that Alan Jones had made contact with the missing persons' charity earlier in the investigation and the volunteer who received the e-mail had the good sense to contact Wrexham rather than the family of the missing couple. It's no secret that a distraught family can often act out of despair and agree to keep police out of a ransom situation, often with disastrous and fatal results for the hostages.

Alan Jones read the message from Phoenix and realised he had a decision to make. Was it possible that the O'Malleys were still alive after six months, or was he looking at a deliberate hoax?

More to the point, Phoenix seemed rather too businesslike in his demands. A chance had to be taken and the senior detective made the policy decision to put the whole weight of a renewed inquiry behind the theory that the missing couple were now the victims of a kidnapper. But who was Phoenix?

Alan Jones and DC James travelled to London on 3 March to seek the assistance of the National Crime Intelligence Service based at New Scotland Yard in Victoria. This unit, which also comprises a national kidnap unit, would open liaison with its Spanish counterpart in Madrid, the crack National Police Anti-Kidnap and Extortion Unit, originally created as a tool against terrorist kidnappings by ETA and now more usually involved in combating the rising number of kidnappings resulting from mass criminal immigration into southern Spain from the former USSR.

Bernard O'Malley, Christine Spruce (Linda's sister) and

Linda's daughters were told of the contact. The news elated them but they also wondered if it could really be possible. If it were a hoax, it would be of the cruellest kind imaginable, but if there was the slightest chance that Linda and Anthony were alive, they would do all that was possible to co-operate with the Wrexham police and bring them home.

Thoughts inevitably turned to raising the ransom money, or at least paying Phoenix his or her fee and waiting for developments. But Alan Jones had other ideas.

By 5 March, a National Crime Intelligence Service negotiating cell had been set up at North Wales Police Headquarters in Colwyn Bay and a police officer acting the role of an employee of the Missing Persons Bureau was in contact with Phoenix. The plan was initially to set up an e-mail link and then hopefully a telephone dialogue with the unknown private investigator. Eventually, a contact would be made with Phoenix, apparently by Bernard O'Malley, but actually in the form of another undercover police officer who would play the part of the distressed brother eager for information and to bring about the return home of his brother and sister-in-law.

Two days later, as a return message was sent to Phoenix asking for more details, DC Dave James and DI Sue Harrop flew to Madrid to liaise on the ground with both Interpol and the National Police Kidnap and Extortion Unit and to supply the élite unit with information from North Wales as it came in.

Back in Colwyn Bay, a reply from Phoenix had come by return. Accompanying Phoenix's reply were the attached scans of Anthony O'Malley's passport, one of his credit cards and a photograph of Linda's wedding ring. The message from Phoenix to whom the sender now thought was Bernard O'Malley contained some intimate details of the missing couple. Both had lost weight and were unwell. Anthony was suffering an eye infection and couldn't wear his contact lenses. He was, Phoenix warned, nearly blind and needed urgent medical attention to his eyes.

The story that the private detective recounted in his early messages was that Anthony, while driving to Málaga Airport on 13 September, had taken a wrong turning on the outskirts of the city and inadvertently knocked down and killed a three-year-old Romanian gypsy child. The police weren't called to the accident. Instead, the parents and close relatives of the dead boy had dragged Anthony and Linda from the car and attacked them in their rage and grief. The car had been taken away to be cut up and sold as scrap. Mr and Mrs O'Malley were taken to an abandoned house where they could never be found and locked in a room. They received a minimum of food and water and were barely surviving.

Phoenix wrote: *'I know these people but they are not friends, you understand, just that I know them. They want £50,000 in cash for Linda and Anthony's release but you don't have to pay that. I can get them out but I'll need my fee of €12,000 paid up front into a Sevilla bank.'*

Other e-mails suggested that the money could be paid in Portugal or that Bernard O'Malley should fly to Sevilla with the money. It seemed Phoenix was based in either Valencia or Andalucía and the e-mail messages were being re-routed through different servers within Spain and across the border into Portugal, making them extremely difficult to trace. The time lapse between dispatch and receipt in Colwyn Bay was anything up to two hours.

Phoenix, it seemed, knew something about computer technology and Alan Jones wondered why the man – Phoenix, the inquiry team had decided, was definitely a male – went through such efforts to conceal himself. Why hadn't the sender made a direct approach? What did this private investigator have to hide?

By 11 March, Dave James had moved from Madrid to Valencia and was in the regional capital working alongside the Spanish homicide unit. There was now no doubt among the Welsh police involved in the reborn Operation Nevada that Anthony and Linda were dead and they were probably dealing with an opportunist killer in the form of Phoenix.

Now it also seemed that, at last, the Spanish police would have to sit up and take notice and, once again, the ponderous route through Interpol was opened. The Spanish were joining the hunt for the O'Malleys at last.

E-mails cannot easily be traced to the sender but rather to the server from which they are forwarded and only then to the individual computer. All e-mail communications are delivered to one of many thousands of servers across the world that then connect to the destination server, identified by the @ symbol in an e-mail address. By rerouting messages through various servers, Phoenix was erecting an almost impenetrable smokescreen. Phoenix, it seemed, to the suspicious mind of Det Supt Alan Jones, had something to hide other than his location.

The interchange of e-mails continued with the focus of the Welsh intelligence team now on a telephone link to the sender. The undercover officer playing the part of Bernard O'Malley was gradually gaining the confidence of

Phoenix and the breakthrough could come at any time. Meanwhile, despite the sender's efforts at diffusion, the Spanish had traced the e-mail source to an Internet café in Valencia.

Meanwhile, Phoenix was being coaxed to the telephone and eventually gave a mobile number to his undercover opposite number. An immediate check was run on the numbers that Anthony O'Malley had telephoned on arriving in Málaga and one surfaced as the number given to the undercover operative playing the part of Bernard O'Malley. There was no doubt that Phoenix was the link to the O'Malley's past. The net was finally closing.

Once the telephone link was established, Phoenix was more than happy to talk to 'Bernard', aka the role-playing Welsh detective. The negotiation was now reaching the significant stage known to professional hostage negotiators as 'proof of life'. This usually requires the hostage to be photographed holding a current issue of a national newspaper. Just how Phoenix planned to pull that off no one can ever tell, although from speaking with those who know the devious mind of Real Sierra well, I suspect he would have protested that his plan to rescue the O'Malleys would be endangered by any attempt to convince their Romanian captors, supposedly unaware of a contact with the family in the UK, to let him take photographs of Linda and Anthony holding up a current newspaper. It might appear risky but the stakes were high and the family would be more anxious to believe their missing relatives were still in this world than to reject that hope on the basis of an inconclusive photograph.

During the first week in March 2003, the following conversation was recorded:

Phoenix: 'They have moved these people two times, you know...?'
WP: 'Right.'
Phoenix: '... from one place to another, you know...?'
WP: 'Yeah.'
Phoenix: '... and they're confined to a room... and then they're confined to a room. These people, they can keep them there for a year if they want to. And I ask, well, for what you going to do with these people – are you going to kill them, are you going to bury them, or what are you going to do with these people... you know? And I start telling them, that's stupid. Another thing they did told [sic] me was Tony has problems with his eyes because he doesn't have his contact lenses. He needs them because he can't see. They even make a joke about that – they tell me, "He isn't going anywhere because he's blind." I ask them, I say, "Listen, the family says to me that Linda is a very strong lady," because you told me that. She has been sitting there day in, day out, you know? And she doesn't move much... '

The conversation then moved to the possible need to pay some of the ransom money in addition to the €12,000 negotiating fee demanded by Phoenix. This was a step expected by Alan Jones, who was now totally convinced that Phoenix was one of the original kidnappers. Jones also knew that the chance of the O'Malleys being alive was minimal. What kidnappers kept their victims alive for six months before demanding a ransom?

The mobile telephone number and a translated transcript of the recorded conversations were now passed to the Spanish national police in Valencia. There, DC Dave James had moved from Madrid to liaise with the Spanish detectives who had been informed that the UK intelligence unit had now traced the calls to an apartment block on Gola de Puchol in El Saler, near the cybercafé from where the e-mails had been sent by Phoenix.

Meanwhile, a Spanish patrolman had sighted the O'Malleys' missing hire car, now carrying false registration plates. As 24-hour surveillance was put into force on the vehicle, DS Steve Lloyd, who had transferred to Madrid to cover liaison with the Anti-Kidnap and Extortion Unit after Dave James' move to Valencia, left the national capital with unit operatives for the journey to El Saler. One hour out of Valencia, they heard that four arrests had been made. Phoenix and three others were now in custody.

In court, Real Sierra's eldest daughter, Estephanie Velázquez, would speak of her terror when armed detectives burst into the three-bedroom apartment with her father and uncle in handcuffs. On his arrival, Steve Lloyd would recall the confusion as shouts and curses in Spanish erupted around him, but the Welsh detective was already following a search team around the apartment to identify any effects of the O'Malleys still present in the apartment. There were plenty.

Among articles recovered were both Linda and Anthony's passports and credit cards, plus Linda's wedding ring. A set of suitcases was also identified as belonging to the missing couple, to emerge later as a clear indication that they had been invited to stay at the Alcoy villa.

A police report issued at the time gave the identities of the arrested men as JRS (53) and JAVG (40). Two women were also taken in custody but no identification was given. The women, I can reveal, were Ana Velázquez Real, the wife of Jorge Real Sierra, and Ana Emilia Velázquez, mother of Ana and José Antonio Velázquez and Real Sierra's mother-in-law.

The women were later released on bail and never charged, much to the horror and chagrin of the O'Malley relatives in the UK. Again, it seemed as if the Spanish authorities were playing 'catch-up'. They had their suspects who would eventually do hard time and the file could be closed with an elaborate slam.

Spanish police sources approached since the trial insist that Velázquez was the first, and last, to break. Real Sierra was reported as saying nothing. The wily older Venezuelan has never gone on record as confessing to the crime or signing a statement.

It seems odd, therefore, that it was Real Sierra whom the police chose to accompany them to the Alcoy villa and who allegedly pointed out the graves in the cellar. Real Sierra insists he was abused and forced to lie on a bedroom floor under guard while detectives searched the villa, eventually breaking through the cellar floor and discovering the bodies. Coming to the conclusion that a newly painted and cemented floor was a probable hiding place is hardly rocket science.

With all apologies due to the Spanish police and never doubting that the Venezuelan knew what the police would find in the cellar, I'm inclined to believe Real Sierra's version of the search. It sounds right.

30

TO DUST RETURNED

NORTH WALES POLICE REPORT TO
CORONER'S OFFICE, FLINT 11
July 2006

Sir,

I respectfully report as follows on the sudden and violent death of the following two persons:

Linda O'Malley (née Bishop) was born on the 26th February 1946 in Liverpool, she has one older sister, Barbara Murphy, who still lives in Liverpool. Her father died some years ago but her mother, Mabel Bishop, is still alive and well, She had previously been married to Kenneth Stewart and from that marriage had two daughters, Nicola Joanne Welch (née Stewart) and Jennifer Louise Stewart. At the time of her death she was fit and well and residing at 38, Market Street, Llangollen and working as a store manager at TJ Hughes, Ellesmere Port since 1995.

Anthony John James O'Malley was born on the 19th June 1960 in Widnes, he has a brother Bernard and a sister Christine who both reside in Widnes. He is described by his brother as a shy person who pretty much kept himself to himself. At the time of his death he was also fit and well and residing with Linda at the Llangollen address and working as a self-employed car salesman.

Linda and Anthony met each other in 1977 when they both worked as cashiers at Burtonwood Services in Cheshire. Although still married at this time, Linda and Anthony formed a relationship; a short time later, Linda and Anthony took up residence with Anthony's mother in Widnes (Mrs O'Malley unfortunately passed away on the 2nd December 2002, whilst the couple were still missing and prior to their bodies being recovered).

The couple eventually married in 1988 and resided at various addresses in North Wales, eventually settling on the Market Street address.

Family members describe Linda and Anthony as the perfect happy couple.

On the 16th September 2002, Barbara Murphy, Linda's sister, reported to North Wales Police that Linda and Anthony had failed to return to the UK from a two-week holiday in Spain.

It transpired that, on the 30th August 2002, Linda and Anthony flew on a JMC flight from Manchester to Malaga, and were due to return on Friday 13th

September 2002. *Their intention in travelling to Spain was to purchase a property for their retirement and they had pre-hired a car, a Fiat Stilo, registration number 85 88 BTT from Malaga airport.*

Shortly after arriving in Spain, Anthony made three unanswered calls from his mobile to a Spanish registered mobile 0034 XXX XXX XXX, and later that same day two further calls to another Spanish registered mobile, 0034 XXX XXX XXX, again believed to be unanswered. These phone numbers eventually turned out to be extremely significant and (one) had been previously advertised in the **Costa Blanca News,** *an English newspaper printed on the Costa Blanca, offering the fated chalet in Alcoy for sale. These mobile telephone numbers together with a telephone call Anthony significantly received at 13.17hrs on the 7th September 2002 from another Spanish mobile number 0034 XXX XXX XXX, which lasted for 3 minutes and 21 seconds, were subsequently linked by North Wales Police to a telephone handset in the possession of the two Venezuelan offenders at the time of their arrest in March 2003.*

Little is known of their movements in Spain and much is dependent on an audit trail of financial transactions from credit card usage, some telephone calls and an encounter with an agent from a Spanish property company. All information was obtained by officers from North Wales Police. It is, however, known that Linda and Anthony stayed in Hotel Ambassador, Benidorm, on the night of the 30th August 2002 and at the Hotel Altaya the following four nights, actually checking out of the hotel at 09.34hrs on the morning of Wednesday 4th September 2002. There appears to have been two additional lawful credit card transactions at a Chinese restaurant in Benidorm on the 6th September 2002 and a petrol station again in Benidorm on the 7th September 2002; after that time, credit card expenditure on all three accounts goes absolutely haywire. [Please see 'Time Line re O'Malley card usage'].

It is also known that Linda telephoned her daughter Jenny at 20.30hrs on the 4th September 2002; the conversation was general in content, mention was made regarding their dogs, properties they had viewed and a reminder for Jenny to post a birthday card to a relative. Anthony also spoke briefly with Jenny and nothing remarkable was said; this was the last contact any family member had with either Linda or Anthony.

North Wales Police also discovered that on the 11th September, Anthony O'Malley contacted the Yorkshire Bank, Chester, and arranged for £18,000 to be transferred to a CAM Bank account Anthony O'Malley had previously opened in Benidorm; this account had been opened during this recent visit and was to facilitate their proposed Spanish house purchase.

It is now believed that Anthony himself, probably at gunpoint, had attended the CAM Bank in Benidorm on Friday 13th September 2002 and withdrew €25,000 in cash.

The matter was reported to the Spanish national

police in Benidorm via Interpol who seemed incredibly disinterested, despite North Wales Police's best efforts to convince the Spanish police that Linda and Anthony had been subject to serious crime, and despite North Wales police officers having visited Benidorm on three separate occasions to meet with their Spanish colleagues and absolutely nothing had been progressed by the Spanish police.

On the final visit to Spain on the 2nd February 2003, Det Supt Alan Jones and DS Steve Lloyd visited all retail outlets in Benidorm, Alicante and Valencia where the O'Malley credit cards had been fraudulently used. The Spanish had previously promised that these enquiries had been undertaken in September 2002; officers took possession, without any assistance from the Spanish police, of original credit card receipts and CCTV tapes.

The receipts were subsequently submitted to a UK forensic expert who compared the signature purporting to be that of Anthony O'Malley's against a controlled sample of a known Anthony O'Malley signature; the result was supportive in the fact that Anthony O'Malley had not signed any credit card receipts after the use at the service station in Benidorm on the 7th September 2002.

Even after being presented with this overwhelming evidence, the Spanish police were still not interested in pursuing a criminal investigation.

After their February 2003 visit to Spain, North Wales Police were in a very disappointing position of not realistically being able to take the investigation any further, their intention at this stage was to submit a final report via Interpol to the Spanish police, in Spanish, outlining all enquiries that had been undertaken by North Wales Police in this matter and urging them to investigate the disappearance of Linda and Anthony O'Malley.

On Wednesday 26th February 2003, the first of three e-mails was received by a missing persons charity in London. The e-mails were purporting to be from a person named 'Phoenix', a private investigator based in Spain, who stated that Linda and Anthony were still alive, that their health was poor and that he could negotiate their release for cash.

Phoenix further stated that Anthony had taken a wrong turning off the motorway and had collided with and killed a Romanian gypsy child and that the family were holding the O'Malleys prisoner since that time.

Also attached to one of the e-mails was a scanned colour picture of Anthony O'Malley's passport, his Barclaycard and a ring taken from the finger of Linda O'Malley. Phoenix, perhaps more sinisterly, was adamant that the e-mails be forwarded to the family of Linda and Anthony.

On the afternoon of Friday 28th February 2003, the matter was reported to North Wales Police. After careful consideration and realising that Linda and Anthony may still be alive, contact was made with other police agencies within UK.

Lines of communication were also opened with the National Police Kidnap and Extortion Unit in Madrid and a technical capability put in place with regard to the e-mails and telephones being used by Phoenix.

A negotiating cell was set up at police HQ Colwyn Bay, with an undercover officer purporting to be an employee of the missing persons charity; the strategy was to establish lines of communication initially via e-mail and then later via phone with a view to tracing Phoenix. Problems initially arose due to the fact that we were able to establish early on that the e-mails were being sent from Valencia, but via a Portuguese server, the implications being that there was a 2-hour delay from the e-mails being sent to them actually being received in Colwyn Bay.

In one of the e-mails, Phoenix wanted Bernard to fly out to Malaga or Seville with the ransom money; who knows what would have happened if the missing persons charity had contacted the family direct and not North Wales Police.

North Wales police officers were subsequently deployed to Madrid and subsequently liaised closely with the Spanish. The breakthrough came when Phoenix actually telephoned the police negotiator and the number used was directly linked to other SIM cards and, more importantly, to one singular handset; for the first time North Wales Police had a direct link between Phoenix and the offenders.

On Monday 24th March 2003, as a direct result of technical enquiries undertaken by North Wales Police, a block of flats in the El Saler district of Valencia was identified.

Further enquiries revealed a Fiat Stilo motor car, partially hidden, now known to be the original Fiat Stilo hired by Linda and Anthony on the 30th

August 2002, now displaying false plates, was discovered nearby.

At 8.15am on the morning of Tuesday 25th March 2003, two males now known to be Jorge Real Sierra, b. 29/1/1950, and José Antonio Velázquez González, b. 8/11/1965, left the flats; one of the males got into the stolen Fiat Stilo and the other into a rented BMW motor car; both men were stopped by armed Spanish police and apprehended. In the glove compartment of the Fiat was found a loaded automatic handgun with a silencer fitted, together with a false police ID.

A search of the flat occupied by the offenders was undertaken. North Wales officers were present during the search. Numerous items of personal property belonging to the O'Malleys were found, including passports, personal documentation and the original number plates for the hired Fiat Stilo. Also recovered were multiple other articles used for forgery and deception.

Later that same day, the two offenders now known to be Venezuelan nationals were questioned by the Spanish police, which resulted later that same day in one of the males, Sierra, taking the police, which again included a North Wales officer, to the fated chalet in Alcoy, a town about one hour north of Benidorm.

In the cellar of the chalet and buried in about 4 feet of earth which was then covered in concrete were recovered the bodies of Linda and Anthony O'Malley; both had their hands and feet tied with plastic ties, Linda's head was covered in a El Corte Ingles plastic carrier bag and sealed with wide packing tape;

Anthony's head was totally wrapped in similar tape; the bodies were placed on top of each other.

On Friday 27th March, both men appeared before a judge in Valencia and were formally charged with the murder of Linda and Anthony O'Malley.

On Friday 5th September 2003, the bodies of Linda and Anthony O'Malley were repatriated to the UK; a second PM was conducted by Mr Brian Rogers, at which he considered the cause of death to have been asphyxiation.

On the 22nd September 2003, the funeral of Linda and Anthony O'Malley took place at Saltney, followed by cremation at Blacon crematorium.

Between Tuesday 28th March and Thursday 5th April 2006, the trial of the two Venezuelans took place in Alicante; the trial was attended by the members of the O'Malley family and officers from North Wales Police.

On Thursday 18th May 2006, the verdict was finally given by the court in Alicante and was as follows: Real Sierra was found guilty on all counts and sentenced to 62 years' imprisonment. José Antonio Velázquez Gonzalez was also found guilty on all charges and sentenced to 54½ years' imprisonment.

DS 41 Lloyd

Following their deaths on 13 September, the bodies of Linda and Anthony O'Malley were almost certainly stored in the cellar of the villa at Carrer Roure 7. No one knows how long the corpses of the murdered couple lay there before burial, other, that is, than the men now imprisoned for their murders, but the hot Spanish climate, even in mid-September, would have dictated a speedy disposal.

The fact that the victims' heads were securely wrapped or bound with plastic demonstrates an unnerving familiarity with the storage of corpses in hot climates where uncovered cadavers are rapidly invaded by calliphoridae, the common bluebottle or blowfly.

While many ancient rituals involved covering the mouth to prevent the spirit escaping and invading the body of a live household member, the secure taping or bagging of the head has a far more practical purpose. In Spain, the law insists on a moratorium on burial for a period of 24 hours to allow for investigation by police and medical professionals into the cause of death; the deceased must be buried as soon as possible after that period. The reason is simple – corruption occurs rapidly at high temperatures and is intensified by insect invasion. The most likely entry points are the nose, ears, eyes and mouth.

Certainly, 4,000 square metres of land would have given ample space for the disposal by burial of two cadavers, but the area was heavily forested by towering pines and evergreen oaks whose roots would have made digging, probably to be carried out after dark, difficult.

The solution was in the cellar itself, with its rough cement floor to be opened with pick and drill. Surprisingly, none of the neighbours in houses just across the street in this tranquil location ever confessed to hearing the sound of drilling equipment being used to break through the cellar floor. A local resident who lived almost opposite the villa told the author that the occupants were 'ideal neighbours, with seldom the slightest noise, even from the children'.

The same man and his wife went on to recall that, after September, no one appeared to be living in the villa, which received only sporadic visits from the two males of the household.

Nonetheless, by whatever effort, 2 square metres of the cellar floor was removed and excavated to a depth of 1.5m. One gets the impression that the minimum of effort was expended in the excavation of the grave. The depth was hardly sufficient for two adult bodies.

Linda's corpse was placed in first, the head wrapped in an El Corte Inglés plastic carrier bag. Anthony O'Malley's body was then placed on top, again face up, with the head swathed in parcel tape, probably for the reasons given earlier.

Once the bodies were barely below the surface – at the disinterment, Anthony O'Malley's foot was found at only 20cm below floor level – a thin layer of cement was laid and later painted a brilliant red. There the bodies would lie until their discovery nearly seven months later.

At their trial, both defendants would insist that the digging of the grave and the interment of the victims was carried out by the mysterious Bradley, whom they claimed had also murdered Anthony O'Malley following Linda's heart attack. Their protestations of innocence would be ignored by the court.

The final interment of the bodies would not take place until a year later when the couple were laid to rest on 22 September 2003 after an emotional service at St Mark's church in Saltney, Chester.

Over 400 mourners packed the small church and graveyard to hear tributes from Anthony's brother Bernard O'Malley and Linda's daughter Nicola Welch. The funeral took place after an inquest held by North-East Wales coroner John Hughes in Flint earlier in July recorded two verdicts of unlawful killing. I sent a wreath from the news desk with a message that I sincerely hoped Linda and Anthony had finally found peace.

In his summary, John Hughes praised the dogged determination of the O'Malley family to discover the truth behind the disappearance of Linda and Anthony and recommended Det Supt Alan Jones, DC Steve Lloyd and DC Dave James to their Chief Constable Richard Brunstrom for the award of a Commissioners' Commendation as officers who had worked in the 'highest tradition' of the police service and who were a credit to both themselves and the force.

However, the Flint inquest merely shadowed the work of Spanish forensic pathologists who had originally examined the remains and had arrived at a different conclusion to that of the British pathologist's findings on Linda O'Malley.

At the trial of David and Matthew, alias Real Sierra and Velázquez González, in March 2006, Spanish pathologist Salvador Giner gave evidence that Mrs O'Malley 'showed no signs of asphyxiation'. While conceding that the subject had received 'three blows to the thorax', Sr Siner said the blows were not fatal.

Instead, he believed that Linda O'Malley, who had no previous history of heart problems, had died of an attack brought on by severe stress. Mr O'Malley, on the contrary, said Sr Siner, showed all the classic signs of death by asphyxia brought about by strangulation.

The result of the Spanish pathologist's evidence was that the panel of judges were forced to consider an alternative charge of manslaughter, or 'imprudent homicide' as it is termed in Spain, in the case of Linda O'Malley. Manslaughter in Spain carries a maximum 12-year jail term.

COSTA BLANCA NEWS, 14 July 2006
'UNLAWFUL KILLING' VERDICT ON MURDERED HOUSEHUNTERS
FLINT CORONER COMMENDS UK INVESTIGATION TEAM
by Danny Collins

THREE NORTH WALES POLICE OFFICERS HAVE RECEIVED A CORONER'S COMMENDATION FOR HELPING TO BRING THE KILLERS OF A NORTH WALES COUPLE IN SPAIN TO JUSTICE.

Anthony and Linda O'Malley from Llangollen were kidnapped and murdered while in Spain looking for their dream home four years ago. An inquest at Flint heard that when Spanish police did not appear to be taking the disappearance seriously, the family turned to North Wales Police. Det Supt Alan Jones, DS Steve Lloyd and DC Dave James made their own enquiries and went out to Spain.

North-East Wales coroner John Hughes, who is to write to the Chief Constable, said, 'They are a credit to themselves as police officers and to the North Wales force.' The coroner recorded a formal verdict of unlawful killing on the couple, who were kidnapped, tortured and murdered on their house-hunting trip to Spain.

It was revealed by pathologist Dr Bryan Rodgers that both deaths were consistent with asphyxiation. The court in Spain heard claims that Mrs O'Malley had died of heart failure, brought on by the shock of her captivity, but in a statement read to the inquest, Dr Rodgers said the bodies had been found under a slab beneath four inches of earth in a villa cellar in Alcoy, near Alicante. Both had plastic bags over their heads, bound with plastic ties.

Jorge Real Sierra, 56, and his brother-in-law, José Antonio Velázquez, 41, were jailed earlier this year for the murders in September 2002 of 55-year-old Linda and her 42-year-old husband Anthony. They received jail sentences totalling more than 100 years between them.

Mr and Mrs O'Malley travelled to Spain in 2002 and transferred £18,000 to a Spanish bank to purchase a property. Conned by the Venezuelans, they were then kidnapped and eventually murdered after their bank account had been stripped of cash.

31

A NEST OF EARTH

Soon after DS Steve Lloyd's arrival at the Valencia apartment with the members of the Anti Kidnap and Extortion Unit from Madrid, he accompanied the arresting officers and their suspects back into the apartment block, identified in the preliminary hearing held at Court Number 3 in Alcoy Court of Justice as Nucleus Five, Tower Five, Door 25, in order to conduct a search of the premises. The Welsh detective was to be present throughout the subsequent interrogations and the gruesome disinterment in Alcoy that would take place later on that same day of 25 March 2003.

In the apartment, detectives found two replica pistols converted to fire live ammunition, blank credit cards and driving licences together with computers and other equipment capable of producing false documentation, and various passports, four of which identified Real Sierra, Velázquez and the two women occupying the apartment as Venezuelan nationals.

In a suitcase, first claimed by Real Sierra as his own but identified by DS Lloyd as the property of Anthony O'Malley, were the British passports of the missing couple along with their now defunct bank cards. Various other items were identified as belonging to either Anthony or Linda O'Malley, including a wedding ring that had been photographed and sent as an attachment to the e-mails of the opportunist Phoenix.

The prisoners, including the two females, Real Sierra's wife Ana Velázquez and her ageing mother, were taken along with the recovered property to the city's National Police HQ and questioned at length. Real Sierra protested his innocence throughout and refused to answer questions without the presence of a legal representative.

Velázquez, mindful that his sister and his elderly mother had also been detained, cracked earlier and admitted that the O'Malleys had been lured to a property near Alcoy and robbed. But Velázquez gave what would prove to be only one of his many versions of events by claiming that Anthony and Linda had been released on 13 September after Anthony had handed over the €25,000 drawn from the CAM Bank in Benidorm. He insisted the couple had been dumped in the countryside and that he and Real Sierra had then gone to the apartment in Valencia. He also admitted changing the registration plates on the hired Fiat Stilo and using it as his own vehicle.

Velázquez's story was to change many times before the trial was held three years later but, through it all, Real Sierra would remain adamant. He knew nothing of the O'Malley's presence in the Alcoy villa since he had been in Valencia the whole time. 'Who are the O'Malleys?' he asked an interrogator, 'I've never heard of them.'

Throughout the interrogations and subsequent trial, the fat Venezuelan would insist the scam had been planned by Velázquez and the Englishman, Bradley, whom Velázquez had met in Alfaz del Pi's once infamous but now dismantled Scrubs Bar.

Real Sierra hinted at an 'abnormal relationship' between the two men and insisted the Englishman had actually murdered the British couple and later sold the Fiat to Velázquez for €2,000. This mysterious Englishman would be named by both defendants at their trial, when the defence of Velázquez began to adopt Real Sierra's storyline.

In any event, that line of defence would be rejected by the Spanish court and the Englishman's name, although pronounced many times in front of the assembled Spanish and UK pressmen, was barely taken up and mentioned in print.

Recognising that their portly detainee was an experienced conman, the Spanish investigators knew they would have to crack him to gain plausible evidence for the state prosecutor. Perhaps it was for this reason that Real Sierra and not Velázquez was bundled into one of a convoy of police cars and driven to the Baradello urbanisation where local officers had roused the owner of the unoccupied villa identified by Velázquez to present himself with the keys. Welsh detective Steve Lloyd stayed close to the Spanish contingent. In court, Real Sierra's version of events at the villa would differ largely from those of the Spanish police.

Meanwhile, I had been roused at my home in the mountain village high in the Sierra Aitana, 15km inland from the coast. It was a call from Nigel Bowden, a good friend and a fine journalist – the original Slippery of the Costas.

Nigel, who, in 2004, was to achieve his lifelong dream of dying in bed in five star luxury in Madrid while intoxicated, was what is known as a red-top journalist, chiefly involved in hunting out sensational stories of scandal and rumour along the Spanish Costas, hence the nickname. Anyone who recalls a highly publicised north-eastern football club scandal, in which two drunken directors were secretly filmed disparaging the club's female fans, should raise a glass to the memory of Nigel Bowden. We had met some years previously when he asked for my help in tracking down a certain UK soap star who had left her TV show to live with her foreign lesbian lover in a resort not too far from my home.

It wasn't my kind of journalism, and I returned Nigel's call from a bar where I had actually encountered the happy couple and told him I had had no luck on the story as I watched the star and her female consort drink coffee together.

I told Nigel the truth about the actress some years later and he smiled through his big moon spectacles and told me he'd guessed I'd lied long ago. There were no hard feelings and we often worked together after that, swapping stories for our mutual benefit.

Now his voice crackled in my ear from over 500km away. 'Take down this address and motor over to Alcoy. They've found the O'Malleys dead. They're digging up the bodies now... '

I later learned that a female relative of a reporter on the Alicante daily *Información* lived on the Baradello Gelat estate and had tipped her cousin off about the massive police activity around the villa at Calle Roure 7. I descended the curving mountain road in record time and arrived at the entrance to the development to find a Guardia Civil vehicle manned by two no-nonsense *civiles* blocking the junction.

I waved my press card and identified myself as *prensa inglesa* and they hauled their metal barrier aside and waved me through.

It never pays to drive right up to a crime scene, so I parked among a huddle of press and police cars and made my way towards the arc lights illuminating the trees and sky two streets down.

The area was like a scene from a production of a Hammer House of Horror spine-chiller, with the late-evening mountain air at 545m above sea level frosting our breaths and creating an eerie swirling atmosphere among the dense pines and evergreen oaks backlit by the police arc lights.

I walked to the far end of the property, following the pierced stone wall, to where I could make out the most activity. I glimpsed the silver-grey flash of DS Steve Lloyd's hair under an arc lamp and saw another figure in overalls scurry up the cellar stairs carrying earth in a black plastic bag.

Cameras popped and flashed around me and hard-nosed journalists swapped comments with the uniformed police guarding the wall. I heard snippets of graveside information that I had long learned to disregard – 'stabbed', 'shot' and *'desgollados'* ('with throats cut') whispered around me. How could they know without an autopsy? But that wouldn't stop wild speculation appearing in the next morning's newspapers.

Without a thought for the victims' relatives, reports spoke of gunshot wounds and the 'fact' that Linda O'Malley's body bore signs of beatings and torture. I later e-mailed Bernard O'Malley in Widnes, assuring him that the first reports of injuries were unsupported by the forensic officers I spoke to, but I feel much of the damage was done. A lesson learned – never believe everything you read in newspapers, many of whose reporters are determined never to let the facts spoil a good story.

As the autumn evening grew even darker, activity ceased around the cellar steps and the group of uniformed and plain-clothes police drifted back to the hidden front of the villa, no doubt to seek some warmth inside and leaving their less fortunate colleagues to man the walls, lest a pressman decided to leap over for an 'exclusive'.

In Continental Europe, the process following the discovery of a body is rather longer and more involved than the British version, which involves a brisk examination by a pathologist or police doctor. In Spain, this demands the presence of an examining magistrate, who might be in the bath or having dinner when the call arrives. It might be a few hours before he or she reaches the crime scene and then it will entail lengthy interviews with the relevant officers or members of the public involved before the order for the *llevantamiento del cuerpo*, or lifting of the corpse, is given.

From Alcoy, the bodies were taken to Alicante for autopsy and the police set a guard and taped off the vicinity of the villa. Bored journalists either headed into town to find a late bar or wandered around the development, tapping on doors and recording quotes from shocked neighbours.

I got to my car and drove home, stopping for coffee at an early opening hostelry perched on a bend before a bridge over a steep canyon as dawn broke. The case had come full circle but we still had a trial ahead.

According to officers' statements to the court, Real Sierra, of his own free will, indicated that the bodies of Linda and Anthony O'Malley were buried under the freshly painted floor of the cellar. The oversize conman's version, which formed part of the appeal lodged on behalf of both prisoners ten days after the hearing, was that he was pinned to the floor of a bedroom by a foot placed on his neck and subjected to a number of indignities as detectives vowed to tear the villa to pieces in search of the bodies.

Whatever the truth may be, pneumatic drills were brought in to break up the cellar floor and detectives removed bricks and slabs used to cover the entrance to a shallow tomb before the first sift of earth revealed Anthony O'Malley's decomposed foot.

The detectives were surprised to see that the head of the corpse was completely swathed in wide parcel tape, resembling the wrapping around an Egyptian mummy. That of Linda was covered by a green-and-black El Corte Inglés plastic carrier bag secured around her neck with the same type of parcel tape that completely covered Anthony's head and face. Psychiatrists would later ponder the bizarre method of burial. Autopsies would discover that Anthony had died either from asphyxiation or a broken spinal column and Linda was judged to have died of a stress-induced coronary embolism. Why then the ritual of covering the faces and, in the case of Anthony O'Malley, literally binding the features of the victim?

Evidently, the judges had the same problem. According to the their summing-up, as declared in the document of sentence issued on 12 April 2006, 'It is logical to assume that if the death of Sra O'Malley was due to a cardiac arrhythmia, the accused wouldn't have found it necessary to tie up the cadaver – nor could it be explained why they had placed a bag over the head.'

But if Linda O'Malley did die of stress, had there been another reason for covering the face so completely?

32

THE KILLERS

Not much is known about Jorge Real Sierra and his accomplice José Velázquez González nor, given Real Sierra's penchant for forgery, even if those are their real names. Court documents, for example, list Real Sierra's aliases as Jorge Argenis Real, Eduardo Besón Vellón and David Velázquez Rodríguez. José Antonio Velázquez seems to have been less flamboyant in his use of aliases, confining himself to that of Matthew Don when placing the false newspaper advertisement.

What is known is that they were both born in Caracas; Real Sierra to Jorge and Laura on 1 January 1950, and Velázquez to Rafael Antonio and Ana Emilia on 8 November 1965.

Jorge Real Sierra was born into a comfortably-off, middle-class family, his father one of the more prosperous professionals of the city. An advantage which allowed the young Jorge, if that was indeed his name in those early years of his development, a college education.

To his duped victims in the petty frauds he was later to engineer in Venezuela and other states of South America that his often failed grandiose schemes forced him to move to, he would boast of a Harvard MBA in business management, a qualification that might well be genuine but which I was unable to verify with the university itself when researching that phase of his life.

His future brother-in-law, José Antonio, was born of much poorer stock and, from the outset, he was fascinated by the flamboyant older man who wooed his elder sister.

Real Sierra was a flashy dresser – later in his criminal career, he demonstrated a penchant for $300 Burberry shirts and $500 calf-leather shoes. The problem was, having taken on Ana Velázquez, he was, as it were, bequeathed the family by fate. He was now inexorably tied to mother Ana Emilia and the worshipful José Antonio, 15 years his junior.

The only advantage was that the younger man was a willing apprentice, never up to Real Sierra's sharp intelligence but always ready to learn and provide a strong back and arm for the more physical side of Real's often ill-fated schemes. One of these, a modest drugs operation in which Real attempted to fleece his suppliers, made the South American climate too unhealthy and the entire family moved to Portugal in the early 1980s, later crossing the border into Spain and settling in the south of the country.

Thus both men arrived in Spain accompanied by the mother and sister of Velázquez – Real's mother-in-law and wife – from Venezuela in the mid-1980s.

The now portly Real Sierra soon gained a reputation as a provider of false documents, driving licences and passports to order among Costa Blanca's underworld fraternity.

Following Real Sierra's arrest in March 2003, an entry in the re-offenders' register revealed he had previously been arrested on the Portuguese border some years before after bailing out of a rented apartment in Benidorm and leaving it stripped of furniture, for which he spent a month in detention in the border town of Badajoz pending further enquiries into his background. Apart from that small 'blip', neither of the suspects had criminal records in Spain.

Renting an apartment and selling the contents before doing a moonlight 'flit' is just about scraping the bottom of the barrel in the world of the confidence trickster. But, as we shall see, in time Real Sierra was to go on to far baser and more lethal activities.

Early reports of the 2003 arrests also gave the nationalities of the women initially arrested with Real Sierra and Velázquez González as Venezuelan. It is now known that they were in fact Real Sierra's partner, Ana Velázquez, and Real's mother-in-law, Ana Emelia. José Antonio Velázquez, now married, was estranged from his wife who was living elsewhere.

Real Sierra's eldest daughter, who gave evidence that her father had left the villa with his family the day before the O'Malleys' arrival, gave her age as 16 in 2006, which assumes a birth date of 1990. Her given nationality of Spanish means she was born after the arrival in Spain, although whether Real Sierra had ever married his partner is in question since his daughter's name was given in her testimony as Estephanie Velázquez. It is always possible, though unconfirmed, that she took her mother's surname after her father was arrested amid extraordinary publicity in 2003. Another possibility is that Real was using his alias of David Velázquez at the time her birth was registered in Spain.

Spanish surnames are confusing to foreigners, and with good reason. A surname in Spain carries the father's family name followed by the mother's. On marriage, a son's surname remains unchanged, while a daughter's will retain her father's family name but drop her mother's, which is then replaced by her husband's, prefixed by the preposition 'of'. Thus, she doesn't change her family allegiance but is identified as the 'property' of her husband.

But the young girl giving evidence had given her first surname as Velázquez, which was the family name of her mother, Ana, who was the sister of José Antonio Velázquez, Real's co-defendant. It caused a brief stir among the Spanish-speaking reporters present but was ignored by the British contingent, who only raised their eyebrows at the sudden whisperings from the local press bench, which soon subsided with the realisation that the men were on trial for murder, so the minor indiscretion of pre-marital hanky panky or name changing was hardly significant.

There were another two younger girls in the apartment in Valencia at the time of the arrests, over both of whom Real Sierra claimed parentage.

According to Real Sierra, his brother-in-law's failing marriage prompted the younger man to plan a return to Venezuela with his new girlfriend, a young Spanish woman called Sandra who dropped from circulation soon after the arrests in which she wasn't involved, and a scam was planned to finance the move.

The plan was to rent a property then advertise it for sale while posing as the owners. This kind of scam, which no doubt evolved from the first confidence man, the one who sold Brooklyn Bridge, would leave the duped buyer holding the keys to nothing while the bogus sellers escaped with the upfront cash.

However, the plan of Real and Velázquez had more the ominous undertones of premeditated kidnap and coercion, since it involved clearing the house and preparing the cellar to hold captives. It was a decision that could have been made after the O'Malley's visit in the afternoon of 7 September, perhaps born of Anthony's boast of funds readily available for the purchase. Or was it a refinement suggested by the shadowy Bradley? Whoever was originally involved, the real estate scam, beloved of expatriate tricksters around the Mediterranean, had taken on a far more sinister aspect.

At the time the plan was hatched, both families lived in the apartment in El Saler, a southern suburb of Valencia City, where the arrests would be made six months later.

On 17 August 2002, the two men found and rented a two-bedroom villa on a 4,000 square metre plot at Calle Roure 7 on the Baradello Gelat urbanisation in the countryside a few kilometres from Alcoy. Javier Silvestre Puig, who rented the villa to the men, recalled, 'a man signed a year's rental contract in the name of David Velázquez and said he was Portuguese. But everyone had left owing a month's rent before the end of September. To be fair, they left the place spotless... they'd even tidied up the cellar and painted the floor, which I thought was nice of them.'

When asked by the prosecution if he saw the man who'd

signed the rental contract in court, Sr Puig turned to stare at Real Sierra on the defendants' bench and then said loudly, 'No, I recognise no one... that isn't the man.'

The fact that someone signed the rental contract as David Velázquez puts even that name in doubt as a true identity, for when the scam was complete, even an over-confident fool would expect the search to begin in earnest. No doubt, El Gordo was already working hard on false passports for the future.

However, the fact remains that he wasn't recognised by the man with whom he was alleged to have signed a rental contract for the villa. Who then had signed it, and supplied their name as David Velázquez? Since Sr Puig had also failed to point out José Antonio Velázquez, we are left with the alternative of Bradley.

Yet Welsh police evidence gathered during the Phoenix phase and the statement of Douglas Eames would tie Real Sierra irrevocably to the scam. Even so, the possibility that not all the guilty parties were in the dock becomes ever more likely.

Not satisfied that the bait had already been nibbled – DS Steve Lloyd would later give evidence to the North Wales coroner that Anthony O'Malley made five unanswered calls to two mobile numbers, later found to belong to the Venezuelans, soon after landing in Málaga Airport – the schemers decided to place an advertisement in the very newspaper through which I at the news desk would keep the public informed of the search for the missing couple.

The mobile numbers would have to have been given to Anthony in Málaga – probably by the hustler whose name would be given to me by an informer on the day my first report of the O'Malleys' disappearance appeared on the front page of *Costa Blanca News*. Yet none of this would emerge at the trial.

33

REVERBERATIONS

COSTA BLANCA NEWS, 16 May 2003

TRAPPING THE O'MALLEY'S KILLERS

HOW COSTA BLANCA NEWS HELPED TO TRACK DOWN THE MURDERERS OF BRIT HOME SEEKERS

CBN Newsdesk Team

A UK television special, broadcast on 12 May and featuring members of the O'Malley family and CBN *News Editor Danny Collins, has revealed the full horror of the investigation leading to the arrests of four Venezuelan nationals for the murder and kidnap of missing British homebuyers Anthony and Linda O'Malley in Alcoy.*

The ITV *programme* Tonight with Trevor McDonald

contained facts already known to investigative reporters Danny Collins and Tom Cain, which had been withheld from publication at the request of North Wales and Spanish police.

The suspects were arrested following a joint 'sting' set up by the UK's National Criminal Intelligence Service and Spanish investigators following a message delivered at the end of February to Bernard O'Malley, brother of Anthony, through a Missing Persons charity.

The sender claimed to have located the missing couple, whom he said were being held by 'a Romanian' who would free them for £50,000. Accompanying the message were photocopies of Mr O'Malley's passport and credit card and a photograph of Mrs O'Malley's ring. However, the sender offered to help the couple escape for a slightly lesser fee paid in advance with a further payment on delivery of the couple to their family.

Doubting that the O'Malleys were still alive, UK and Spanish officers immediately set about tracing the sender through contacts opened by the O'Malley family.

CBN investigators Collins and Cain, who had already traced the missing couple to within a few kilometres of Alcoy, were asked to temporarily suspend their enquiries for fear of compromising the operation. The suspects were traced to Valencia and proved to be four Venezuelans already under surveillance for computer crime and fraud. Two men and two women were arrested on 25 March after a link was established between the gang and the

O'Malleys' missing hire car, re-plated and parked in a nearby street. After confessing to the crime, a male gang member gave officers details of the murder site in Alcoy, where the bodies were buried under a concrete floor in the cellar of a rented villa on the Baradello Gelat estate. Forensics revealed that the O'Malleys had been killed within two weeks of their abduction on or around 8 September 2002.

In the documentary programme, Bernard O'Malley thanked Danny Collins and Tom Cain for their support and collaboration in keeping the story in the public eye and for their help in bringing the killers to justice.

Part of the CBN investigation involved tracing the newspaper advertisement which put the O'Malleys in contact with their killers and establishing police contact with a local British resident who had also answered the classified ad and met the killers, but escaped with his life when he decided the villa was not for him and drove off without entering the property.

The response to news of the murders and the arrest of the Venezuelans was felt strongly both across the region and nationally. As I wrote in an earlier chapter, Spain relies heavily on tourism as its major industry. The idea that a pleasant, middle-aged couple could fly in and be murdered within a week was the worst form of public relations for the provincial, regional and national ministries of tourism. Although it has to be accepted that murderers can and will strike in any environment where influences exist from other cultures that place less value on life, the O'Malleys hadn't disappeared in the Masai Mara game reserve, neither did they drop out of circulation while on a trek through the Andes. They were in a region regarded as a safe haven, an area people gravitate towards because of all the good things in life, and personal security would have been high on the list of the O'Malleys' requirements in their latter years.

The problem facing the Spanish tourism promotional departments was that the couple had booked flights with a charter company used by thousands of British holidaymakers during Spain's extended summer season. It was totally unthinkable that a middle-aged couple seeking a home on the Costas could end up as victims of murder. Unthinkable, indeed, but it had happened.

Matias Pérez Such, then provincial tourism chief and now head of regional tourism for the Valencia autonomous region, was horrified at the news and immediately called together his committee to discuss ways of containing the damaging waves of publicity that were sure to ensue from the UK press.

In the regional capital, José Luis Olivas Martínez, the newly elected Valencian president, was similarly engaged in damage control.

Thousands of holidaymakers were forced to think long and hard about future travel plans, when faced with the horror of suffocation and burial in the cellar of a Spanish villa. Rumours began to abound and expatriates suddenly recalled sensationalist stories of highway robberies, murder and rape culled from the pages of *El Caso*, a particularly gruesome read itemising Spain's more horrific crimes.

I received telephone calls from radio stations as far away

as Cape Town, South Africa, anxious to learn of local expatriate reaction to news of the murders. Even more vociferous was the sinister voice of Stormfront, an Internet website that boldly declares white supremacy and 'Spain for the Spaniards', to which some wag once posted 'And UK waiters' jobs for the English'. Neither of which took in the need for the tourists' euros, nor for someone who knew how to serve paella in Earl's Court.

Stormfront's web banner declared 'IMMIGRANTS MURDER TOURISTS' and the argument was that foreign immigrants from Venezuela – Spain has its own cross to bear from its colonial past – had committed the crime that belied Spain's traditional warm welcome to visitors.

It would later emerge that Real Sierra and his partner in crime Velázquez were very bad apples indeed in the Spanish barrel. Although intensive enquiries were made concerning similar crimes both in Spain and the suspects' native Venezuela, little was learned due to Real Sierra's criminal expertise at document forgery.

My own enquiries in Caracas and Maracaibo through contacts established in that part of the world back in the late 1950s were hampered by the enigma of the men's backgrounds, and information was sparse. As we have learned, the podgy Venezuelan has a number of aliases including Jorge Argenis Real, Eduardo Besón Vellón and David Velázquez Rodríguez. Many investigators believe that the latter is more than likely to be his correct name, but it's doubtful that, after so many years of deceit, even Real himself remembers his true identity. Whatever crimes he committed elsewhere in Spain or in the land of his birth and elsewhere, it is likely the mysteries and possibly the victims will forever remain unknown.

It would be foolish to believe that a 53-year-old fraudster – for that was the age of Real Sierra at the time of the O'Malley's murders – had not committed similar crimes before. Certainly, my own enquiries brought forth a sketchy history, but one wonders how far the South American police stretched themselves.

Unless the unlikely event should occur that Jorge Real Sierra, aka David Velázquez, confesses his past, we shall never know. There has been little investigation into his history while in Spain. Given the furore that engulfed Spain's tourism industry following the discovery of the O'Malley's fate, it was no surprise that the Spanish authorities were anxious to distance themselves from two Venezuelan immigrants who had disgraced their hosts.

A month after the discovery of the bodies, I was invited to Valencia by regional TV's Canal Nueve – Channel Nine – to take part in a programme aimed at discerning a foreign journalist's view on the murders. No doubt, it was also to highlight the fact that it was foreign immigrants, and not Spaniards, who had committed such a heinous double murder.

Already, the UK press was advertising its protest that the two women arrested with the men, Real's wife, Ana Velázquez, and her mother Emilia Ana, were released within a few days and allowed to collect the younger woman's three daughters who had been placed in temporary care. This was a move that didn't sit well with the grieving O'Malley relatives. Linda's eldest daughter Nicola Welch made those feelings clear when she spoke after the trial, stressing that 'much of the family's bitterness is concentrated on the wives [sic] of the killers.'

Mrs Welch's mistake in believing that both women were the wives of the accused men was because she was unaware that Velázquez and his wife had been separated for some weeks before the kidnap was planned.

Eccentric Spanish national legislation often allows those over 70 a moratorium on prison due to their advanced old age.

Thus, in theory, even Real Sierra could expect the State's consideration for early release on achieving his three-score-and-ten. Indeed, it worried the life out of many UK journalists, anxious for a definition of the new Penal Code. They needn't have bothered. A sympathetic prison officer, who was attending the Alicante trial as part of his advanced study of penal law, assured me that septuagenarian murderers were simply transferred to a special prison unit for the elderly when their time came, a sort of Old Lags' Home within the prison walls.

Non-payment of relatives' indemnities is also a common reason to ignore pleas for parole. Sr Real, it would seem, is in there for his duration.

It was also not forgotten in an auspiciously Catholic country that it was Velázquez's broken marriage that had prompted his plan to return to Venezuela. To fund this, it is believed that he initiated the plot to rob their eventual victims, the plot that was to cost Linda and Anthony O'Malley their lives.

34

POINTS OF LAW

Following the drama of the arrests of March 2003, the O'Malley case sank into the mire of forgetful memory. Everyone recalled the story of the two Welsh (sic) house-hunters who had been strangled, shot or poisoned by South Americans... or was it Mexicans? But few were clear on the details. The fact is that news today is so transient that even the most horrific events soon become briefly recalled fragments of memory. The newspapers move on to more recent outrages and yesterday's newsprint becomes no more than the faded surface of a drawer liner or the discoloured particles in repulped paper.

But for Alan Jones in Wales and the O'Malley family spread between Liverpool and Aldershot, there remained a trial and the hope of justice being meted out to the murderers of Linda and Anthony. By this time, I had also tracked down the man whom both Real Sierra and Velázquez claimed was the true villain of the piece.

I eventually managed to contact the mysterious 'Bradley's' sister, warning her that her brother had been named in a notorious murder trial in southern Spain and asking her to get him to call me. Whether that message was passed on, I'll never know, but I believe the man eventually became aware of the accusations levelled at him by the convicted Venezuelans. Finally, receiving an address from a contact, I wrote to the man himself. He never replied.

Perhaps to the criminal mind – for 'Bradley' is a known criminal with significant past convictions – it was better to ignore the warning, but it can't be denied that, throughout my investigation, the Englishman was a nebulous figure on the periphery of events.

His friendship with José Antonio Velázquez is supported by letters between the two men after the trial; a man fitting his physical description was seen with Velázquez visiting the villa in Alcoy during the time of the O'Malleys' incarceration; and his rapid departure from Spain occurred soon after the murders. Probably, most damning of all, is his continued refusal to answer the charges made against him.

There is no doubt in my mind that Real Sierra and his brother in-law, while ultimately guilty of the crimes for which they were imprisoned, did not act alone. While I am convinced that the fingers around the throat of Anthony O'Malley on that fateful day of 13 September 2002 were those of Jorge Real Sierra, alias David Velázquez Rodríguez, I still sense the shadowy, smirking presence of the Englishman who accompanied the O'Malleys to the smallholding in Els Parrals.

Both the Welsh and Spanish police are fully aware of the

true name and location of the Englishman known by the alias of Matt Bradley, but I do not foresee any further action in that direction without additional proof. The files remain locked in the basements of Colwyn Bay and Madrid. The case is closed.

★　★　★

In June 2005, I received a call from Bernard O'Malley, who was planning a trip to Alicante to visit a Belgian human rights lawyer who was offering to find the family pro bono legal representation for the private prosecution, a process of Spanish law conducted concurrently with the state prosecution wherever claims for compensation are applicable.

I met Bernard and his delightful wife Georgie at the Hotel Meliá in Benidorm, parking my car opposite the hotel in the forecourt of the Plus supermarket, where Anthony and Linda were last seen alive by Joanne Miles two-and-a-half years earlier.

Bernard O'Malley drove his hire car as I directed him towards Alicante city and the Avenida Maisonnave where the Belgian lawyer had his office. I remarked it seemed unfair that the victim's brother should need to make an expensive journey to Spain to arrange legal representation when the consulate is normally obliged to assist in such matters. Bernard told me he had received little help from the consul and would prefer to make such arrangements himself.

The meeting with the obliging Belgian lawyer went well, as a promise of representation was forthcoming with the usual proviso of a percentage of any compensation awarded by the court, permissible under the pro bono concept where a court can order a private prosecutor's fees to be paid by the unsuccessful defendants. Bernard O'Malley finally accepted the conditions of representation over lunch at the 'four fork' restaurant of El Corte Inglés.

Months later, the Spanish lawyer earmarked for the trial suffered a road accident and the O'Malleys accepted a lawyer from the consulate list, asking for the help of the Belgian lawyer, who was not licensed to represent clients in a Spanish court, and the help of myself only in finding a licensed interpreter.

On the advice of their new lawyer, each of the legal heirs of Linda and Anthony O'Malley, represented by brother Bernard, sister Christine, and daughters Nicola and Jenny, claimed €300,000 for each murder relevant to their status. The court would eventually award €80,000 each to the daughters of Linda and €50,000 each to the heirs of Anthony.

Given the perpetrators' declared insolvency, it is extremely unlikely that the family will ever see a euro cent of the awards. Although Spanish legislation provides for a private prosecution lawyer to be appointed by the State through the *Colegio de Abogados* in cases of financial hardship, this option was not taken up by the family.

A method that was open to their lawyer but, again, not put into use was, by the strangest of coincidences, the same Spanish procedure of embargo that had brought Anthony and Linda O'Malley to Spain in pursuit of a property for sale at auction. For while the embargo is implemented to seize property from debtors, it can also be used to prevent a potential debtor disposing of assets before a court action that could see the same assets confiscated.

A legal embargo could have been sought on the financial assets of both the accused and would have prevented their disposal or transfer before the case went to trial. It was not done and the family had to pay the eventual price for the justice they sought.

At the time of the Alicante meeting, no date had been set for the trial as defence pleas and challenges set before the examining judge in Alcoy's Court number 3 delayed the proceedings. The eventual trial was still nine months away.

35

THE RELUCTANT
WITNESS

Despite records of earlier mobile telephone contacts undisclosed at the trial, the advertisement on page 79 of *Costa Blanca News'* small ad property section dated 6 September 2002 has been accepted as the bait that lured Anthony and Linda O'Malley to their appointment with death. Through that advertisement another witness was to appear who would directly implicate both suspects and place them at the villa in Alcoy on the morning of 7 September, the Saturday of the weekend of the victims' disappearance. That witness and his wife would later reflect with horror on how close they had come to a similar fate as the O'Malleys.

Retired businessman Douglas Eames had spotted the advertisement while browsing through the *CBN* ad pages at breakfast. Fifty-five-year-old Eames lived with his wife in the Sierra Bernia mountains on the outskirts of Jalón, the town that gives its name to a fertile valley famous for its wine co-operatives and the splendour of its early blossoming olive trees.

Wondering, as most readers would, whether the quoted price of €30,000 was a clumsy misprint, Eames telephoned the mobile number accompanying the advertisement and was assured it wasn't. A man giving his name as David Velázquez arranged a meeting for 11am that morning outside a newspaper shop in the town of Alcoy. Bocairent, explained 'David', was the only genuine misprint in the advertisement.

Doug Eames drove his 4x4 to the rendezvous and met up with the smartly-dressed, portly individual called David, who led the way to Baradello Gelat in a late series BMW saloon.

Eames would later relate to me his misgivings. 'I found the man too unctuous... there was something repellent about all the dry hand-washing. I just felt uncomfortable in his presence. And when we got to the house, I didn't like the setting. The building was boxy and there were too many trees. I saw another man working in the garden in a cleared area at the back of the house but decided it wasn't for me. I just thanked the man called David and drove away.'

It was the luckiest break of Doug Eames' life, for he would surely have been invited back with his wife should he have shown any interest. Real Sierra and Velázquez had lost their first intended victims but, by nightfall, there would be two more in their grasp. Eames and his wife Susan would not realise just how near they had been to robbery, death and an unmarked grave until the arrests were made six months later.

I had been given a list of mobile telephone numbers by

the now alerted national police in Benidorm and asked to check if any had been used in property advertisements. I handed what could have been an onerous job over to the ultra-efficient Kay Jones, the *CBN* staff member who managed the small ads sections.

Using a database search programme, within minutes she identified a mobile number, 667319463, as that carried in the Bocairent advertisement and handed me the original classified form, number Z564.

The advertisers were named as Matthew Don and David Velázquez, the latter the alias used by Real Sierra and found on identification documents, including a Venezuelan passport and driving licence, in the search of the apartment in Valencia.

I ran the story on the following Friday, feeling a little self-conscious that the tragic story we had run for six months had originated in our own office. I tried to recall the day the advertisement had been placed on 2 September, 2002, and wondered if I'd caught a glimpse of the killers. Would I have remembered them if I had? I doubted it.

The following Monday, I was passed a call from Susan Eames. This wasn't unusual since Susan is a travel writer and her articles were often featured in the newspaper travel section for which I sometimes took ex officio responsibility. But this time we weren't going to discuss a fortnight on safari.

She told me her story and, as soon as she was off the phone, I called Benidorm police station. There, an inspector called Antonio asked if I could bring the Eameses in to make a statement. I obliged and the statement was taken from Douglas Eames at 5.15pm that day. Shown a mug shot of each suspect, he immediately identified Real Sierra as the man who called himself David Velázquez.

Real Sierra's insistence at trial that he had known nothing of the scam until tragedy struck would be refuted by the testimony of Doug Eames and the ad booking form carrying the name of David Velázquez.

Jasmin Rokadia, the receptionist who took the advertisement, would later recall that the man calling himself Matthew Don, who originally attempted to place the advertisement, didn't have any identification, which was then supplied by the man accompanying him.

Thus a forgotten ID card by the absent-minded Velázquez had caused Real Sierra, alias David Velázquez, to place himself firmly in the frame at the time the advertisement was placed, destroying his later excuse that he was an innocent bystander to the plot.

Even as I listened to Tom Cain translating Doug Eames' statement for Inspector Antonio, my mobile rang. Slippery of the Costas, aka Nigel Bowden, was in town and seeking a return for his original favour of alerting me to the discovery of the bodies. Who was the mystery witness?

I guessed someone in the newspaper office had been talking when they shouldn't, an occupational hazard of working in a newspaper office with untrained and garrulous staff. This had caused me problems six months earlier when the distressed young woman had attempted to contact me with her version of the sighting of the O'Malleys' hire car. Since I had left the office, the contents of the call were passed around and discussed before someone rang me at home.

The result was that somebody talked to a persuasive TV

reporter and the news of the sighting, together with the circumstances, appeared on the BBC website the next morning. It was a distressing breach of an informant's confidence and that same morning I received a very heavy, telephoned threat from the woman's partner. If she should come to harm because of my [sic] disclosures, I would be next. My complaints to my editor were met with a philosophical shrug. Basically, it was a case of *fait accompli*. Where did I think I was – Langley, Virginia?

Nigel, however, was less prosaic – where did my new witness, he or she, live? I'd already asked the Eameses if they would consent to their names and photographs appearing in the press, and they had firmly refused. On that, I couldn't fault them. They might well become key witnesses in a murder trial and no one knew what friends of the accused were out there.

I refused the information to Nigel who, I learned later, promptly headed for the Benidorm police station and followed the Eameses home when they left. Old Slippery, God rest his soul, never missed a trick.

But it wasn't through reluctance or a fear of testifying that Doug Eames' testimony finished up as a statement read out by the court clerk. No one in the Alicante judicial system had thought to tell him of a trial date.

The result was a panic on day three of the hearing, when a confused interpreter summoned for the occasion was told there was no witness present. The Spanish shrugged and Steve Lloyd and Dave James, the Welsh family liaison officers, reached for their mobiles. Meanwhile, as soon as the court recessed until the following Tuesday, 4 April, I drove home and got on my computer.

When I found Doug and Susan Eames, they were island

hopping in Thailand and were worried enough to wonder whether they should return. I passed on a message from the Public Prosecutor telling them not to bother.

36

THE AFTERMATH

Spanish penal law dictated a preliminary examination of evidence by the examining judge in Alcoy. This process is referred to as the 'Oral Hearing', in which defendants are questioned exhaustively in the presence of their counsels, who are allowed to present their arguments to the court.

What this process means is that, by the time the examining magistrate decides there is a case to be heard, all evidence has been presented and the subsequent grand hearing in the provincial court has the effect of a rubber stamp on the process.

Evidence not presented to the examining magistrate cannot be entered in argument at the provincial hearing. The result is, once the case moves on, the verdict is practically assured. Not that there was any doubt of the guilt of the two accused when the provincial court finally assembled in Alicante almost three years after the arrests, give or take a few days.

The three-year delay between the arrests and the trial, which was eventually scheduled for five days, 28–30 March and 4–5 April 2006, had caused some consternation among the UK press due to a reporter misinterpreting Spain's four-year rule concerning detention before trial. The revised Spanish Penal Code of 2000 dictates that no one can be held in custody for more than 48 calendar months before being brought to trial, whatever the offence. After the four years had elapsed with no movement to trial, the prisoner would have to be released on very restrictive bail. However, the reporter concerned had counted from the month of the offence, September 2002, rather than of the arrests on 25 March 2003, which put the bail year as 2007.

The erroneous report concluded that the trial date in March 2006 would see the defendants released on bail a few days before the hearing and added a panicked forecast that they would abscond. It gave the UK press something to write about but was soon refuted by a release issued by the Alicante court press office that left one over-eager reporter feeling rather embarrassed at launching the furore.

The report first came to my knowledge in early 2004 when I was approached by an anonymous caller and asked if I wished to hear, and presumably publish, the Venezuelan's version of events. I didn't. I had no intention of giving anyone a public springboard before the trial.

Disturbing reports then began to flood back to me through prison contacts. Real Sierra was being taken from his cell in Fontcalent under guard but un-handcuffed for unrecorded visits to a prominent and influential jurist.

A report was made by a concerned party to the court in

Alicante and the unofficial visits were curtailed, although neither prison officials nor the jurist concerned were ever disciplined.

A human rights lawyer who had helped Real Sierra out in the past also found himself the victim when the Venezuelan used the lawyer's number which – unbeknown to the lawyer – had been installed on the SIM card of a mobile telephone which had again been smuggled in to him. It was plain that Real Sierra had friends both inside and outside prison walls.

37

CONFUSED EVIDENCE

COSTA BLANCA NEWS, 27 JANUARY 2006
O'MALLEY MURDER SUSPECTS
GO TO TRIAL

VICTIMS' FAMILY WILL ATTEND SIX-DAY
COURT HEARING

By Senior Correspondent Danny Collins

ACCUSED VENEZUELAN BROTHERS-IN-LAW JOSÉ ANTONIO VELÁZQUEZ GONZÁLEZ AND JORGE REAL SIERRA WILL SIT BETWEEN PRISON GUARDS SCANT METRES FROM THE FAMILY OF THEIR ALLEGED VICTIMS, ANTHONY AND LINDA O'MALLEY, WHEN ALICANTE PROVINCIAL COURT Nº 3 CONVENES TO HEAR THE CASE AGAINST THEM ON 28 MARCH.

Both are jointly accused of kidnap, robbery, illegal detention and murder following a four-year investigation by detectives from North Wales and Spanish national police following the disappearance of the couple in early September 2002.

Anthony and Linda O'Malley had flown to Málaga on the Costa del Sol on 30 August with the intention of bidding for a property advertised in a Costa Blanca auction by UK-based Spanish Properties Ltd.

From Málaga, the couple hired a car and drove to Benidorm, where they contacted a representative of the company and proceeded to make arrangements for the purchase. They were last seen alive together on 6 September.

Their bodies were recovered from a cellar in Alcoy where the victims were allegedly held and tortured to reveal credit card details. Mr O'Malley was also forced to arrange a large transfer of cash from the UK. The couple were murdered by their kidnappers when their accounts were exhausted.

The trial of Jorge Real Sierra and José Antonio Velázquez González took place in the spring of 2006 and was scheduled to last five days. The court convened from 28–30 March and then recessed until 4–5 April. The charges were kidnap, illegal detention, robbery, extortion, misuse and falsification of public and commercial documents, grand larceny, illegal possession of firearms, assault and murder.

Although UK press reports had forecast a trial by jury, a process introduced in Spain under the penal code reforms of 1995, due to the nature of the charges the trial would be heard by a panel of three judges. The chief judge Doña Virtudes López Lorenzo was assisted by judges Don José Daniel Mira-Perceval Verdú and Doña María Dolores Ojeda Domínguez.

Trial by jury in Spain is permitted only in cases of crimes in office by civil servants, crimes against the environment, crimes against the person, and the embezzlement of public funds. In those cases, nine jury members are sworn in, along with two substitutes, and the trial is presided over by one judge only. In the case of Real and Velázquez, the inclusion of other charges such as robbery and kidnap precluded trial by jury.

Trials in Spanish courts are also quite distinct from the UK and USA in that there is no grandstanding by attorneys and witnesses face the judges, not the spectators. The accused also sit facing the bench throughout, usually book-ended by two burly prison officers, standing only to give their evidence or answer questions from the judges. Defence and prosecution sit on opposite sides of the court facing each other.

Time spans for the cases of the prosecution and defence also seem absent, since both sides of the court are allowed to question witnesses and accused at will, with the odd question thrown in from the bench. The atmosphere created is one of conversation rather than accusation or denial, with voices kept at a low register and decorum observed throughout.

Near the end of the first day of the hearing, I noticed a colleague slip out through the doors at the back of the court after beckoning to me that he had some important information. I rose to follow him and paused to bow respectfully to the bench before leaving. Nonetheless, within minutes, I was being admonished by the court clerk who had followed me out on the instructions of the deacon judge Doña Virtudes López Lorenzo. Would I be attending court tomorrow? Yes, I hoped so. Then would I, in future, pay respect to the bench and not leave until I was told I could do so? Yes, of course, and my apologies. Evidently, nobody had noticed the earlier escape of my colleague.

A reawakening of interest in the O'Malley story saw many foreign journalists outside the ornate baroque façade of Alicante's Palace of Justice on the morning of 28 March. Interest centred on a passageway between the courthouse square and the narrow Calle San Fernando from where the defendants would enter the court building.

Among the scribes and photographers poised for their first sight of the accused in the flesh was the *Daily Telegraph*'s venerable Nigel Bunyan and the award-winning photographer Eddie Mulholland, who was to pull off a pictorial scoop days later when he cannily caught Real Sierra's left profile complete with expression of petulance as the Venezuelan avoided other photographers crowding in on his right.

I was also fascinated on the second day of the trial to see Eddie doing a frantic moonwalk across the court forecourt in an effort to take a photograph of Real's daughter Estephanie as she was escorted weeping from court by her father's defence counsel, who kept her face hidden behind his briefcase. I swore the celebrated photographer had eyes in the back of his head as he reversed at a rapid rate of knots, eerily swerving around obstructions and pedestrians with not a glance over his shoulder.

Another face in the crowd was my old friend Arthur

Mills, veteran reporter of the *Shropshire Star*, known for his persistent coverage of the news surrounding Trevor Rees-Jones from Oswestry following the bodyguard's horrific involvement in the Paris car crash that killed Princess Diana and Dodi Al Fayed.

Parting the crowd like Moses' staff over the Red Sea was a BBC TV team who shepherded the O'Malley family through to the court anteroom where they stood guarding their charges as if escorting royalty.

Oddly, mostly absent from the gathering were Spanish journalists, for whom the case had long lost interest. Many members of the Spanish press openly resented the implications of the UK newspapers that Spain was bandit country for foreigners, where tourists were robbed and murdered for the contents of their wallets.

But there were enough UK journalists and freelancers like myself present – I had retired from full-time employment in journalism in the autumn of 2004 – to forestall the use of the small Court number 3 on the third floor that had been originally allocated for the trial. Instead, the court would convene in the grander and much larger Court number 1 on the ground floor.

A previously issued pass was necessary to walk through to the lobby where a metal detector frame was monitored by two members of the Guardia Civil. The prisoners would descend stairs from the floor above and enter the court through a rear door. Another photo opportunity would present itself as the defendants took their seats in chairs placed on the raised podium in front of the right-hand tier of benches where they sat between two guards and from where they would give their evidence when called upon.

The prisoners and the opposing counsels would be seated when the *civil* guarding the main doors announced the court was open and allowed the waiting journalists and spectators to enter. There we were allowed to take a few somewhat pointless photographs of the prisoners' hunched backs before the judges' entourage entered.

The O'Malley family, represented in court by Anthony's brother Bernard, sister Christine Spruce, and Linda's daughters Nicola and Jenny, together with Christine's husband and Bernard's wife, sat with their female interpreter in the first two benches on the left, almost immediately opposite Real Sierra and Velázquez.

The use of a private female interpreter had been requested by the family because they jointly felt a woman would be more sensitive to the distasteful physical details of evidence and would temper her translation accordingly. No headphones were provided for translation and the interpreter spent her time in court scribbling in a notebook and passing it around to family members.

The interpreter had been found and recommended by the Belgian human rights lawyer whose earlier offer to find representation for the family had finally been refused. No official translation was provided by the court, much to the consternation of visiting UK journalists, who had to rely on local bilingual Spanish speakers such as myself for an account of what had been said in court.

Real Sierra was represented in court by Don Gonzalo Martín Cano and Velázquez by Don José Soler Martín. The defence team sat on the left of the courtroom, the state and civil prosecutors to the right.

The trial opened with the defendants' declarations of innocence and it was at this time that both men implicated the Englishman whom they referred to as 'Bradley'.

Velázquez was the first to be called to stand and face the judges' bench. He wore a red shirt under a black zipper jacket and was seen wearing spectacles for the first time since his arrest. Each time he ran the gauntlet of photographers at the back of the court, he also wore a red or black bandana tied across the lower part of his face, giving him the bizarre look of a bank robber from a Wild West film set. His brother-in-law demonstrated more sobriety with a well-pressed, dark-grey pin-striped suit, white shirt and red tie.

Velázquez, who had originally confessed to the murders, stood with hunched shoulders and stared at the floor. He now insisted his original confession had been given under duress to obtain the release of his sister and mother. The Judge Deacon, Dona Virtudes López Lorenzo, took up the preliminary questioning. Had Velázquez murdered Anthony and Linda O'Malley some time in September 2002?

Velázquez lifted his head and looked the judge in the eye. 'No.'

Who thought up the plot?

Velázquez used his head to indicate his brother-in-law standing next to him. 'Jorge,' he told the court, 'he told me what to do. There was also another person involved with us. His name is Bradley.'

When asked who killed Linda and Anthony, he shrugged his shoulders and continued, 'I went Valencia the day they came and Bradley later told me all had gone well. When I left, they were both in good health.'

The judge waved him back into his chair and called Real Sierra. The fat Venezuelan stood to sloppy attention and gave off the air of an owlish Billy Bunter accused of raiding the tuck shop.

He told the court, 'I went with my family to Valencia and left my brother-in-law at the villa. I never saw the O'Malleys arrive.' Again the name 'Bradley' emerged as an English acquaintance of Velázquez, but Real Sierra was more lavish with his accusations against the mystery man.

Who had placed the advertisement in *Costa Blanca News*?

'Bradley and José Antonio. I believe Bradley is Matthew Don.'

Matthew Don is the other name, along with Real Sierra's alias of David Velázquez, that appears on the form used to book the newspaper advertisement on 2 September 2002. If, as I believe, it was Real Sierra and Velázquez who actually placed the advertisement, then the man playing the part of Matthew Don that day was José Antonio Velázquez himself, the one who hadn't remembered to bring his identification.

When the name 'Eames' was mentioned by the judge in reference to the expatriate Englishman who had kept an appointment to view the villa on the morning of 7 September, Real Sierra said he'd never heard of the name nor met the man. His denial would be exposed as untrue by Douglas Eames' statement, made before me in the office of a Spanish detective in Benidorm three years earlier. Eames, whose statement would be read to the court the following day, claimed to have met Real Sierra by appointment in Alcoy on that morning and identified him from a police photograph taken after the arrests.

The court then moved to the matter of who had rented

the Alcoy villa. Up to this time, all questions had been put by the judges with the public and private prosecutors keeping respectfully silent throughout the preliminaries. A look around the court brought me raised eyebrows from many of the British correspondents unfamiliar with the workings of a Spanish court.

Real Sierra was now asked if he had spoken to the owner of the villa. He denied any knowledge of the rental contract and was not questioned further on the matter. Instead, the questioning moved to his part in the removal of €25,000 from the CAM Bank in Benidorm. The judge deacon read out to him the prosecution's contention that he had accompanied Anthony O`Malley to the bank in the Fiat Stilo hire car driven by Velázquez. Real Sierra now acknowledged his part in the stripping of the victims' accounts, but insisted he was only trying to get his brother-in-law out of a hole.

'He called me in when it all went wrong,' he told the judge. 'José Antonio told me Mr O'Malley had agreed to buy the villa and to sell him the car. He had left Bradley there with the man and the woman and a week later he told me they were dead. As for the cards, yes, I admit I used them on some occasions in Valencia and Alicante, but not all. The police have never used a handwriting expert to examine the signature on the sales slips.'

This particular piece of information from Real Sierra was true. Although Welsh detectives had submitted the signed receipts for examination by a calligraphy expert in the UK, this had proved only that Anthony O'Malley had not signed for the purchases made on his credit card.

Evidence of who had signed the receipts was never produced and not even the Welsh findings were submitted to the court. The public prosecutor seemed to be working on the premise that the bodies of Anthony and Linda O'Malley had been found in Real Sierra's rented cellar and all incriminating proof followed accordingly.

Although my own investigation had convinced me the two men in the dock were guilty and that Real Sierra had undoubtedly signed the receipts, I felt uncomfortable and pretty sure that an English jury would not be totally convinced of Real Sierra's guilt by the way the case was being presented.

Questioned now on the Phoenix e-mails with regard to the attempted extortion of ransom money from the family while posing as a private investigator in February and March 2003, Real Sierra denied sending the e-mails to the Missing Persons' Bureau asking the organisation to contact Anthony's family.

The last question related to the semi-automatic pistol found in the glove box of the car he was driving on the day of arrest, when his movement towards the weapon had sent the Spanish detectives reaching for their own sidearms. Was the gun his?

'Yes', he told the court. The firearms charge would later be dropped on appeal – no firearms expert was ever called to verify the prosecution's assertion that a conversion had been made to fire live ammunition – and the overall sentence subsequently reduced by three years.

The task facing the prosecution was that while both men tacitly admitted to either planning or being aware of the deception involving a third party, and to one or the other or both placing an advertisement in *Costa Blanca News*, they firmly denied taking part in the actual kidnaps and murders.

No mention was made by the prosecution of the telephone calls to Real Sierra's mobile made by Anthony O'Malley from Málaga Airport in the early hours of 31 August. I recalled the words of Alan Jones' e-mail: *'I have no idea how much of the real story will be given at the hearing.'*

However, it should be understood that, under the Spanish Penal Code, the entire case had already been heard by the examining judge in Alcoy, who had passed the case to the Provincial Court once satisfied that a crime had been committed and that the defendants were guilty.

No evidence unspoken before the Alcoy judge was admissible at this later date in the proceedings. The three judges sitting in Alicante were merely rehearing the spoken evidence in order to ratify the Alcoy court's findings.

In doing so, they had no hesitation in putting their own questions, often interrupting counsels to do so. But both of the accused had raised the spectre of the third man, who according to them both was the true assassin. Real Sierra had been questioned about who had actually placed the newspaper advertisement and he indicated his brother-in-law, claiming Velázquez had been accompanied by Bradley. This was at odds with my own recollection of the second man producing a Venezuelan ID in the name of David Velázquez, a known alias of Real Sierra.

When prompted, Real Sierra cannily denied meeting Douglas Eames, the first caller to the villa, which would have implicated him deeper into the plot. Eames' statement would negate his denial.

Real Sierra did, however, admit to using Anthony O'Malley's credit card on 'a few occasions' but denied making all of the purchases and, again, complained that his handwriting had never been examined against those on the payment slips. He also admitted ownership of the allegedly converted firearm found in the car he was driving on the day of his arrest. A sprat to catch a mackerel?

He returned to his main defence that an argument with his brother-in-law on the afternoon of 7 September 2002 had led to him leaving the villa with his mother-in-law and children and returning to Valencia before the O'Malleys arrived. He said he had later seen Velázquez driving the Fiat, but accepted his brother-in-law's story that he had bought it from a girlfriend. Velázquez later changed his story to say that Bradley had sold him the car for €2,000.

Real told the court, 'I was only alerted when everything had gone wrong. I know nothing about these people or their murders.'

The court's next question was obvious. If he knew nothing of the O'Malleys' deaths, how had he been able to take officers to the Alcoy villa and show them where the bodies were hidden? Real Sierra gave the court the look of a beaten puppy. 'I was subjected to an attack by the officers, who threw me to the floor and held me down with a boot to my neck. They said they would rip the house to pieces to find the bodies. I didn't tell them where they were because I didn't know.'

On my own earlier examination of the cellar, which runs parallel to the foundations of the villa under the front veranda and had one central window at ground level visible before remodelling by the present owners, I had noticed that no breaches had been made in the brick wall leading to the interior of the foundations. I wondered at the time why such an obvious place for disposing of the bodies hadn't been examined before starting on the back-breaking task of digging up the cellar floor. Either the searchers already knew that the grave of Linda and Anthony O'Malley was under their feet from information received during interrogation, or someone had made a lucky guess.

But if Real was telling the truth when he said he hadn't pointed out the grave – a statement that would not clear him of the murders, since not admitting where the bodies were buried didn't mean he had no knowledge of the site – and this were a fabrication by the Spanish police, it pointed towards a careless and slapdash compilation of evidence in which the end was seen to justify the means. It was a conclusion that didn't surprise me in the least.

The defence counsels then took their clients over a brief rebuttal and the British journalists in the spectators' benches put their heads together and helped each other clarify points that had been missed. No one picked up on the mention of Bradley. The court rose at 2.30pm until the next morning.

38

MYSTERY WITNESS

Interest among journalists on the second day of the trial was stirred by the appearance of two names alongside that of Douglas Eames on the witness list, relating to Real Sierra's 16-year-old daughter Estephanie and her mother Ana Velázquez. In the event, it was only the daughter who took the stand, a centrally placed lectern-like arrangement before and facing the judges' panel.

I had noticed a court interpreter when I entered the court building and was told he would be interpreting the evidence of Doug Eames, the other house-hunter who had barely escaped the fate of the O'Malleys those long months ago. The problem was that I knew that both Mr and Mrs Eames were out of the country, a fact of which no one else, including the prosecution who were calling Mr Eames as a witness, was aware.

Panic ensued among the prosecution since Doug Eames testimony was vital in placing Real Sierra in Alcoy on the day of Mr Eames' visit to the villa and identifying the older Venezuelan's involvement in the early stages of the scam. Eventually, after a long delay, it was decided that Mr Eames' statement as dictated to Spanish police in Benidorm would be read out in court while efforts were made to find the witness and bring him to court in person.

It is worth remembering that it was largely due to the English-language press that Douglas Eames' statement had ever been taken, since it was Tom Cain and I who had escorted both Mr Eames and his wife to Benidorm national police station after they had telephoned me on seeing my article on the mobile telephone numbers used by the arrested Venezuelans.

That night, I e-mailed the Eameses and learned they were island hopping in Thailand. While both were anxious to return to Spain and attend the trial, I was eventually given a message to pass on to them telling them not to bother. So much for key witnesses.

Real Sierra was again the first to be questioned by the female prosecutor, Dona María Illán Medina. 'Do you now admit to making all purchases and cash withdrawals recorded on the credit cards?'

'No.'

'Do you speak English?'

'Yes, but I didn't make all those purchases.'

'Your involvement in the kidnap and murders was for financial gain, isn't that true?'

Real Sierra became almost apoplectic in his hurry to reply. 'No, that is absolutely untrue. I simply wanted to help my brother-in-law who had just broken up with his wife and needed cash to return to Venezuela. He had family problems and was constantly backwards and forwards to the villa from Valencia. I discovered he was even taking women to the villa to help him pacify the O'Malleys. He told me Bradley was also staying there to keep an eye on them.'

'What did you think when your brother-in-law appeared with the stolen car?'

'I'd never seen the car before, because I had left for Valencia before the O'Malleys arrived. José Antonio told me it was on loan from a girlfriend. Then he later told me he had bought it from her.'

The story would later change to the purchase of the Fiat Stilo from Bradley, who was now becoming the alleged mastermind of the plot *in absentia*. All through the five days of the trial, journalists would meet in huddles before the court was in session to try and clarify what was the current story of the constantly changing defence.

In truth, the defendants had been kept in separate prisons since the arrests and one can only assume they hadn't had time to synchronise their mental watches. The obvious plan seemed to be for Velázquez to pick up on Real Sierra's testimony, but he was failing miserably and his brother-in-law was floundering as a consequence.

The prosecution now called a Spanish detective who claimed to have worked with the technical team responsible for tracing the mobile telephone used by Phoenix to the El Saler area of Valencia, although I was aware that the trace had been made by the Welsh police. This was yet another example of the way Spanish law enforcement had come from behind to hijack the prosecution evidence gathered by Alan Jones and his team.

As far as the Spanish were concerned, once they had a location focused on the El Saler apartment block, and had found the falsely-plated car, all they had to do was wait and arrest whoever approached the vehicle as the driver.

The detective briefly explained the approach in February 2003 to the British charity by the e-mailer calling himself Phoenix. He told the court the e-mails had been re-routed through Sevilla and Portugal by someone with obvious knowledge of computer technology. No mention was made in his evidence of the part played by the Welsh police in the tracking of Phoenix, nor that the person who had gained the confidence of Phoenix enough to disclose a mobile phone number by posing as a family member of the O'Malleys was an undercover detective of the UK National Intelligence Service. In fact, no mention was made of the work of the Welsh police throughout the investigation.

The implication to those who didn't know better was that it was a Spanish national police operation from September 2002 until the arrests in March 2003. Fans of George Orwell's concept of 1984 Newspeak might have applauded the audacity but what, I wondered, must the three Welsh detectives present in court have thought of that glaring omission? Try as I might, not one of them could be later drawn to comment.

Before the court heard the testimony of Estephanie Velázquez, another detective identified only by his shield number gave evidence of the arrests and of the incriminating evidence found both in the search of the vehicles and the apartment in El Saler. Found in the car was a receipt from a mobile phone company listing calls made to Anthony O'Malley's mobile. Upstairs in the apartment, police found the registration documents for the Fiat Stilo and of another car, a Seat Ibiza that had been reported stolen by an Alcoy car hire company in November 2002. Another pistol allegedly converted to fire live ammunition and fake passports were discovered alongside the original registration plates of the O'Malley hire car, plus computer equipment and card embossing machines used to clone credit cards.

At this point, Real Sierra, who was emerging as the main villain of the piece, was questioned by his defence counsel and denied knowledge of everything found, including the passports, the origin of which, he told the court, he had no idea.

In summing up on the last day of the trial, his counsel would accuse the police of planting the evidence found in a last desperate attempt by Sierra to convince the court of his innocence. After her father had given evidence, Estephanie Velázquez took the stand. She was a thin, not particularly pretty 16-year-old, who visibly shook as she took the witnesses' lectern. In a hushed voice, little more than a whisper, she told the defence counsel of the day of the arrests, which she termed as 'the worst day in her life'.

The 'second-worst day' of her young life, she claimed, had been 7 September 2002, when her father and uncle had had a tremendous argument that also involved her mother and led to them all going back to Valencia. According to Estephanie Velázquez, her mother and father, her grandmother and she and her two younger sisters had returned to the El Saler apartment on Saturday afternoon and remained there until the arrests of March 2003. Oddly, she made no mention of the later arrival of her uncle, José Antonio, who claimed to have followed his sister and his irate brother-in-law to

Valencia later that day, leaving the O'Malleys to the mercies of the alleged Bradley.

Her testimony supported Real Sierra's contention that he had left Alcoy before the supposed arrival of the O'Malleys, but left a gap in which her uncle could have met up with the Englishman and kidnapped the O'Malleys. Certainly, although Real Sierra insisted he had left after his wife to drive with his mother-in-law and children to Valencia before the O'Malleys arrived in Alcoy, there is no reason why he couldn't have driven back after an interval in which the British couple could have been met in Alcoy by either Velázquez or, if we are to believe the existence of a third man, by the elusive Bradley. The A-31 that runs south-east from the regional capital links up with the N-340 to Alcoy and the journey can be made in less than 90 minutes.

Velázquez had again changed his story from the release of the O'Malleys on 13 September to leaving them with Bradley on 7 September. While, if it is to be believed, this new version of events meant that neither of the accused had anything to do with the tragic fate of the O'Malleys, other than to exploit their credit cards and bank balance, investigators had proof that a webcam link, using the wireless video camera bought by the kiter from El Corte Inglés in Alicante two days after the O'Malley kidnap, was used to monitor the couple's captivity from a computer in the Valencia apartment.

There may well have been an accessory, but anyone in Valencia would have been aware of events unfolding in the cellar at Alcoy simply by switching on the monitoring equipment.

The court adjourned for lunch, during which the BBC

TV team held interviews against the grey stone façade of the Palace of Justice with the O'Malleys' relatives and the Welsh detectives who had flown in to attend the trial as family liaison. I also noticed the presence of the latters' chief officer throughout the investigation, Det Supt Alan Jones, who had also flown in for the last days of the trial.

As opinions and family statements were made and recorded for fickle posterity, I and other Spanish-based freelancers helped out our UK colleagues with the translation of evidence that they may have missed.

The last prosecution witness of the day was a Spanish patrol officer, on surveillance duties in the search for the O'Malley's Fiat Stilo in Valencia on the day before the arrests. Here I wish to clarify an important point. The patrolman's presence in the southern suburbs has been widely reported as a direct result of the conversation held between Alan Jones, Steve Lloyd, Tom Cain and myself a few weeks earlier. We had set before the Welsh police our theory that the O'Malleys were either in the hands of or had been robbed and murdered by cash point fraudsters based in the south of the regional capital. I doubt that is so. As I have stressed previously, the Fiat Stilo was more likely discovered as a direct result of the Welsh police handing over the location of the mobile phone calls from Valencia.

After the officer gave evidence of having seen and identified the car near the apartment on the day before the arrests, the court adjourned for the day at 3.30pm.

The following day, we would hear evidence from the brother of the landlord of the villa and learn who had – or more correctly, possibly, who hadn't – signed the rental contract that was the first step in the spider's web that snared Linda and Anthony and led to their deaths.

39

SPINNING THE WEB

Costa Blanca News, 31 March 2006

O'MALLEY KILLERS SHIFT THE BLAME

BROTHERS-IN-LAW POINT THE FINGER
AT EACH OTHER
By Senior Correspondent Danny Collins

A COURT PACKED WITH FOREIGN AND SPANISH JOURNALISTS IN ALICANTE THIS WEEK HEARD EACH OF THE ACCUSED LAY THE BLAME FOR THE WELSH COUPLE'S ABDUCTION AND MURDER FIRMLY ON TO THE OTHER.

In the larger, ground-floor court allocated to the case, José Antonio Velázquez told the court with bowed head that his brother-in-law, Jorge Real Sierra, had first come up with the idea of luring prospective home-owners into the net with an advertisement for cheap property. In his turn, Real Sierra took the stand to deny any involvement, claiming he was living in Valencia during the week of the kidnaps and subsequent murders and putting the blame on the shoulders of his brother-in-law, who remained cowed throughout the hearing.

Real Sierra's protests of innocence were dulled by evidence from two national police inspectors who described the arrests in El Saler, Valencia, and the disinterment of the bodies in a cellar in Alcoy. One inspector told the court that Anthony O'Malley had apparently died of asphyxiation and that a plastic bag covering Linda O'Malley's head and tied with a cord at the neck bore the fingerprints of Real Sierra.

CCTV footage also showed both men contacting the victims' family from an Internet café in an attempt to extort more cash for their safe return, although both victims were dead at the time of contact.

ADJOURNED

The hearing, which opened on Tuesday, was scheduled to run until yesterday, when evidence was heard from the owner of the Alcoy villa, the landlord of Real Sierra and Velázquez's Valencia apartment, and shop personnel who identified Real Sierra as the user of Anthony O'Malley's credit card. The court has now adjourned until next Tuesday when pleas will be entered by public and private counsels.

Javier Silvestre Puig was the first prosecution witness of
the day. Sr Silvestre, a tough-looking elderly man in his
seventies, told the court that he was not the owner of the
villa but had acted for his brother who was in poor health.
In answer to the prosecution's questions, he recalled that
a man who signed the rental contract as David Velázquez
had paid one month's rent and one month's deposit in
August 2002. The rental contract was for one year but, by
the end of September, the villa was abandoned and the
only sign of a month's occupancy had been a newly-
painted cellar floor. The contract would have been
cancelled in November and the month's deposit against
rent default confiscated. He did not recognise Real Sierra
as the vagrant tenant when he saw him handcuffed to a
policeman after he himself had been contacted by the
police to attend the villa with the keys on 25 March 2003.
When asked if he recognised Real Sierra on the prisoners'
bench, Silvestre again shook his head.

The chronology of witnesses was confusing the UK
press benches whose occupants were used to much more
ordered proceedings. Instead, they were left to unravel a
constantly changing thread of evidence in which
continuity played no part.

Witnesses whose names were printed on sheets
dutifully handed out each morning by Ana Belen, the
obliging court press secretary, were never called or
mentioned and the judges' bench had a habit of extending
lunch adjournments far beyond the hour announced in
court, even, on one occasion, cancelling the afternoon
hearing all together but neglecting to tell the press waiting
to re-enter the courtroom.

Following this bizarre pattern, a detective who had

appeared earlier was recalled to give evidence of purchases made on the O'Malleys' credit cards, in particular and for reasons never explained by the prosecution, of a pair of shoes size 45, or UK 9½.

This officer also now gave evidence of CCTV footage of Real Sierra and Velázquez seen separately in an Internet café near the Valencia flat when, it was alleged, e-mails were sent by Phoenix. Although the destination of those e-mails was a link set up by Welsh police in Colwyn Bay and monitored by a Welsh police officer, this wasn't mentioned and one was left to assume that the operation that had brought Phoenix to discovery was masterminded by the Spanish.

Another apparently useless piece of evidence was that a fingerprint on the plastic bag covering Linda O'Malley's head was identified as that of Real Sierra – an all too obvious and not impossible consequence of someone living in the villa where the bag was kept. Such trivia entered in evidence by a prosecution that already had its miscreants undeniably linked to the O'Malleys and their murders gave the impression to the sophisticated UK pressmen that both the prosecution and police were acting out of desperation.

It seemed the prosecution was more interested in nailing the defendants with a welter of often inconsequential evidence that went nowhere, rather than presenting the hard facts that proved their guilt. It might have made sense in a trial before a jury when trivia can swing the emotions, but it wasn't working before a judge deacon and her two colleagues in a hearing attended by sophisticated and hard-nosed professional journalists. The press was beginning to fidget.

Other witnesses of this seemingly interminable day included Carlos Pechuán, manager of the Internet café from which some of the Phoenix e-mails were sent. The young manager, whose evidence was given with a bright smile and an obvious desire to please, identified both Real Sierra and Velázquez as regular users of the café's computers but explained that it was impossible to identify from which apparatus a particular e-mail had been sent. E-mails carry the source of the message but, in the case of Phoenix, this was the identification number of the Internet café server.

The time the message was sent could tie in with a recalled or CCTV recorded visit of a particular person or persons, but it was not conclusive since other clients were also present. Did he recognise anyone in court who was a regular client of his establishment? Pechuán turned and faced the prisoners' bench and smiled apologetically at Real Sierra and Velázquez. Yes, he believed it was these gentlemen.

A last question from the prosecutor, 'Did these *gentlemen*... '– there was a definite stress on the third word – '... did these *gentlemen* attend the Internet café together and how often?'

Pechuán shook his head. 'No,' he said, 'I've seen them separately on a number of occasions, but I've never seen them together.'

It was a lesson for the prosecution – never ask a question to which you don't already know the answer.

40

A LETTER TO
THE PRESS

The following letter, shown here translated from the Spanish by the author, was written by Jorge Real Sierra and sent to the Spanish daily newspaper *Información* in Alicante on the fourth day of the interim adjournment. It was never published.

Dear Sirs,
As one presumed guilty of taking part in the murders of British citizens Anthony and Linda O'Malley, and having read in various newspapers what has been published of the case without reference to the evidence heard in court and the daring to speculate, even more, over the tenor of the offence so that it seems to be 'vox populi', I must thank you for the impartiality you have demonstrated throughout the proceedings, recording with clarity and without judgement the reality of what has been said and heard in court.

I am certain that, at the end, the truth will emerge and my innocence be proven, putting an end to all this speculation. The judges of Court number 3 are the only persons who can pass judgement on the case and, if proven, pass sentence.

During the summary hearing, my lawyers requested of the examining judge in Alcoy a number of submissions that were automatically denied. Some of these regarded the obligation of the police to have acted sufficiently to clarify much of the confusion generated in this case.

The police did not carry out the following procedures:

Handwriting tests to determine who had used the credit cards.

Take from the villa in Alcoy (Baradello) a single fingerprint, something inexcusable in a case as grave as this. (The only fingerprints taken were from the cars.)

Voice tests to determine the person who called to England and an NGO [Non-Governmental Organisation, the Missing Persons' Bureau in London], because the British authorities refused to disclose the information in spite of that, at the request of the British, the Spanish carried out the interception of some telephone numbers after it being made clear that there would be no reciprocity. (I attach a copy of that communication.)

Assisted by British law, which blocks the dissemination of information on its citizens to other countries, they have protected in this case any British subject who might be involved.

For more than three years, suspicion of involvement in this case has centred on at least two Englishmen, Matthew Don and Bradley [real surname deleted by author], the latter of whom has been named in evidence given by my co-accused. There still exists proof of a relationship between these two but this line of investigation was not pursued...

As there is no reciprocity, investigation in Britain is impossible. Meanwhile, I am accused of having taken part in these recorded conversations (of which there are no transcriptions or copies) and of having sent e-mails. Those who know of the way English is spoken in England would know that only an Englishman could deceive another Englishman through speech. The person or persons who contacted the NGO were English and that is recognised in one of the documents.

The presumption of innocence has ceased to be a right and has been converted into an empty phrase if it does not incorporate the simple phrase, 'What if...?' 'What if this is true and this one and the other are innocent...?'

I can still hear the words of one of the witnesses who was asked by the public prosecutor if he recognised me. He turned and looked, then exclaimed, 'No, he's not there. That isn't the man!'

I admit I am far from being a saint nor anywhere near, but I can say in truth that not in my mind nor conscience nor heart do I carry regrets for having caused physical damage to anyone, let alone death. I have written this letter because if something has been understood, an example is the case of Dolores

Vázquez, it is that the truth will out sooner or later in the manner least unexpected. I am sure that will be true in this case.

With respect,
Jorge Real Sierra

PS – As an example of the many irregularities in this case, I am enclosing a photographic police report. Please study the date that the camera records on the photographs. In all of these I do not appear and the date is 24 March 2003.

How can this be? According to the police, we were arrested on 25 March and only on that day did anyone become aware of the existence of this case. Date of arrests 25 March 2003.

[Author's note: In fact, no evidence produced in court by the prosecution was acknowledged as the results of an investigation by the Welsh police.]

Throughout the hearing, the part played by Alan Jones, Steve Lloyd and Dave James was singularly ignored, neither were their names ever mentioned. Real Sierra was also wrong in his assertion that the calls from Phoenix were never recorded. They were and the transcript of one is reproduced in the relevant chapter of this book.

The 'Dolores Vázquez' referred to in Real Sierra's letter was imprisoned for the murder of Dutch student Rocio Wanninkof in Mijas Costa in 1999. She was pardoned and released when 'Costa Killer' Tony King was later found guilty of the crime.

The refusal to acknowledge the work of North Wales Police is fairly typical of the attitude of Spanish law enforcement generally. An example of this was when I received a telephone call in my office from a real estate agent who had discovered a young woman's body while taking a client to view a property. The body was lying amid undergrowth near a development known as La Mascarat, built at the foot of a huge chasm where the Sierra Bernia reaches the Mediterranean coast at the leisure port of Luis Campomanes near Altea.

I agreed to report the cadaver to the Guardia, since the estate agent feared a large part of his working day would be taken up making pointless statements, a procedure not unknown in officious Spain where even a good Samaritan who reports a hit-and-run accident can be detained and questioned for hours as a possible suspect. I was interrogated at length over the telephone.

Was I certain it wasn't a hoax? No, I wasn't. Had I checked the site? No, I hadn't. Why not? Because I was 10km away and I thought it was a job for the police. Who had called me? I hadn't the foggiest notion, a man who had spoken in English. What did he look like? It was difficult to know over the phone.

Eventually, I was promised a visit that never came, but I did see the press report that rolled off the office fax the next morning. Two alert officers while on patrol had discovered the body of a young Belgian woman near La Mascarat...

To round the story off, it finally appeared that the woman had been throttled by her boyfriend and her body dumped where it was found. No other details were forthcoming. It was a police matter, not for the press.

The mention of the third man in court had particular meaning for me. It was the same name I had heard from Glasgow John almost three years before when I had assumed El Gordo of Valencia was spreading an alibi in advance. It was during the adjournment that I went back to the villa at Carrer Roure 7 in Alcoy to speak to neighbours. I had already returned earlier in October 2004 with a film crew from ITV Wales with presenter Jonathon Hill and producer Judith Davies, plus a cameraman and sound crew, to make a documentary for a series called *Crime Secrets*. The once dowdy house with its stained white walls was now painted a deep rich terracotta. The roof had been extended over the veranda and was now supported by four thick white columns.

There was no sign of the cellar window and steps led down centrally from the veranda to the garden, covering where it had been. At the far end of the villa, steps still led down to the cellar well and the door was visible, but whether the cellar was in use or permanently kept locked I had no way of knowing, other than approaching the new owners, a young couple from Alcoy who use the villa as a summer retreat and who would hardly appreciate such macabre interest.

Given the harsh winters of Alcoy, when drifting snow can pile up to 2m high, much of the urbanisation of Baradello Gelat consists of summer residences, with the owners preferring to wait out winter in the towns nearer shops and humanity. As such, doing the rounds in late March resulted in unanswered knocks on doors that guarded empty houses. However, I found some locals willing to speak about *la tragedia*. One old couple agreed to offer their thoughts about *los venezuelanos*, provided they themselves were not identified in print. I'll call them Toni and María, which are far enough away from their own names to keep them happy.

'Sure,' Toni told me, 'I remember the Venezuelans. They didn't stay long. I remember the young girls who used to play among the trees. They were perhaps six and eight years old. There was also an older girl, about 12 or 13, called Estephanie, I think.'

María chipped in. 'There was also an older lady who would smile and nod as I passed the wall.' María was diminutive and admitted she could hardly see over the pierced wall. 'Not', she insisted, 'that I would ever be so nosy with neighbours as to stand on tip-toe.'

There seemed to be regular visits from a younger male relative and his male friends who often used the pool and lit barbecues, but the older man, they both assured me, was much more conservative and seldom joined in. He always wore a smart suit and they had assumed he was a manager of a store or that he worked somewhere in an office. 'They only seemed to stay for a few weeks, then they left,' Toni told me, 'I thought they were vacationers until the police brought him back.'

Had either Toni or María ever seen the O'Malleys?

They exchanged glances and Toni lifted his shoulders and rolled his head from side to side in a 'perhaps' gesture. 'We've been asked that question so many times and I'm honestly not sure. Do I remember a blue car? Perhaps I do, but who remembers cars well if they aren't one's own? Certainly, we never heard a sound from the villa after the family had left. But I can tell you one thing. There were visitors.'

I asked him what he meant by 'visitors'?

'Men... and women, too. Sometimes separately, sometimes with the younger Venezuelan. They'd be there most of the day and sometimes late at night. That was in

September and October. Then the older man came back with the younger one in November and we never saw him again until their photographs appeared in the newspapers. What a horror that was.'

María nodded. 'Those poor people,' she said and she crossed herself. 'To think they suffered there and we didn't know about it. I pray for their souls every night.'

'We both do,' Toni assured me. 'What else is there left to do?'

I walked around the perimeter of the villa in question, and took a few more photographs. Would Linda and Anthony have thought the villa in its original state a bargain for €30,000? I didn't doubt it, especially as they had no reason to doubt that the sale was genuine.

At that price, someone more experienced in Spanish property prices might have looked for hidden subsidence or searched the town hall archives for news of a road to be built across the property, but to the O'Malleys it must have seemed like Lady Luck was smiling down on them. How tragic is that?

It was while I was daydreaming in the road that I had the luck to meet possibly the last person to see Linda and Anthony O'Malley alive other than their killers. I shall call my elderly new acquaintance by the sobriquet of Don Alejandro, although he never asked me for anonymity. Indeed, he dismissed the very idea with an elegant swirl of his walking cane which he tended to wave around to accentuate his speech, rather like a conductor's baton. He was dapperly dressed in a lightweight, lovat-green caped overcoat over a woollen shirt and corduroy slacks, despite the warmth of early spring. He was accompanied by a magnificent and friendly long-haired German Shepherd that sat obediently near us and watched with approval as we talked.

'Did I know of *la tragedia?*' Don Alejandro asked me, tapping dust off his fine Oxford brogues with his cane. I nodded in reply.

'Yes, it's an awful thing,' I agreed. 'The men are now being tried in Alicante. Did you ever meet them?'

Don Alejandro wagged his head up and down sadly. Indeed he had done, at least to nod to. He believed they were from South America. The older man, Don Jorge, had seemed such a gentleman. And the young girls were such sweet children. Whatever had led to such a terrible occurrence?

I couldn't help him on that without getting into the evil that men do – my sort of work doesn't attract many philosophers to the trade. I asked him about the O'Malleys. Nobody I'd spoken to, except the old farmer at Els Parrals and Joanne Miles, had ever had close contact with them in those last days before their disappearance, and here was a man who might have seen them on the very day of their deaths.

Don Alejandro nodded back at me a few times. 'Yes, I did see those unfortunate people, although nobody has ever bothered to ask me except you. It was on a fine Sunday morning last fall when they drove by me as I walked Diana. They stopped their car and the man got out to look at the urbanisation plan on the board.'

At her name, the German Shepherd wagged her bushy tail and nudged herself against the old man's legs. Don Alejandro went on, 'I asked if I could help but the man obviously had no Spanish and just tapped a point on the board as if he'd remembered where he was supposed to be.'

I nodded in return, 'If it were a Sunday, I believe he would have also been here the day before.'

My companion nodded, 'Quite so, I wouldn't know. But I particularly remember because the woman got out of the car and was fussing Diana, who craves attention and isn't at all bothered from whom it comes. The lady pointed to herself and then to Diana and smiled at me. I took it to mean she either liked dogs or had one similar.' He smiled apologetically, 'I don't speak English; there was never much of a call for it in my youth. I later saw the car parked here.' He gestured with his stick to indicate the drive at the side of the villa that was shared by the property at the rear. 'I assumed they were visiting the South Americans.'

He had later seen both Venezuelans driving the car but couldn't recall seeing either of the English couple again. I took down some notes and took a photograph of his dog, which he didn't object to.

As for my elderly friend himself, I have never revealed his identity for the same reason that the Eameses were reluctant to speak to the press. When someone grows older, their sense of paranoia and danger often diminish, in the way that the same may have been true for the O'Malleys. Mine, on the contrary, has increased with age and I don't regret that one iota.

I also didn't know whose friends were prepared to go to criminal lengths to keep talkative old men quiet. Although the trial was in progress, I didn't doubt that someone could still be out there. It wasn't a time to tempt the gods.

41

FORENSIC EVIDENCE

When relatives of the O'Malleys who were attending the trial asked for a 'sympathetic' female interpreter, they were expecting detailed forensic evidence from which they might well be spared. No interpreter was provided by the court and it was left to the Belgian human rights lawyer who had offered free legal advice in the early stages to ask among his many contacts.

This was explained to the final candidate for the job, who took on the task and dutifully transcribed the more palatable evidence into a notebook which she passed to the relatives sitting on the front benches.

Throughout the fourth morning, the court was to hear evidence from toxicologists Miguel Angel López, María de la Mar Pastor, Soledad Sanchez and forensic pathologist Salvador Giner, all from Alicante's Institute of Legal Medicine. DNA expert Josefa Gómez would give evidence via video link from Madrid.

The various specialists spoke of their individual examinations of bone and tissue and gave their conclusions. All agreed that Anthony O`Malley had met his death through asphyxiation, pointing to a fracture of the hyoid bone which is always indicative of that form of death. Mention was also made of two distinct fractures of the 3rd and 4th vertebrae that could have occurred in a violent struggle and would almost certainly have caused eventual death due to paraplegic failure of the vital organs. It was noted that Anthony O'Malley's head had been bound tightly with parcel tape post mortem.

The cause of death of Linda O'Malley was discussed at length and caused a stir on the defence table when forensic pathologist Salvador Giner was unable, despite constant prompting from the public prosecutor, to give the cause of death as asphyxiation.

Much was made by the prosecution of the department store carrier bag placed over the woman's head and taped at the neck and of a subdural haematoma in the upper right rear quadrant of the skull, but Sr Giner was adamant in that the victim's lungs were clear of any residue naturally formed during a struggle for breath and lack of oxygen and that the blow that resulted in the haematoma would not have been immediately life threatening.

Instead, the pathologist pointed out deposits of calcium in the vena cava and aorta indicative of preliminary heart disease and gave his opinion that death was due to a heart seizure, probably brought on by stress.

This evidence was later to be used by the defence in an attempt to reduce the charge of first degree murder in the case of Linda O'Malley to *homocidio inculto*, involuntary homicide, which would hopefully lead to a reduction in the sentences handed down to both of the accused. It would prove unsuccessful. The appeal court would rule that both O'Malleys had been murdered.

A video link was then set up with Madrid. The location of the monitor made viewing impossible for the assembled journalists and spectators who had to be content with occasional words heard from the inadequate sound system that barely survived the shuffling and murmurs from the pressmen and the public prosecutor's annoying habit of rattling her microphone across her desk every time she wrote a point on her legal pad.

The video link introduced Dr Josefa Gómez from the Madrid Institute of Forensic Pathology. Dr Gómez, an expert in DNA identification of corpses through bone and marrow scrapings, said that a jawbone sent to her for examination corresponded in DNA testing to blood samples taken from members of the victims' family. The jawbone, she had no doubt, belonged to Anthony O'Malley. The jawbone had also played a part in the matching of dental records of the deceased male.

Could she ascertain the cause of death, asked the judge deacon?

'Not from a jawbone, *su excelencia,*' was the reply.

The defence counsels for both defendants were at odds to challenge the findings of the medical experts, although the reasons were never made clear in cross examination. After all, it was never in doubt that the bodies discovered in that shallow grave in the Alcoy cellar were those of Anthony and Linda O'Malley. Neither in the case of Anthony O'Malley was the cause of death in dispute, and pathologist Giner had already conceded that Linda

O'Malley's death had not been at the immediate hands of the accused.

However, the State questioned how Linda's corpse in particular could have allowed such forensic detail after lying in the soil for six months. Dr Giner explained, 'Many of the internal organs, including the heart and lungs of the female, had been preserved due to the position of the bodies in the grave, in as much that liquid escaping from the corpse of the male during dehumidification had soaked into the body of the female below, humidifying the tissues and leaving them in an extraordinary state of preservation.'

There were no more questions from the defence.

Following the forensic evidence, during which the O'Malleys' relatives had read the interpreter's notes impassively, hardly taking their eyes of the profiles of Real Sierra and Velázquez, both the public and private prosecutors declared the sentences sought.

The State asked for consecutive sentences totalling 62 years for Real Sierra and 56 years for Velázquez, who had not been indicted on the falsification of documents and firearm charges.

The public prosecutor addressed herself directly to the accused, as would private prosecutor Don Enrique de la Cruz Lledó, and sought indemnities of €120,000 for the brother and sister of Anthony O'Malley and €180,000 for each of Linda's daughters.

The private prosecution, brought by Bernard O'Malley, Anthony's sister Christine and Linda's daughters Nicola Welch and Jenny Stewart, sought 54 years for each of the accused and individual indemnities of €300,000 for each of the murders. It also sought the repayment of

€28,186.20, which was the total amount of cash withdrawn from the couple's accounts by direct transfer and credit card fraud.

Oddly, Spanish law had allowed the public prosecution to seek a three-year sentence for each of the accused for the illegal possession of firearms, although this could only relate to the pistols found in the stolen hire cars and the apartment in Valencia and did not relate to any firearm being used in the actual murders.

The defence counsels were shuffling papers at their table and muttering to each other as the private prosecutor finished his speech. There seemed reluctance on the part of the defence to proceed. Finally, José Soler Martín addressed the judges' bench. 'Sus excelencias, the defence for both parties humbly beg more time to present their arguments due to the conflicting evidence we have heard from the medical experts.'

Judge Deacon Dona Virtudes López Lorenzo checked her wristwatch and then indicated the court clock with a magisterial wave of an elegant hand. 'It's now 12.15. We'll adjourn until 12.45.'

Both defence counsels looked decidedly unhappy but nodded in courtroom-required obeisance. The court rose.

I crossed over to the Rincón Gallega, a small bar and restaurant opposite the Museum of Contemporary Art set on the corner of Calle Mayor. There I drank coffee and discussed the case with some of the court staff who were taking a short break while I waited for Arthur Mills to call in his story by telephone to the copy desk of the *Shropshire Star*. As its freelance Senior Correspondent, I was covering the story for the weekly *Costa Blanca News* and didn't have to file until Thursday afternoon.

At 12.40, we walked back towards the court entrance and noticed the majority of the journalists and TV crews were lounging around the square and showing no sense of urgency. The adjournment, we learned, had been moved forward to 1.30pm. At 1.15pm, we heard from the *civil* guarding the door that the prisoners had left and the court was now adjourned until 10.00am the following morning. As I crossed to the underground parking to collect my car, I noticed the three judges lunching in the restaurant of the Hotel Mediterranea Plaza.

They seemed to be enjoying their meal.

42

'JORGE!'

On Thursday, 5 April, the Alicante sun shone as fiercely as ever as I crossed from the parking area under the marine boulevard towards the Palace of Justice. Today would see the defence present the case for their clients. I couldn't help feeling that, as guilty as I believed them both to be, the Venezuelans in the hypothetical dock were being thoroughly railroaded by the prosecution. I hadn't heard any conclusive proof in court that either of the men had actually met the O'Malleys.

According to telephone records, Real Sierra had spoken with Anthony O'Malley on at least two occasions but there were no eye-witnesses to the presence of either Anthony or Linda at the villa, other than my recently discovered eye-witness to their arrival. He was unknown to the prosecution and I had no intention of involving him in the case even if there had been time to do so. In any event, late evidence from the prosecution not presented in the disclosure process represented by the preliminary oral hearing is equally inadmissible.

I thought a British jury might have had problems with this, but perhaps I was forgetting that the case had already been tried by the examining judge in Alcoy. Perhaps that was why crucial points of evidence seemed to be ignored and, just as the canny Welsh Detective Superintendent Alan Jones had forecast, the full story wasn't coming out in court.

Once the trial restarted, the defence counsel for Velázquez came into his own. José Soler Martín had a way of stopping in mid-flow and almost literally plucking words out of the air with his expressive hand gestures. This was, he told us, not a trial by media. The police were anxious to close the file but their evidence proved nothing of murder.

Yes, his client admitted profiting from the credit cards; yes, he was at the bank in Benidorm when Anthony O'Malley withdrew €25,000 in cash; but he knew nothing of the subsequent murders. He had given the police and the court a name. Where was Bradley, the assassin? But never mind about another man in the plot, his client was blameless in the murders. It was, according to counsel, a ploy by the police to close the file. His client had confessed under duress and was guilty only of two minor charges involving fraud and misappropriation of funds, worth no more than six months incarceration for each.

For all the spirit of his defence, Soler Martín's plea fell on deaf ears. Counsel for Real Sierra, Martín Cano, fared no better. The searches had been illegal and his client had been pinned to the floor by a policeman's boot while his home and former home were ransacked. The kidnap and murders had been carried out by a man known as Bradley, alternatively identified by the co-accused as Matt Bradley, who had co-plotted the deception, stayed at the villa while Real Sierra was with his family in Valencia and had acted alone in killing and burying the O'Malleys. Bradley had even sold the co- accused the victims' hire car for €2,000.

Martín Cano also conceded fraud and misappropriation on behalf of Real Sierra and pleaded for no more than six months' imprisonment on each charge. It was the only possible defence left to either counsel and none could fault them for their spirited advocacy, but no one doubted the eventual verdicts.

The court gave the accused a last opportunity to speak before the court adjourned for sentencing. Velázquez managed a wordless shrug and stared at his boots. Real Sierra rose and faced the judges' bench.

'Your excellencies,' he began, 'I stand here as a man falsely accused of a crime of which I am incapable. I am a fraudster, a thief and a cheat, and I have made my living by deceiving my fellow man, but I have no remorse for any other action. I have never harmed man nor beast. I couldn't hurt a living soul.'

His counsel, Martín Cano, had one last question for his client. 'Could you believe your brother-in-law would drive around in the car of two people he had murdered?'

Real Sierra turned to look at the huddled form of Velázquez and shook his head. 'There is a limit even to his stupidity,' he replied.

Judgments of major cases in Spanish courts are not announced on the day. This was a matter for deliberation and the verdict and sentences of Summary Number

1/103 Court Roll Number 6/03 would not be announced for two months.

The court was now told to rise and the judges filed out. Then it was the turn of the prisoners. I watched the O'Malley bench and could sense the tension in the shoulders of Bernard O'Malley.

Something was going to happen and I prayed none of the family would be moved to violence, for the punishment by Spanish courts for disrespectful behaviour is both harsh and swift. Suddenly, Bernard O'Malley reached under his jacket and called to Real Sierra. I tensed. 'Jorge!'

The fat man stopped and turned on his heel towards the voice.

Facing him, each family member was holding up a photograph of either Linda or Anthony. Real Sierra stared impassively at the display then spun away, followed by the hunched figure of Velázquez, both shielded from the family's contempt by the prison escorts. It was a moment that no journalist would have missed at any price. A poignant rebuke from the family for the man they believed had robbed them of a beloved brother, sister-in-law and mother.

Outside the court, Bernard O'Malley was asked on camera to explain the family's action in the courtroom. Each family member refused photographers' inevitable pleas to repeat the action with the photographs and Bernard, who was to face severe bouts of depression in the months following the trial, said simply, 'As a family, we have always acted with dignity. In five days, that is the first time we looked into the eyes of Real Sierra and José Antonio Velázquez. I cannot fully explain what was in our hearts.'

The sentences were handed down on 12 April but not made public until 18 May. Jorge Real Sierra was jailed for 62 years and José Antonio Velázquez received a sentence of 54 years. The court awarded indemnities of €90,000 each to the daughters of Linda O'Malley and ordered the return of €28,173.20 stolen from their mother and stepfather's accounts. Bernard O'Malley and Anthony's sister Christine were awarded €50,000 each. Costs of both prosecutions were also ordered against the prisoners, both of whom lodged appeals within ten days of the hearing.

Under Spanish law, an appeal once lodged, if allowed by the Supreme Court in Madrid, renders the trial court's verdicts and awards null and void. Thus the appeal would have to be heard and lost in the nation's capital before the family of Linda and Anthony O'Malley could receive compensation for their loss, if indeed they ever did.

Both prisoners are without funds and lived in rented accommodation. It is doubtful that the compensation or court costs will ever be paid.

However, there is a downside to non-payment of indemnities and costs for Real Sierra and Velázquez. Non-payment of compensation means no parole. Jorge Real Sierra will certainly die in prison. Should José Antonio Velázquez González live so long, he will be 98 years old on his release.

This was confirmed on 23 January, when Spanish news agency Efe published the following communiqué:

The second Chamber of the Supreme Court has ratified the sentences of the Alicante Court that condemned two men for the kidnap and murder in

2002 of a Welsh [sic] married couple in Alcoy. The bodies were found buried in a cellar of a villa.

In May 2006, the Alicante Court imposed a sentence of 62 years and 56 years on the Venezuelan nationals Jorge Real Sierra (55) and José Antonio VG (41) respectively as those responsible for the murders of the Welsh couple, Linda and Anthony O'Malley, and also decreed an indemnity of €280,000 in favour of the family.

After a period of considering the appeals presented by the convicted parties, the sentence of the Supreme Court is to agree only to annul the accusation against Jorge Real Sierra of the illegal possession of arms and to reduce by one month's imprisonment the sentence imposed for falsification of an official document, and the unauthorised appropriation and possession of equipment used in the said falsification.

The reduction in the sentence is made because these offences are independent of the actions that affected the Welsh couple and results in a total reduction of two years and ten months, with the final sentence adjusted to 59 years' imprisonment.

For the other accused, José Antonio VG, the sentence is raised by two years and eight months for the offences of falsification of an official document and unauthorised appropriation, with the full sentence now totalling 57 years.

The Supreme Court affirms that it has rejected any defects in the original categorisation of the charges and confirms that the married couple were both murdered.

AFTERWORD

Throughout this book, I've asked the question many times as to why the Spanish police hadn't come to same conclusions as I, given the evidence that we shared. But the truth is, we shared nothing.

From the first request from North Wales Police for assistance in their missing persons' inquiry up to Det Supt Alan Jones' decision to treat the inquiry as a case of kidnap following the emergence of Phoenix, there was no Spanish participation. There can be no doubt that it was due to the Spaniards that the source of the Phoenix e-mails was traced to a Valencian suburb, and that the help given by Madrid's Kidnap and Extortion Unit was invaluable in the closing stages of Operation Nevada. But it is wholly appropriate to criticise the Spanish authorities for their earlier failure to collaborate with the Welsh police.

There can also be no doubt that it was the efforts of the UK National Crime Intelligence Service that made the final contact with Phoenix and brought the investigation to its conclusion. The onus was never on the North Wales Police to pursue a murder inquiry in Spain. Their Missing Persons' Inquiry was successfully, if sadly, brought to its conclusion with the discovery of the O'Malleys' bodies under the cement floor of the Alcoy cellar. Neither the alleged participation of the individual named as Bradley nor the intercession of the tout 'Hal' at Málaga Airport is anything other than a matter for the Spanish investigators to pursue and the file is closed. I suspect it will never be reopened.

Giving evidence at the Flint coroner's inquest, DS Steve Lloyd made the remark that must have been in every Welsh officer's mind: 'If two Spaniards had gone missing in Wales, I hope we would have done a better job.'

It couldn't have been the attitude of every Spanish detective that Anthony and Linda O'Malley were having a senior moment and had simply forgotten to phone, or even return, home. Somewhere along the chain of command, someone had decided the case wasn't worth the bother.

That attitude wouldn't have been helped by the arrival of a determined and irascible senior detective from North Wales and his faithful sergeant and constable. The national police in Benidorm had been so astounded when these officers arrived back in Spain for the trial that they interrogated them for hours to satisfy themselves of their intentions.

It is not my intention to knock the locals. The Costa Blanca is a hotbed of crime ranging from street muggings – mainly, it must be said, carried out by North African immigrants, many of the perpetrators having entered the country illegally – to the organised crime of the ex-Eastern bloc *mafiya*. While the former are victims of circumstance and subject to the poverty that always stalks the lower castes of the developing world, the latter enjoy the freedom of a democratic state and an overworked policing system that is now the major sickness of Europe.

The newly arrived criminals work in prostitution, protection, housebreaking, drugs and bank robbery. Drugs have a ready market on the southern Costas of Spain, sold along the infamous *ruta de bacalao*, the nickname for the string of nightclubs and late-night bars that infest the coastline from Marbella to Denia.

The force pitted against organised crime is the undermanned and overworked Unit against Drugs and Organised Crime, UDYCO. I count many friends among its courageous ranks.

I also know many fine Spanish policemen who serve the community with dedication but even they yawn at the constant flow of foreign visitors who, to coin a phrase, leave their brains on the tarmac when they arrive at the airport. Many disappear and most pop up again, having come to their senses and flown home without bothering to alert the Spanish authorities to whom they've been reported missing.

However, there's no doubt in my mind that serious errors occurred on the Spanish side of the O'Malley investigation. No one, frankly, other than the Welsh police at Wrexham, was interested in their disappearance until large, uncharacteristic withdrawals and purchases were made against the couple's credit cards. Even then, the Spanish end of the inquiry was sluggish to say the least. Only when Alan Jones's squad in North Wales alerted the Spanish authorities to the presence of Phoenix in their midst did the inquiry become a matter of urgency.

There is no doubt that, once the suspects were traced to Valencia, the Spanish police in the form of its Madrid-based Kidnap and Extortion Unit moved swiftly, but it was far too late for the O'Malleys.

If my highly anxious female witness from La Nucía – who had insisted to me that she saw a known scallywag's wife driving the missing hire car – had been believed, the link might well have been traced to Real Sierra, Velázquez and the Alcoy villa much sooner.

It is plain from this book that I believe Anthony and Linda O'Malley met their deaths on 13 September, over three weeks before my witness appeared, but the young woman had seen the vehicle on 1 September. Who knows if an earlier alarm to the press wouldn't have brought her forward while they still lived?

It was the UK National Crime Intelligence Service working from Colwyn Bay that identified the Gola de Puchol apartment block as the location of the mysterious Phoenix. It was the corresponding surveillance that spotted the O'Malley's hired blue Fiat Stilo partly concealed nearby.

This case of the missing house-hunters was solved by the hard work and diligence of three North Wales detectives, headed by their dedicated boss Alan Jones and backed by the skills of the UK Criminal Intelligence Service, whose incessant search for the O'Malleys in Spain led to the discovery of their murderers. There is no call for false heroes. I played my part and I am proud to have done so, as I am sure are those who were my colleagues at that time.

References to the Englishman Bradley, who cannot be fully identified here for legal reasons, the man whom Real

Sierra and Velázquez claim was the mastermind and main perpetrator of the tragic scam as well as the cold-blooded murderer of both victims, are made purely because they are records of fact. But nothing in my enquiries, which have included correspondence with both the man and his family, has led to any direct proof of his involvement. There is only that vague suspicion in the air that surrounds the case.

There is no doubt that 'Bradley' was on the Costa Blanca at the time of the O'Malleys' kidnap and murders, and that he was a known acquaintance of José Antonio Velázquez, and frequented the Scrubs bar where Real Sierra claims the two of them met. But that has only given the man the opportunity to commit the crime that was open to anyone else in the area at the time. What has never been made clear is motive, again open to anyone who happened to be in dire financial straits at the time.

If it were provable, it might well have made a good defence, but the fact that I heard the name from Glasgow John, with El Gordo as the source, could mean that Real Sierra, who more than fits the bill as El Gordo, the forger of documents from Valencia, was already preparing his alibi. He was supported by a convenient argument with his wife and brother-in-law on the afternoon of 7 September, which was used as an excuse to move his wife, children and mother-in-law out of the villa in preparation for Linda and Anthony's visit and subsequent captivity. What a pity for him that he had not discussed it as a defence with his lawyer and brother-in-law before the arrests.

There is no doubt that the Englishman and José Antonio Velázquez knew each other and that their friendship was known to Real Sierra, but I find the older Venezuelan's insistence that the two plotted the kidnap and murders without his knowledge unconvincing. A photograph of the Englishman and Anthony O'Malley before a 'well-known Benidorm *cafetería*' might have convinced the prosecution to the contrary but, although promised to me, it never materialised, with the excuse that it had been destroyed as 'incriminating evidence'. Against whom, I wonder?

Of José Antonio Velázquez, I have no doubt that he was a hesitant yet willing accomplice in the plot with his brother-in-law to imprison and rob their victims, with the possible tacit assistance of Matt Bradley.

It is also clear through copies of correspondence in my possession that he and Bradley were close friends. As for them meeting in the Scrubs bar in Alfaz del Pi, that, given my own experiences there, would seem a likely venue. The Scrubs, now sold and renamed, was in 2002 a popular meeting place for local scallywags, a few of whom I, nonetheless and without apology, count among my friends.

Most importantly, I do not believe that either of the men convicted of the killings of Linda and Anthony O'Malley intended for their scam to end in the tragic way it did. As I made clear earlier in this book, property rip-offs by bogus owners are recurring stories on the Spanish Costas.

I was also informed that an extensive search of records of this sort of crime was made in Venezuela following the arrests of Real Sierra and Velázquez, and that their fingerprints were circulated throughout South America, but with what result I have never learned. Earlier convictions would have been known to the trial judges but not pronounced publicly in court and thus we, the public, shall never know.

It is my belief that it was the intention of Real Sierra and Velázquez to flee with the money on that fateful day of Friday, 13 September and to leave the O'Malleys to be found by the police following a telephone call from either of the robbers. Their plan came to nothing through the untimely death of Linda O'Malley from a heart seizure.

In no way should these men escape punishment for her death, which the Alicante court if not the Court of Appeal recognised as 'imprudent homicide', the Spanish equivalent of manslaughter brought about by their actions, nor for the deliberate and cruel murder of her grieving husband Anthony. They are both paying for their crimes with life sentences that make it likely that both will die in prison. If there was a third man, and that possibility still exists, I know where and who he is and he lives with his own conscience.

The case has done irreversible damage to tourism on the Costas and I, as a long-term resident of Spain, think that a pity. Spain is a beautiful and friendly country and the pitfalls of buying property are few.

The rules are simple and apply in Spain as they do anywhere else in the world: don't be taken in by glib talkers and never wave your money around; don't talk of your plans to strangers you meet in bars; find a registered estate agent and get yourself a good English-speaking lawyer. I can't help thinking that if Linda and Anthony O'Malley had stuck to those few simple rules, they would be living happily in Spain today – and this book would never have been written.

Of the other minor players in the tragedy, I believe 'Hal'

and his wife were paid a sizeable commission by the scam operator to forget the introduction of the O'Malleys when it ended in their deaths. Certainly, they became suddenly wealthy around Christmas 2002. They now live somewhere in England, as does Bradley, the English ex-bar owner named to me in Benidorm.

An e-mail from Eileen Proctor in April 2006 read, 'There should be at least four men standing trial (in Alicante).'

I'm inclined to agree with her.

APPENDICES

Time Line of the O'Malleys' Card Usage

31/8/02	13.31	Yorkshire Bank	Hotel Ambassador, Benidorm	81.74
2/9/02	10.08	CAM Bank	Opening Balance	300.00
3/9/02	22.59	Yorkshire Bank	Pizzeria Benidorm	34.07
4/9/02	09.34	Yorkshire Bank	Hotel Altaya, Altea	297.83
6/9/02	22.38	Yorkshire Bank	Chinese Restaurant, Benidorm	25.00
7/9/02	13.55	Yorkshire Bank	Service Station, Benidorm	30.00
8/9/02	15.55	Yorkshire Bank	ATM-Santander (0579) Finestrat	200.00
	16.14	Yorkshire Bank	ATM-Santander (0579) Finestrat	300.00 (Attempt-Incorrect pin no.)
	17.04	Yorkshire Bank	ATM-Santander (0579) Finestrat	120.00
		Barclays Bank	ATM-Santander (0579) Finestrat	150.00
		CAM Bank	ATM-Carrefour, Finestrat (420)	250.00
9/9/02	15.31	Yorkshire Bank	Carrefour, Alicante	244.59 (General goods)
	17.40	Yorkshire Bank	Centro Mail Alicante	49.95 (Video Game)
	17.52	Yorkshire Bank	Footlocker, Alicante	119.80 (Mens sportswear all XL size)
		Yorkshire Bank	ATM-Alicante	300.00
	18.10	Yorkshire Bank	ATM-CAM Bank Alicante	120.00
	19.34	Yorkshire Bank	Carrefour, San Juan	266.06
		Barclays Bank	ATM-CAM Bank	15.00
		Yorkshire Bank	Road Toll-Valencia District	2.18
10/9/02	10.38	Yorkshire Bank	CIMA-Benidorm	394.90 (Computer equipment)
	12.10	Yorkshire Bank	El Corte Inglais-Alicante	180.38 (D/phone)
	12.17	Yorkshire Bank	El Corte Inglais-Alicnate	195.00 (Camera)
	12.24	Yorkshire Bank	El Corte Inglais-Alicante	36.90 (Alarm)
	12.33	Yorkshire Bank	ATM-CAM Bank Alicante	300.00
	12.34	Yorkshire Bank	ATM-CAM Bank Alicante	200.00 (Attempt-Strip Worn)
	15.30	Yorkshire Bank	Perfumeria Gala-Alicante	129.15
	16.36	Yorkshire Bank	Carrefour-Alicante	267.52 (General goods)
	16.54	Yorkshire Bank	Mayordomo-Alicante	72.00 (Shoes x 2-ladies 40 gents 43)
		Yorkshire Bank	ATM-BBVA Alfaz-Benidorm	300.00
		Yorkshire Bank	Bank Popula Alfaz-Benidorm	200.00
		Yorkshire Bank	Road Toll-Valencia District	2.53
		Barclays Bank	ATM-BBVA Alfaz-Benidorm	200.00
11/9/02	15.39	Yorkshire Bank	Carrefour-Finestrat	554.39 (Computer Modem, Scanner, DVD disc and other computer items)
	16.51	Yorkshire Bank	Carrefour-Finestrat	134.77 (Dremel multi tool and household goods)
	16.00	Yorkshire Bank	Offtienda, Finestrat	190.00 (Nokia)

Time Line of the O'Malleys' Card Usage

11/9/02	16.57	Yorkshire Bank	Radio Castilla, Alicante	1,900.00 (Attempt Lap top Computer)
		Yorkshire Bank	ATM-Santander (5939) Benidorm	300.00
		Yorkshire Bank	Road Toll-Valencia District	2.53
		Barclays Bank	ATM-Caixalt-Benidorm (304500149)	100.00
		Yorkshire Bank	STATUS REMOVED BY BANK	
12/9/02	15.27	Yorkshire Bank	ATM-Alicante	250.00 (Attempt)
	15.28	Yorkshire Bank	ATM-Alicante	250.00 (Attempt)
	16.03	Yorkshire Bank	ATM-Alicante	180.00 (Attempt)
	17.01	Yorkshire Bank	ATM-Alicante	130.00 (Attempt)
		Yorkshire Bank	Transfer to CAM Acc	28,186.20
		CAM Bank	ATM-Alicante (0172)	300.00
		CAM Bank	BATA-Alicante	148.00 (Shoes)
		CAM Bank	Carrefour-Alicante	473.57 (General goods)
		Barclays Bank	ATM-C.A.Val Spain-Alicante	100.00
		Barclays Bank	ATM-C.A.Val Spain-Alicante	100.00
13/9/02		Yorkshire Bank	Road Toll-Valencia District	2.18
		CAM Bank	Cash Withdrawal-Benidorm	25,000
		CAM Bank	ATM- CAM Bank Alicante	300.00
14/9/02	13.25	CAM Bank	El Corte Inglais-Valencia	169.50
	13.26	CAM Bank	El Corte Inglais-Valencia	157.00
	13.36	CAM Bank	EL Corte Inglais-Vale.ncia	222.00 (3 x Burberry shirts XL)
	13.51	CAM Bank	El Corte Inglais-Valencia	199.00 (Shoes x 2 size 45)
	14.00	CAM Bank	El Corte Inglais-Valencia	11.34 (School books)
	14.01	CAM Bank	El Corte Inglais-Valencia	57.20
	14.20	CAM Bank	El Corte Inglais-Valencia	267.80
	14.37	CAM Bank	EL Corte Inglais-Valencia	65.90
		CAM Bank	ATM-Sistema (4b/7507390)	300.00
		CAM Bank	Carrefour-Valencia	359.90
		Barclays	ATM-Bank Popula-Valencia (0739)	100.00
15/9/02	15.19	Yorkshire Bank	ATM-Ullera-Valencia	100.00 (Attempt)
		Barclays Bank	ATM-Bank Santander(0093)	100.00
16.9.02	11.19	Yorkshire Bank	ES Servipetrol-Valencia	6.00 (Attempt)
		CAM Bank	ATM-SERVIRED (1308730) Alfafer-Valencia	150.00
		Barclays Bank	ATM-Caixa D Spain (201311229) – Valencia	100.00
		Barclays Bank	ATM-Santander Spain (5883)	100.00
19/9/02	14.05	Yorkshire Bank	ATM-BBVA Valencia	40.00
		Barclays Bank	ATM-C.A.Val Spain (207707559) Valencia	100.00

Incriminating Booking Form

CB NEWS S.L. - CLASSIFIED ADS FORM

CB NEWS S.L.
Edificio Ensenada, 2ⁿᵈ Floor D,
Calle Dr. Pérez Llorca 9,
03503 Benidorm (Alicante)
Tel. 96 585 52 86/7
Fax 96 585 83 61/96 680 59 75
N.I.F. B-03959244

Office/Desk/Agent: HEAD OFFICE
Date: 02 / 09 / 2002 : Albarán Number: Z 564
Name: MATHEW DON, (DAVID VELAZQUEZ
Address: C/ PAIS VALENCIANO 32.
Town: VALENCIA NIF/GB: X 2933969 V.
Post Code _____ Tel: 667319413 Fax:
News: ☒   Post: ☐   Both: ☐ (Please Tick the Appropriate Box)

PROPERTY	FOR SALE X	WANT BUY	TO LET	WANT LET	EXCHANGE	BUS OPP	SERVICES	ACCOMM
GENERAL	GENERAL	SITS. VAC	SITS. WAN	ITEMS WAN	HEALTH&B	PERSONAL	MOTOR M	DEATHS

PRICE PER WORD: COSTA BLANCA NEWS, 0'30 €uros. WEEKLY POST, 0'25 €uros. BOTH, 0'36 €uros.

Total Number of Words: 16   CBN: X   POST: ___   BOTH: ___   €uros: 4,80

N° of Insertions: 2   Start: 06/09/02 Finish: 13/09/02   €uros: 9,60
Box N° Required: Yes ☐   No ☐   (1'50 €uros): €uros: ___
                                    Discounts: €uros: ___
Additional Information: _____   I.V.A./V.A.T. @ 16%: €uros: 1,54
                                    TOTAL CHARGE €uros: 11,14

Costa Blanca News
Small Ads

House for Sale

TEXT:

**2 BEDROOM HOUSE IN 4.000M2 LOT. BOCAYRENT,
PINE TREES, WATER, ELECTRICITY. NO AGENCIES.
30.000 EUROS. 667-319463**

Mathew Don
Calle Pais Valenciano 32
Valencia

KAY	CUSTOMER	DESK/AGENT	JOSE

*The newspaper advertisement booking form
carrying the aliases of Velázquez as Matthew Don and
Real Sierra as David Velázquez.*

NIGHTMARE IN THE SUN

Fatal Newspaper Advertisement

COSTA BLANCA NEWS, September 6-12, 2002

CALPE VILLA WITH Peñon- and sea views, 960/200sqm, oil heating, pool garage. Price: 334.500 Euros Daniel Tel. ███ ██ ██ ██ www.real-estate-costa-blanca.com (SE6)

LA SERELLA SERVICES/ Mountain Concepts. Building plots in Vall d' Ebo, Vall de Gallinera and surrounding areas. Many have own water and power services can be supplied by alternative energy systems Tel ██ ███ ██ ██ (SE13)

MORAIRA BENIMEIT. Private sale. 3 bed/3 bath villa (180m2) in beautiful gardens (1000m2). With views to the sea, Moraira and country side. House and pool refurbished and tastefully decorated for comfortable, year round living with A/con, and heating. Arranged as two, self contained apartments. Ground floor: sitting room, fitted kitchen, dining room with full width sliding doors to pool. Large, master bedroom suite, doors to terrace, full height fitted wardrobes and bathroom. First floor sun/dining room with views over the palm shaded pool to the sea and surrounding hills, sitting room with fireplace. Kitchen. Storeroom. Double bedroom (en suite) and double bedroom with bathroom. Easily maintained garden, water deposit, mature trees, driveway and car port. No agents please £318.000 (UK pounds) Tel ███ ███ ███ (SE13)

JAVEA/MORAIRA - HAVING PROBLEMS SELLING YOUR HOUSE? WE ARE A UK PROFESSIONAL COMPANY WITH MANY CLIENTS VIEWING ON INSPECTION TRIPS WHO ARE EAGER TO PURCHASE DURING SEPTEMBER. LOW COMMISSION RATES, NO SALE NO FEE. PLEASE CONTACT ANDREW TUCKETT BSC FRICS Tel. ███ ███ ███ (SE13)

HEALTHY CONSTRUCTION WORKS and healthy living at Costa Blanca. We are a German builder with experience in using healthy materials for houses. Protect your highest value, your health, three times: with "breathing" materials. With "natural" heating of your rooms, with "energy saving" usage of raw materials. We would like to inform you about your personally "health house". Please do not hesitate to call us at ███ ███ ███ for any further information (SE27)

BENIARBEIG NEW DETACHED villas available for occupation right now! Plot average 400m2, build size 125m2, 3 bedrooms, 2 bathrooms. Own 8x4m pool + car port. Select south facing location, only 6 properties. Price 237,300 Euros. Call A2Z Properties (Benissa) on ██ ███ ██ ██ (SEP6)

OPPORTUNITY!! SITUATED in a wonderful province (19Km to the sand beaches) south facing Valle de Laguart (near Orba) house 300m2 with 3 separate floors even with 100m2 built in 1988 fantastic free view to the sea, Ibiza and mountains. Garage 50m2 roof terrace 45m2 central heating air conditioning part of furniture price Euros 195,000 Tel/ Fax: ██ ███ ██ ██ Mobile 696 ██ ███ 272 (*)

BOCAYRENT, TWO BEDROOM house in 4.000m2 plot. Pine trees, water, electricity. No agencies. 30.000 euros Tel: 667 319 463 (SE13)

LUXURIOUS NEW flat 2 bed (85m2) 2 bath, in urbanisation pool Denia Las Marinas. 138.000 Euros Tel: ███ ███ ███ (SE13)

LOVELY RUSTIC VILLA in Denia, very quiet and private area. Completely renewed. 3 bedrooms (one outide), main

MORAIRA BENIMEIT villa with magnificent sea view. South facing as new (built in 1997-99) 3 beds, 2 baths, lounge, dining Americna kitchen, big porch, pool nice garden with grass and palm trees all on one level (95/ 1100m2) heating and air condition, fully furnished 680.000 Euros LA TORTUGA IMMOBILIEN S.L. Tel. 96 574 84 ██, ███ ███ ███ e-mail: ███████████████████ (SE6)

ELS POBLETS attractive, south facing town houses (3 beds, 2 baths, separate fitted kitchen, lounge, storage room, pre installation air con warm/ cold) communal pool and garden, parking space and lock up storage room in underground garage. Prime location in quiet and sunny residential area with green zones. Wide illuminsted streets just around the corner from the town centre Euros 149.652 K&K Property Consultants Tel. ██ ███ ██ ██ Fax: 96 ███ ██ ██ (SE6)

PLOTS, PLOTS HUNDREDS of Plots. www.thelandregister.com 661 746 663 (NO10)

FINCAS EL PORTAL S.L. DENIA villa built on a flat plot of 680m2 in a very quiet cul de sac, close to shopping facilities, the house is in a very good condition, partially renovated and consists of 2 bedrooms, bathroom, closed kithen, living room with old wooden beams and chimney terraces. A beautiful well maintained garden Euros 215.000 www.API-Inmobiliaria.de Tel ███████ ██ ███ ██ ██ or ███████ ███ ███ ███ (*)

SUPERBLY RESTORED FAMILY home in medieval quarter of market town. An immaculate dwelling. 4 double bedrooms, lounge, fitted

The location is given as Bocairent (misspelled as Bocayrent) rather than Alcoy to avoid alerting the owner of the rental property

286